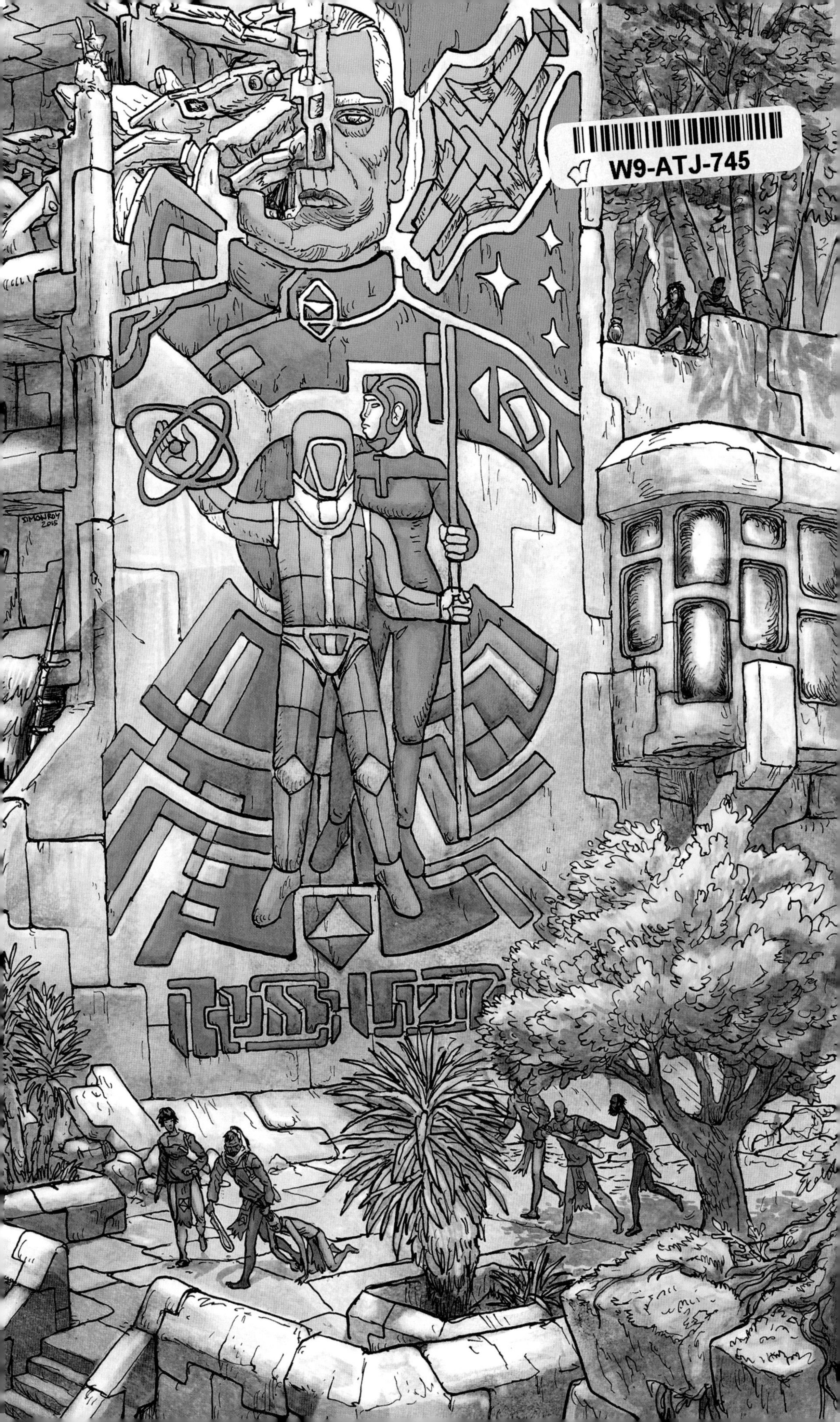
SIMON ROY
2015

IMAGE COMICS, INC.
Robert Kirkman – Chief Operating Officer
Erik Larsen – Chief Financial Officer
Todd McFarlane – President
Marc Silvestri – Chief Executive Officer
Jim Valentino – Vice-President

Eric Stephenson – Publisher
Corey Murphy – Director of Sales
Jeff Boison – Director of Publishing Planning & Book Trade Sales
Jeremy Sullivan – Director of Digital Sales
Kat Salazar – Director of PR & Marketing
Branwyn Bigglestone – Controller
Drew Gill – Art Director
Jonathan Chan – Production Manager
Meredith Wallace – Print Manager
Briah Skelly – Publicist
Sasha Head – Sales & Marketing Production Designer
Randy Okamura – Digital Production Designer
David Brothers – Branding Manager
Olivia Ngai – Content Manager
Addison Duke – Production Artist
Vincent Kukua – Production Artist
Tricia Ramos – Production Artist
Jeff Stang – Direct Market Sales Representative
Emilio Bautista – Digital Sales Associate
Leanna Caunter – Accounting Assistant
Chloe Ramos-Peterson – Library Market Sales Representative
IMAGECOMICS.COM

HABITAT

BY SIMON ROY   STORY EDITORS: DANIEL BENSEN + JESS POLLARD

SPECIAL THANKS TO JESS,
DANIEL, AND BRANDON, WITHOUT
WHOM THIS BOOK COULDN'T
HAVE HAPPENED.

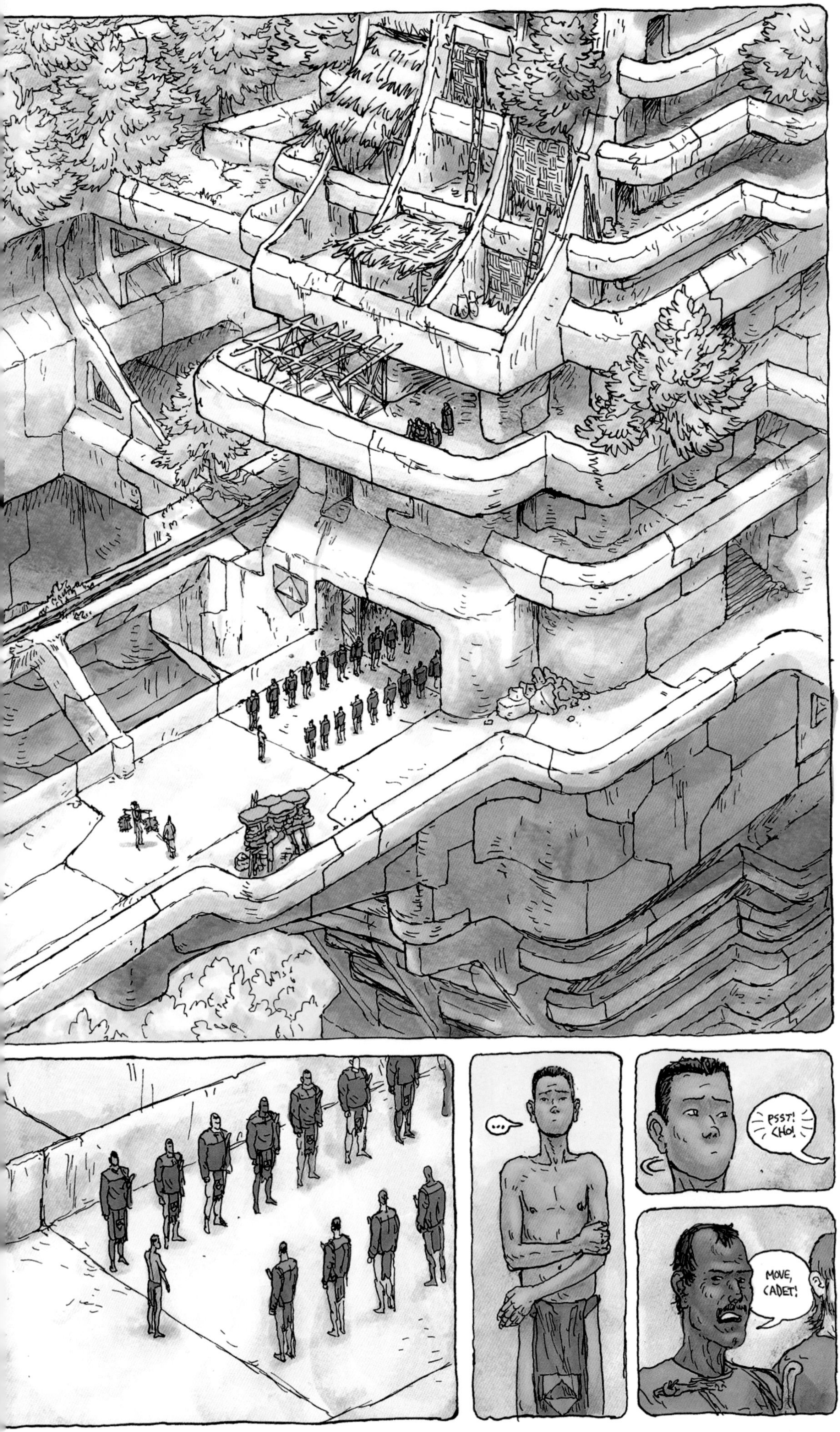
...
PSST! CHO!
MOVE, CADET!

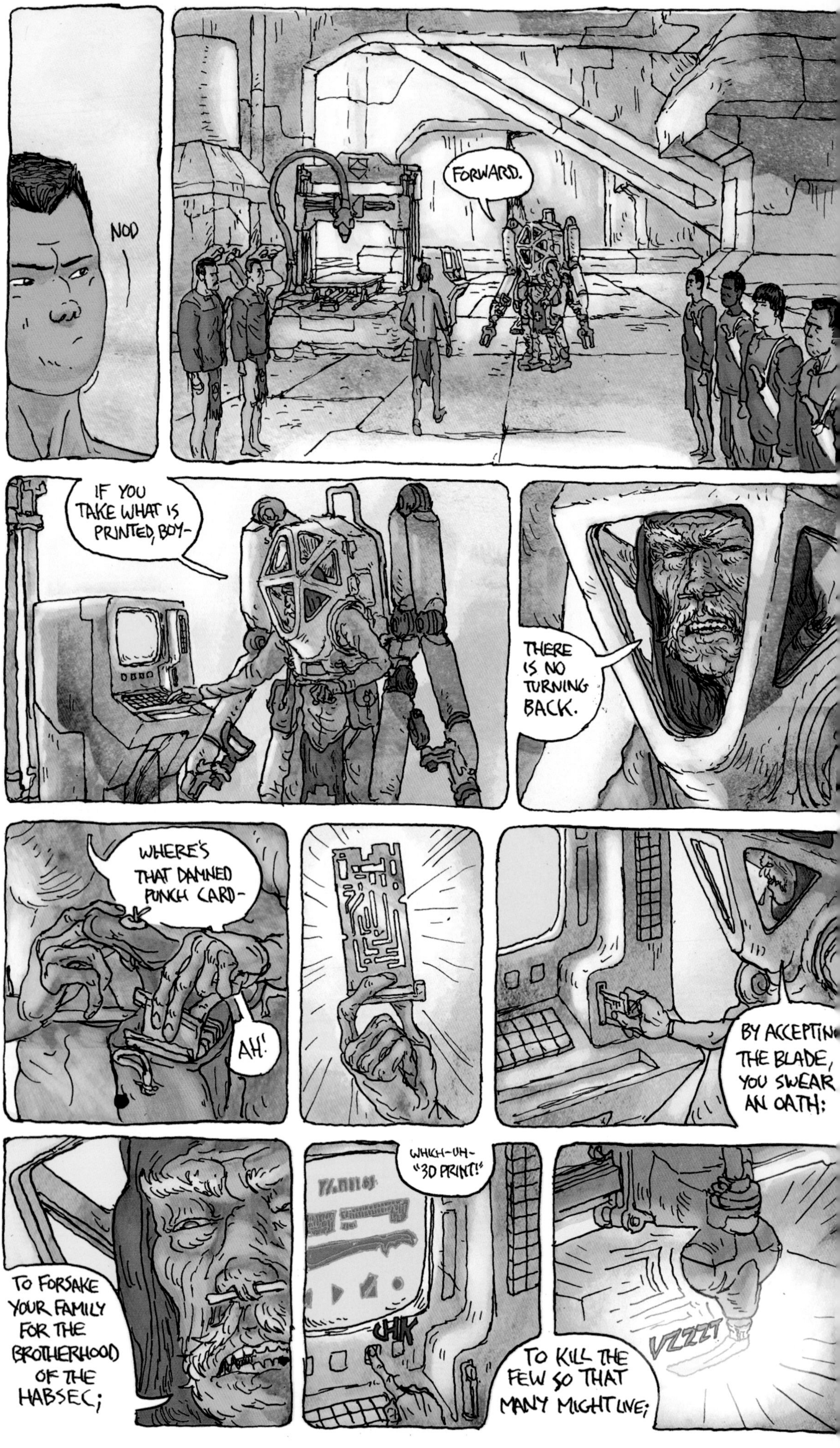
NOD
FORWARD.
IF YOU TAKE WHAT IS PRINTED, BOY-
THERE IS NO TURNING BACK.
WHERE'S THAT DAMNED PUNCH CARD-
AH!
BY ACCEPTING THE BLADE, YOU SWEAR AN OATH:
TO FORSAKE YOUR FAMILY FOR THE BROTHERHOOD OF THE HABSEC;
WHKH-UH- "3D PRINT!"
CHK
TO KILL THE FEW SO THAT MANY MIGHT LIVE;
VZZZT

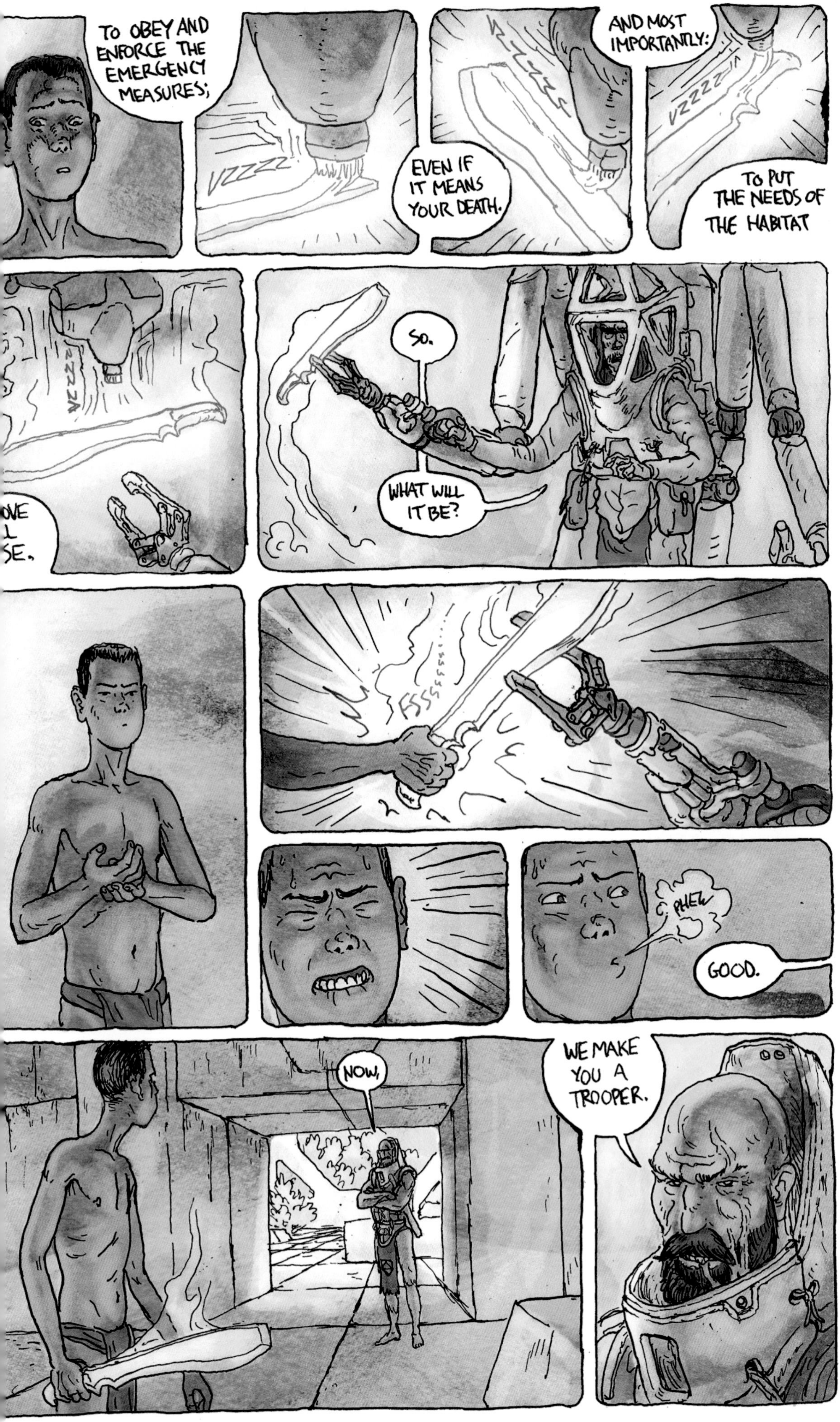
TO OBEY AND ENFORCE THE EMERGENCY MEASURES;
VZZZZ
EVEN IF IT MEANS YOUR DEATH.
VZZZZZ
AND MOST IMPORTANTLY:
VZZZZ
TO PUT THE NEEDS OF THE HABITAT
ZZZZ
OVE
L
SE.
SO.
WHAT WILL IT BE?
FSSSSSSS
PHEW
GOOD.
NOW,
WE MAKE YOU A TROOPER.

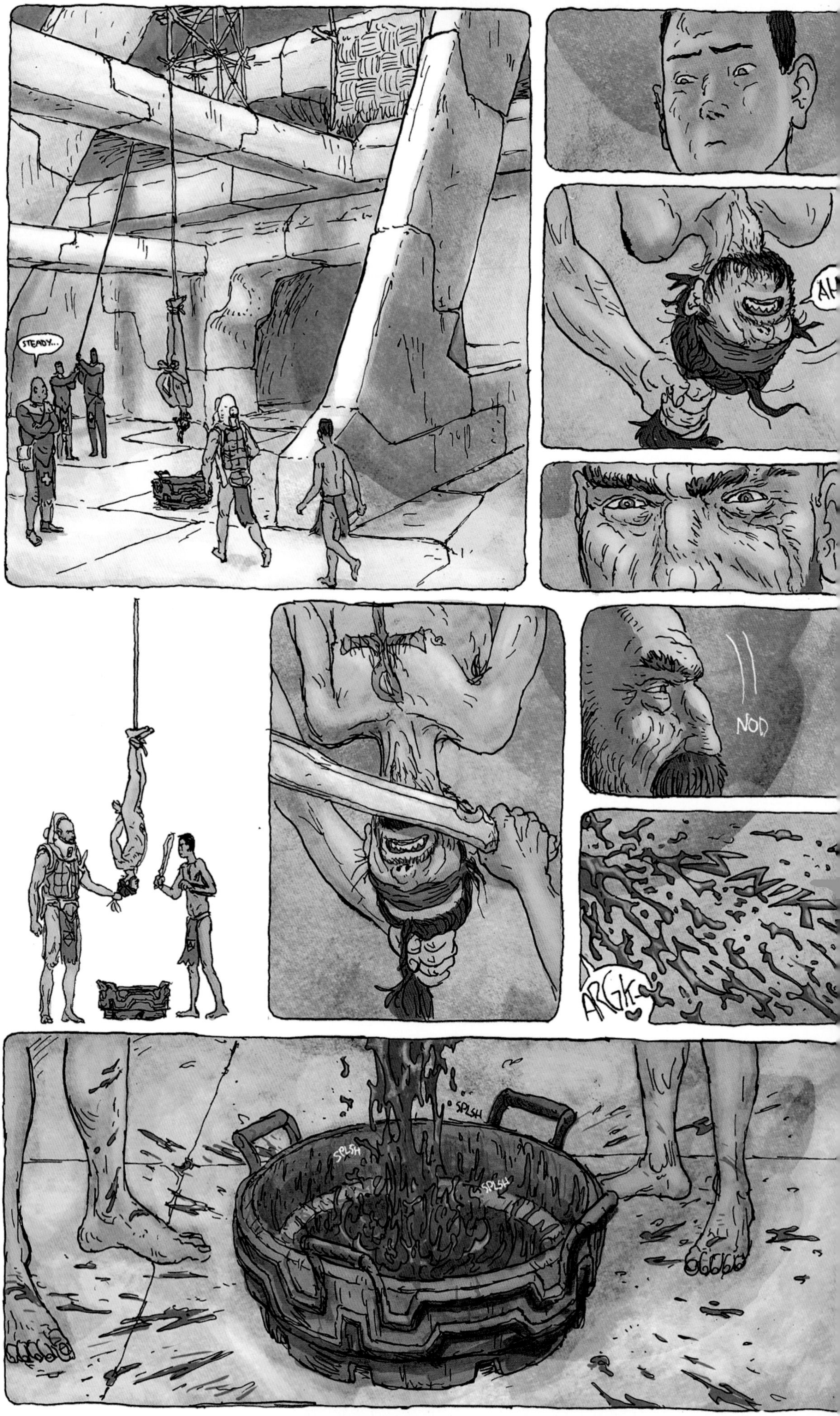
STEADY...
NOD
ARGK-
SPLSH
SPLSH
SPLSH

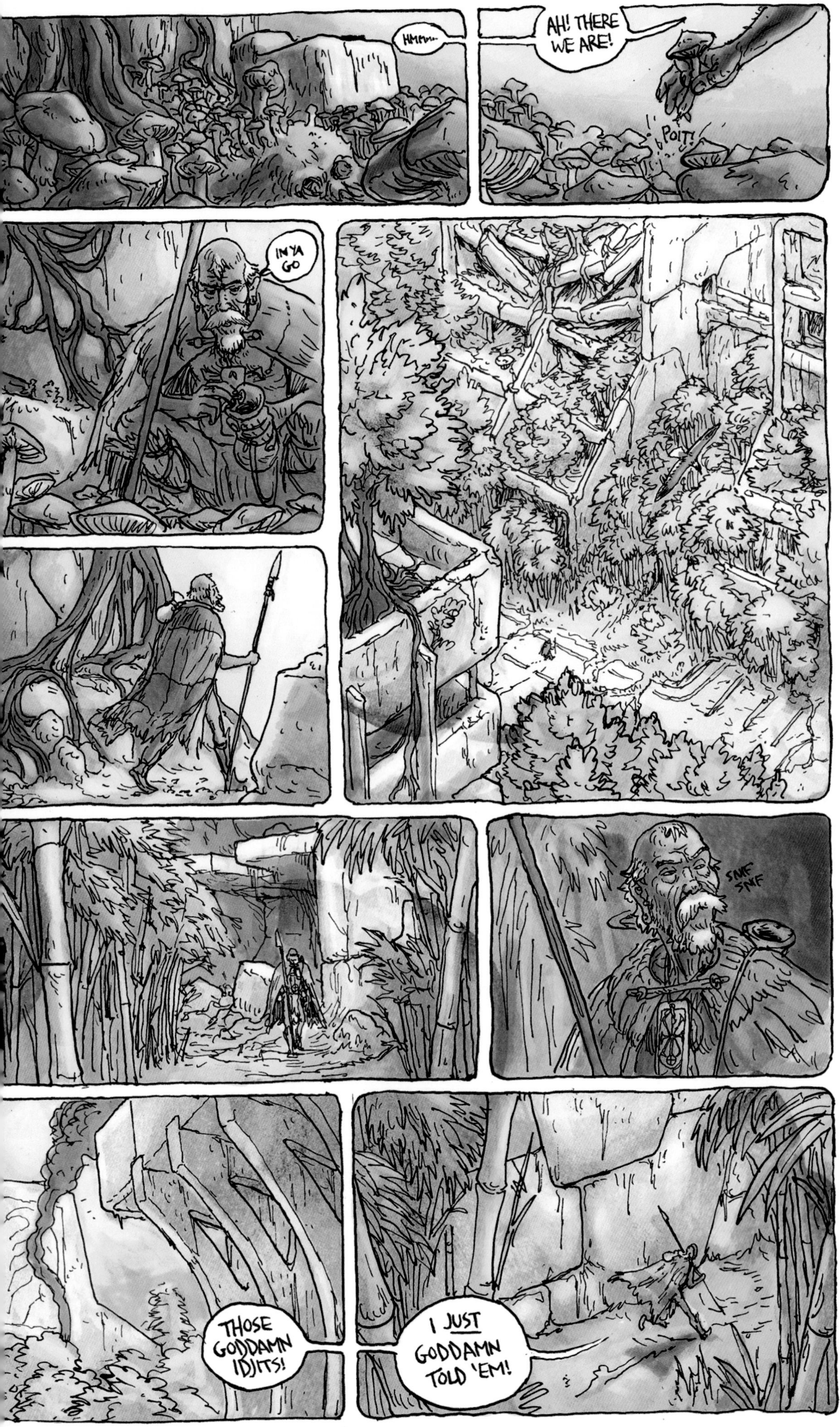
HMMM...
AH! THERE WE ARE!
POIT!
IN YA GO
SNIF SNIF
THOSE GODDAMN IDJITS!
I JUST GODDAMN TOLD 'EM!

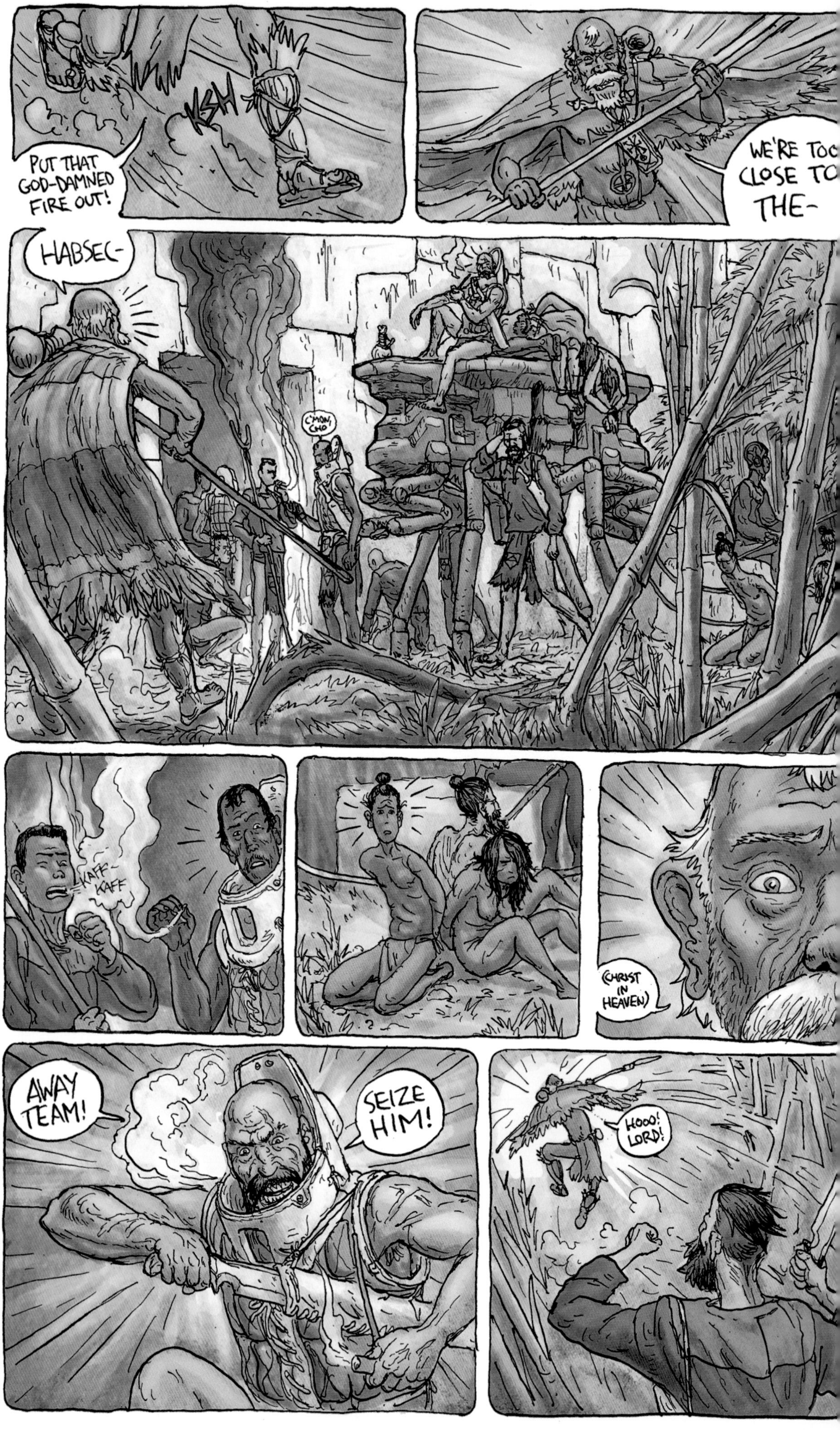
KSH
PUT THAT GOD-DAMNED FIRE OUT!
WE'RE TOO CLOSE TO THE-
HABSEC-
C'MON, CHO
KAFF KAFF
(CHRIST IN HEAVEN)
AWAY TEAM!
SEIZE HIM!
HOOO! LORD!

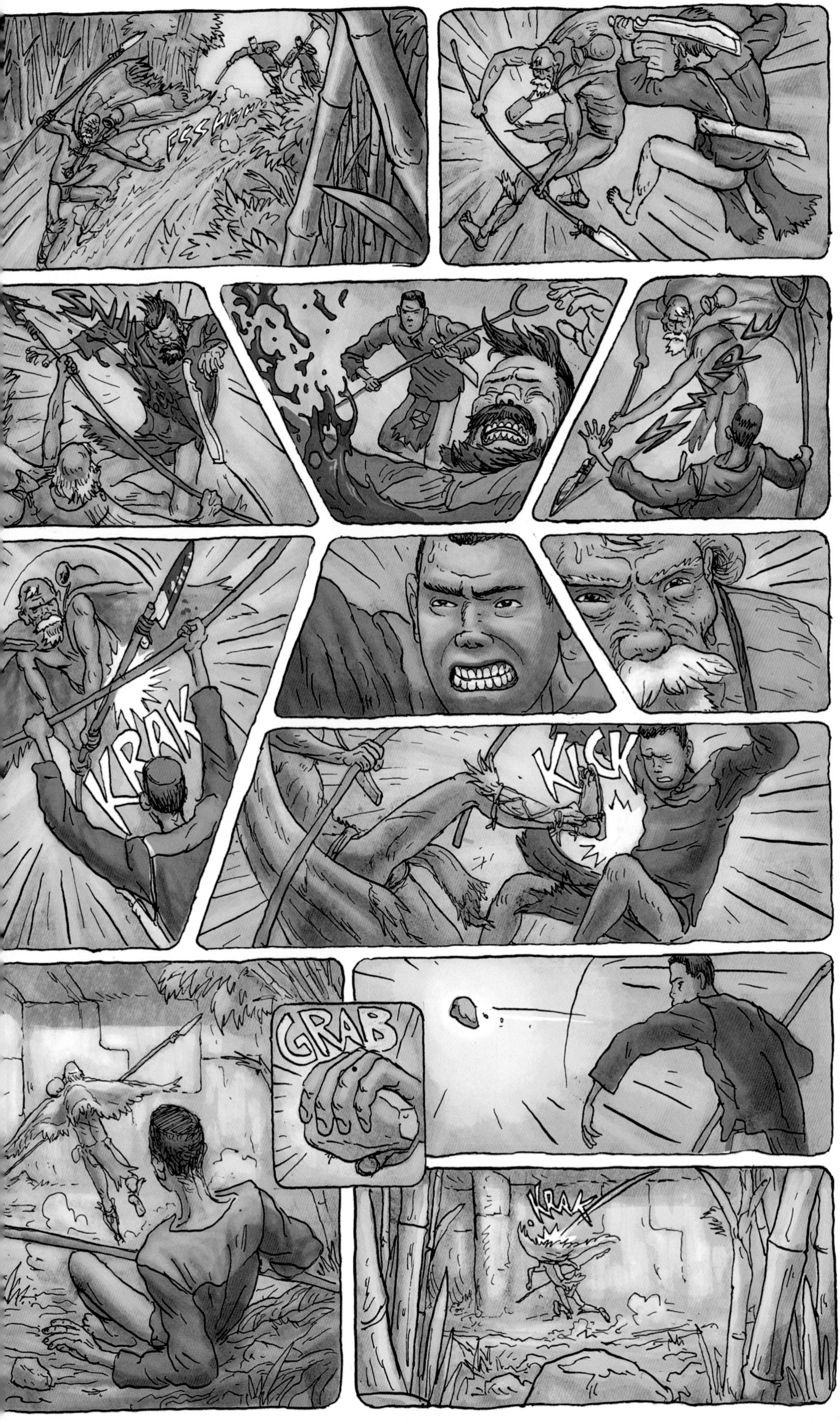
FSSHHHH
KRAK
KICK
GRAB
KRAK

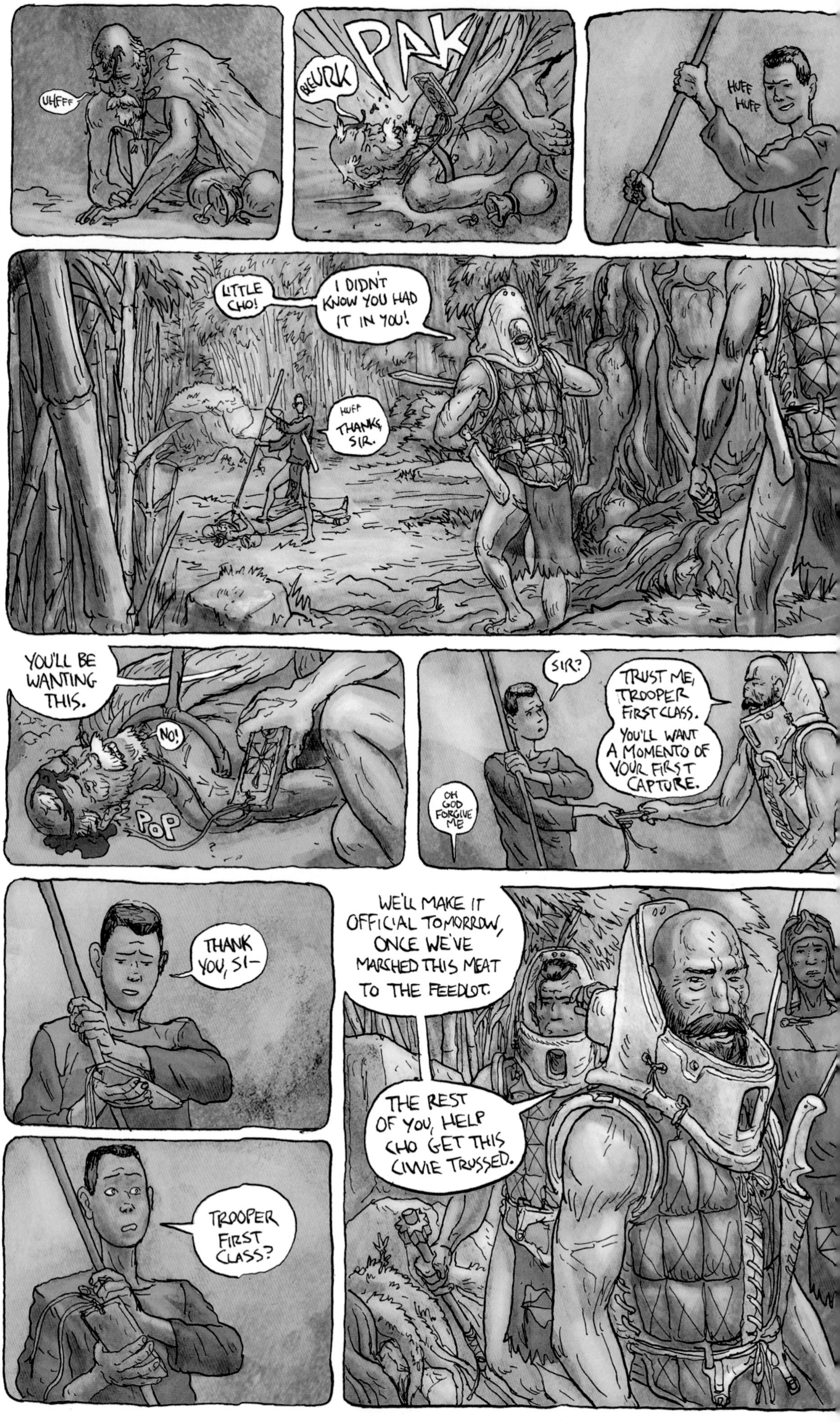
UHFFF
BLEURK
PAK
HUFF
HUFF
LITTLE CHO!
I DIDN'T KNOW YOU HAD IT IN YOU!
HUFF
THANKS, SIR.
YOU'LL BE WANTING THIS.
NO!
POP
SIR?
TRUST ME, TROOPER FIRST CLASS.
YOU'LL WANT A MOMENTO OF YOUR FIRST CAPTURE.
OH GOD FORGIVE ME
THANK YOU, SI–
TROOPER FIRST CLASS?
WE'LL MAKE IT OFFICIAL TOMORROW, ONCE WE'VE MARSHED THIS MEAT TO THE FEEDLOT.
THE REST OF YOU, HELP CHO GET THIS CIVVIE TRUSSED.

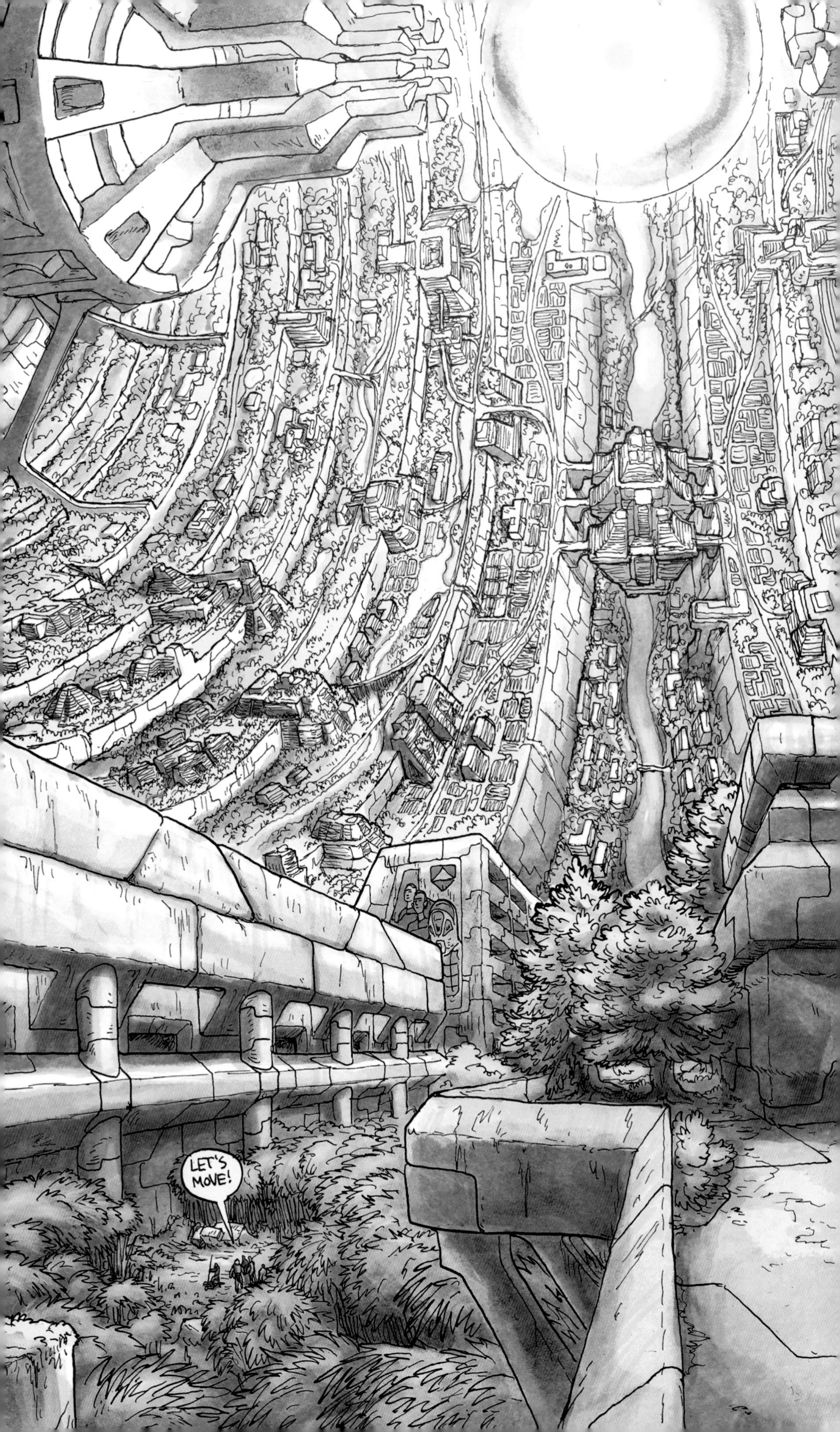
LET'S MOVE!

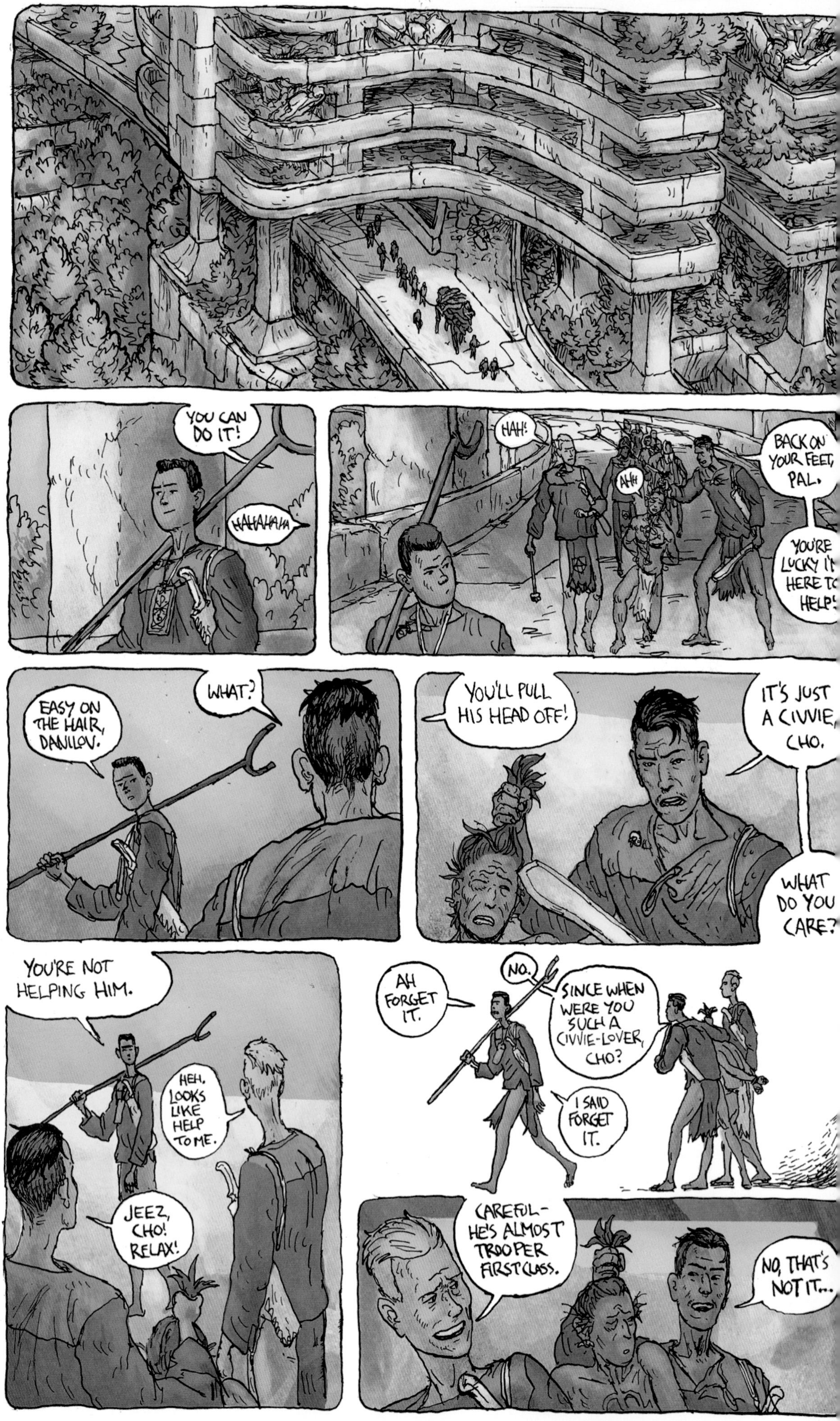
YOU CAN DO IT!
HAHAHAHA
HAH!
AHH
BACK ON YOUR FEET, PAL.
YOU'RE LUCKY I'M HERE TO HELP!
EASY ON THE HAIR, DANILOV.
WHAT?
YOU'LL PULL HIS HEAD OFF!
IT'S JUST A CIVVIE, CHO.
WHAT DO YOU CARE?
YOU'RE NOT HELPING HIM.
HEH. LOOKS LIKE HELP TO ME.
JEEZ, CHO! RELAX!
AH FORGET IT.
NO.
SINCE WHEN WERE YOU SUCH A CIVVIE-LOVER, CHO?
I SAID FORGET IT.
CAREFUL- HE'S ALMOST TROOPER FIRST CLASS.
NO, THAT'S NOT IT...

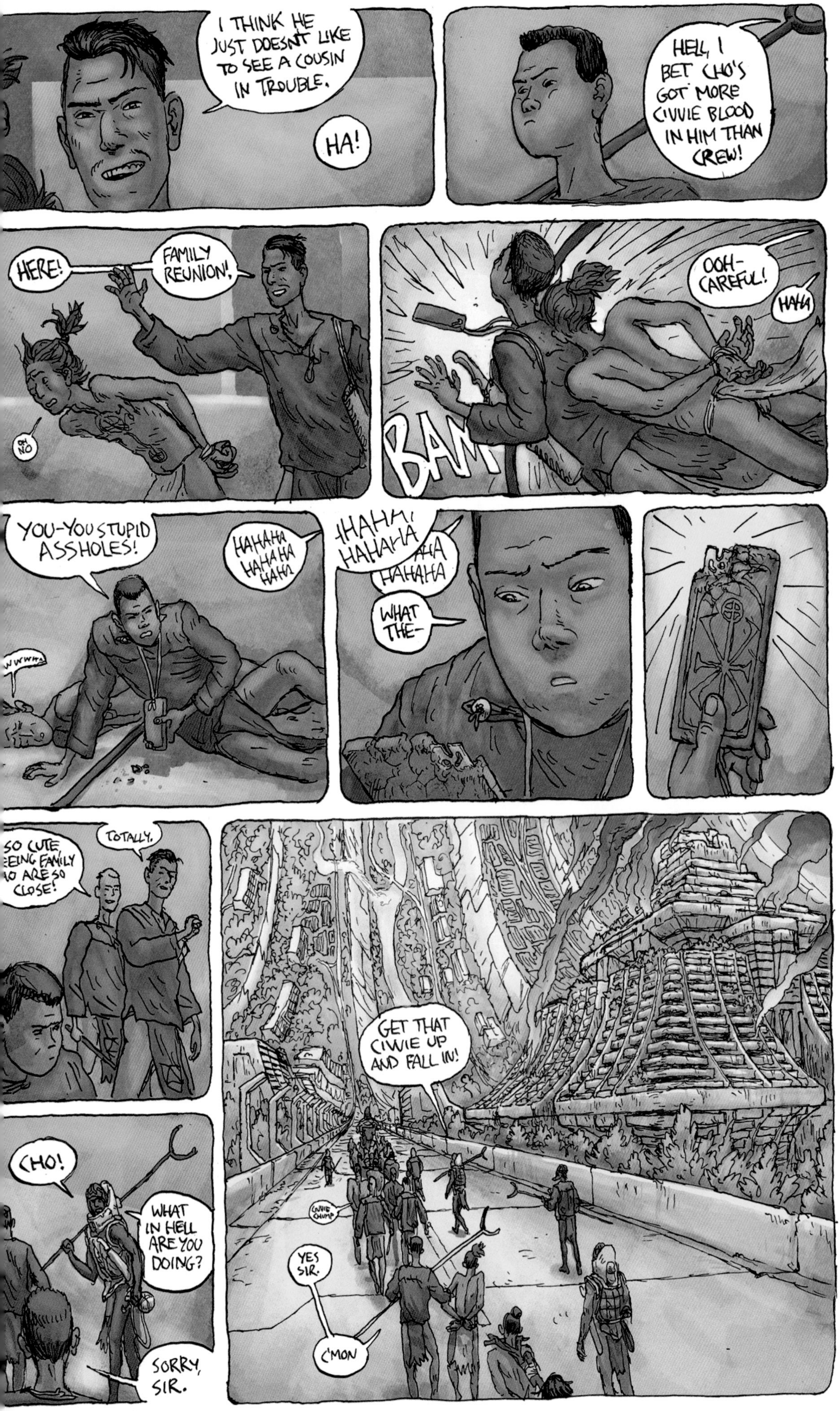
I THINK HE JUST DOESN'T LIKE TO SEE A COUSIN IN TROUBLE.
HA!
HELL, I BET CHO'S GOT MORE CIVVIE BLOOD IN HIM THAN CREW!
HERE!
FAMILY REUNION!
OH NO
OOH- CAREFUL!
HAHA
BAM
YOU-YOU STUPID ASSHOLES!
HAHAHA HAHAHA HAHA
WWWHA
HAHA HAHAHA HAHA HAHAHA
WHAT THE-
SO CUTE SEEING FAMILY WHO ARE SO CLOSE!
TOTALLY.
CHO!
WHAT IN HELL ARE YOU DOING?
SORRY, SIR.
GET THAT CIVVIE UP AND FALL IN!
CIVVIE CHUMP
YES SIR.
C'MON

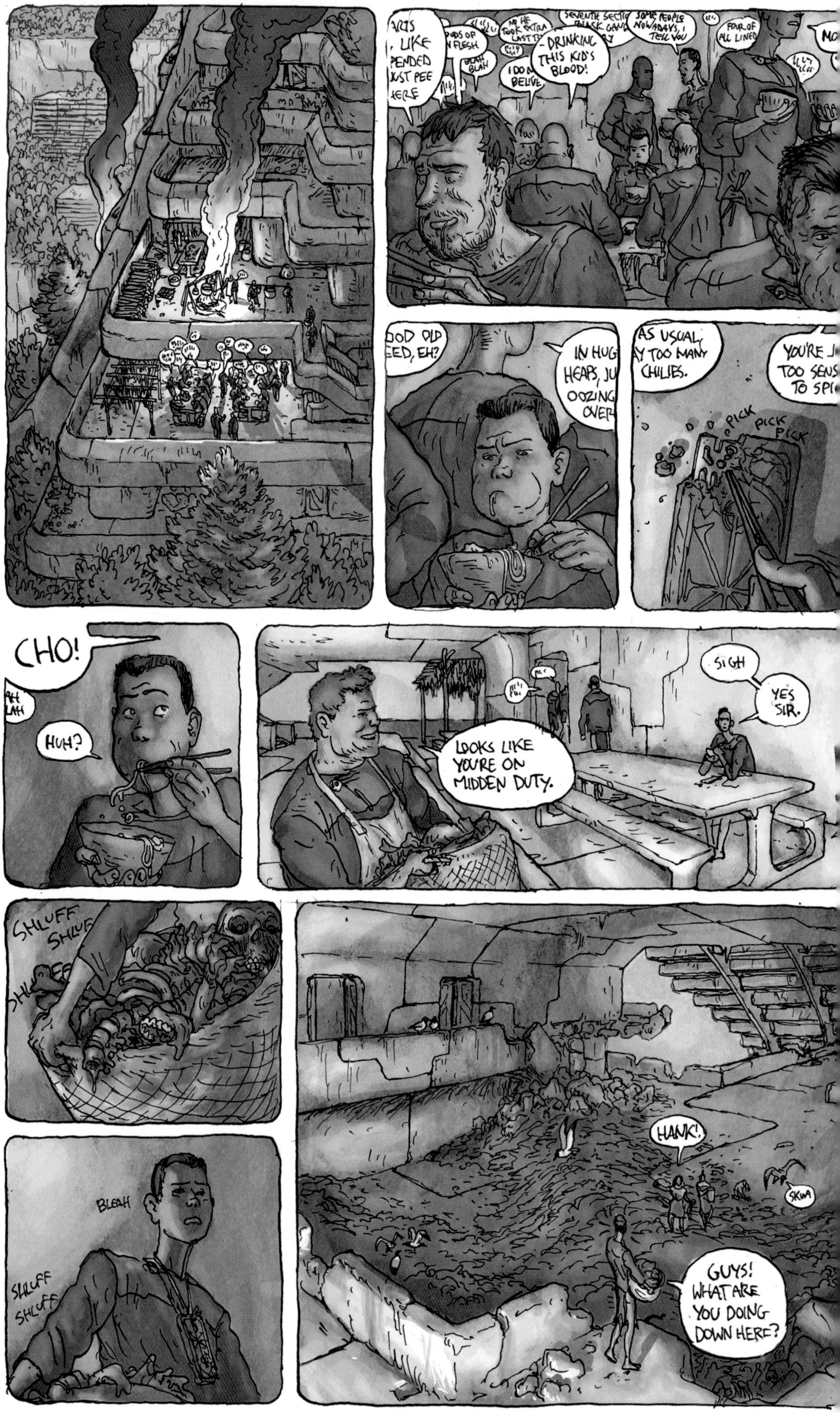

ARTS
, LIKE
PENDED
JUST PEE
HERE
PODS OF
N FLESH
BLAH
BLAH
NO HE
TOOK EXTRA
LAST TI
I DON
BELIVE
- DRINKING
THIS KID'S
BLOOD!
SEVENTH SECTIO
BLACK GANG
SOME PEOPLE
NOWADAYS, I
TELL YOU
FOUR OF
ALL LINED
MO
OOD OLD
EED, EH?
IN HUG
HEAPS, JU
OOZING
OVER
AS USUAL,
AY TOO MANY
CHILIES.
YOU'RE J
TOO SENS
TO SPI
PICK
PICK
PICK
CHO!
HUH?
SIGH
YES
SIR.
LOOKS LIKE
YOU'RE ON
MIDDEN DUTY.
SHLUFF
SHLUF
BLEAH
SHLUFF
SHLUFF
HANK!
SKWA
GUYS!
WHAT ARE
YOU DOING
DOWN HERE?

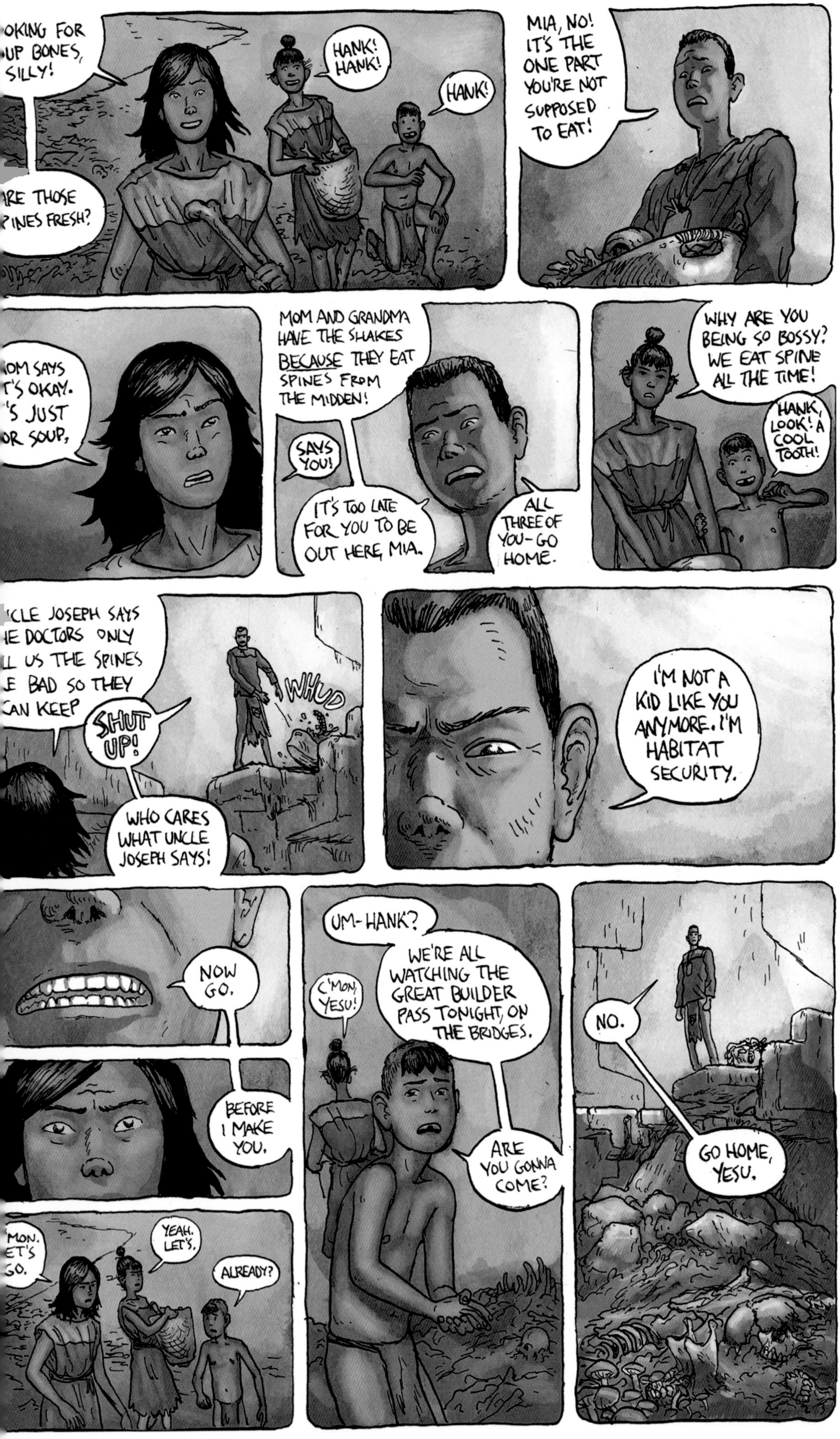

OKING FOR
UP BONES,
SILLY!
RE THOSE
PINES FRESH?
HANK! HANK!
HANK!
MIA, NO! IT'S THE ONE PART YOU'RE NOT SUPPOSED TO EAT!
OM SAYS
T'S OKAY.
'S JUST
OR SOUP,
MOM AND GRANDMA HAVE THE SHAKES BECAUSE THEY EAT SPINES FROM THE MIDDEN!
SAYS YOU!
IT'S TOO LATE FOR YOU TO BE OUT HERE, MIA.
ALL THREE OF YOU- GO HOME.
WHY ARE YOU BEING SO BOSSY? WE EAT SPINE ALL THE TIME!
HANK, LOOK! A COOL TOOTH!
ICLE JOSEPH SAYS
IE DOCTORS ONLY
L US THE SPINES
E BAD SO THEY
CAN KEEP
SHUT UP!
WHUD
WHO CARES WHAT UNCLE JOSEPH SAYS!
I'M NOT A KID LIKE YOU ANYMORE. I'M HABITAT SECURITY.
NOW GO.
BEFORE I MAKE YOU.
MON.
ET'S
GO.
YEAH. LET'S.
ALREADY?
UM- HANK?
C'MON, YESU!
WE'RE ALL WATCHING THE GREAT BUILDER PASS TONIGHT, ON THE BRIDGES.
ARE YOU GONNA COME?
NO.
GO HOME, YESU.

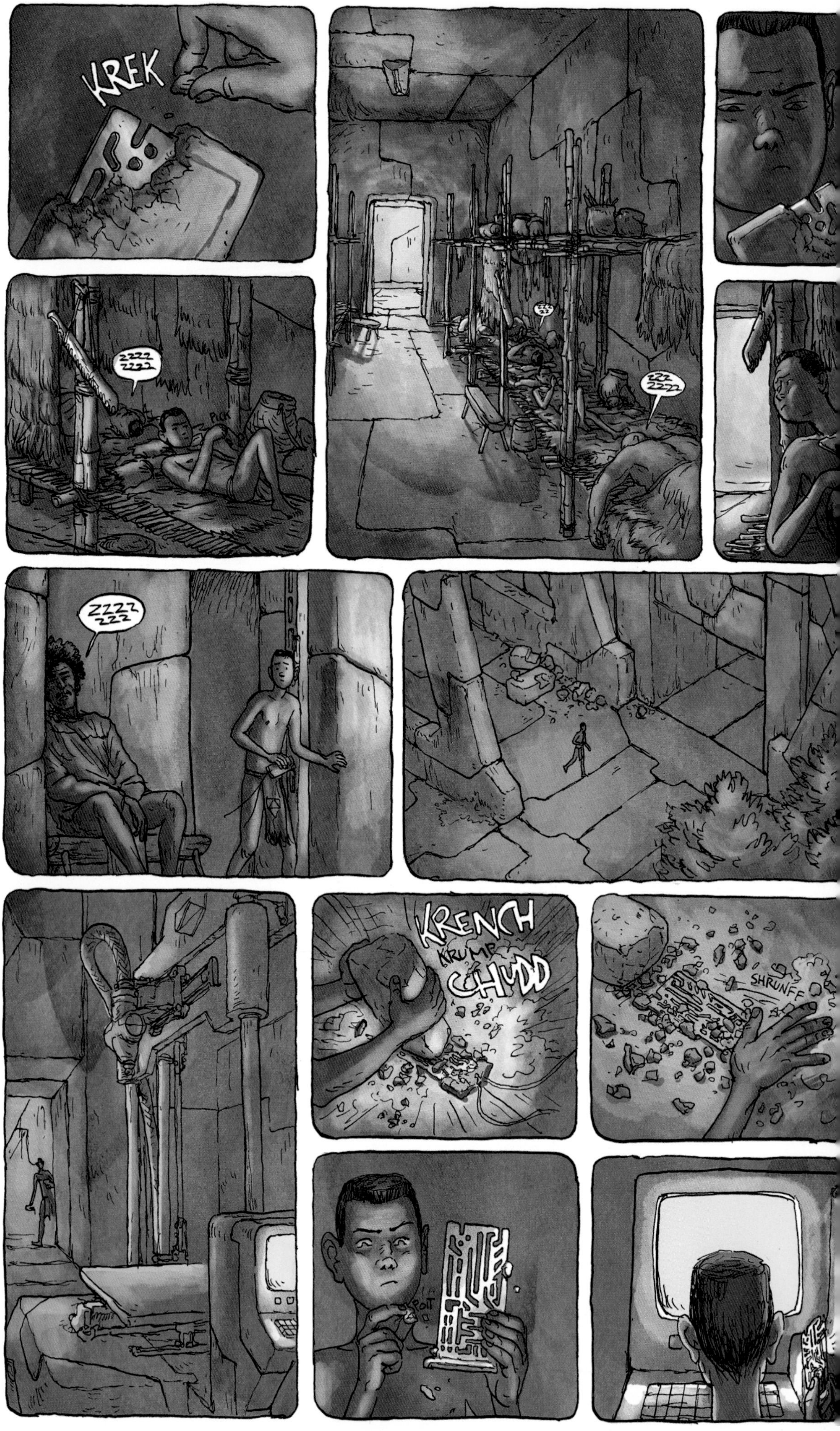
KREK
ZZZZ ZZZZ
PICK
ZZZ ZZ
ZZZ ZZZZ
ZZZZ ZZZ
KRENCH
KRUMP
CHUDD
SHRUNFF
POIT

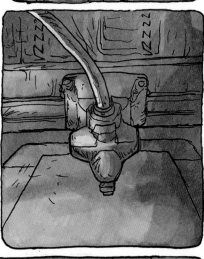

KLIK

KLIK

KLIK

ZZZZ ZZZZ

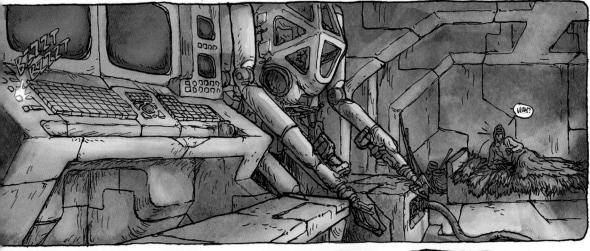

BZZZT BZZZT

KLIK?

DOCTOR, WHAT IS IT?

WAKE THE LIEUTENANT.

BZZZT

BUHHHH

DOCTOR, WHY AM I AWAKE?

AS IF YOU DON'T KNOW!

FRANKLY, I WILL PUT UP WITH THESE PRANKS NO LONGER!

MEDICAL DOE NOT EXIST T BE THE BUT OF SECURIT JOKES!

WHAT IN HELL ARE YOU BABBLING ABOUT?

THE PRINTER, MAN! ITS USE IS FORBIDDEN TO ALL BUT SENIOR MEDICAL STAFF!

YET SOMEONE, I'D BET ONE OF YOUR BOORISH REDSHIRTS, IS RUNNING IT RIGHT NOW!

WHAT? WHY WOULD A REDSHIRT USE YOUR DAMNED PRINTER?

I'M NOT THE BLOODY JOKESTER!

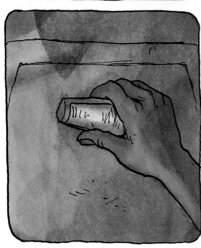

CLIK

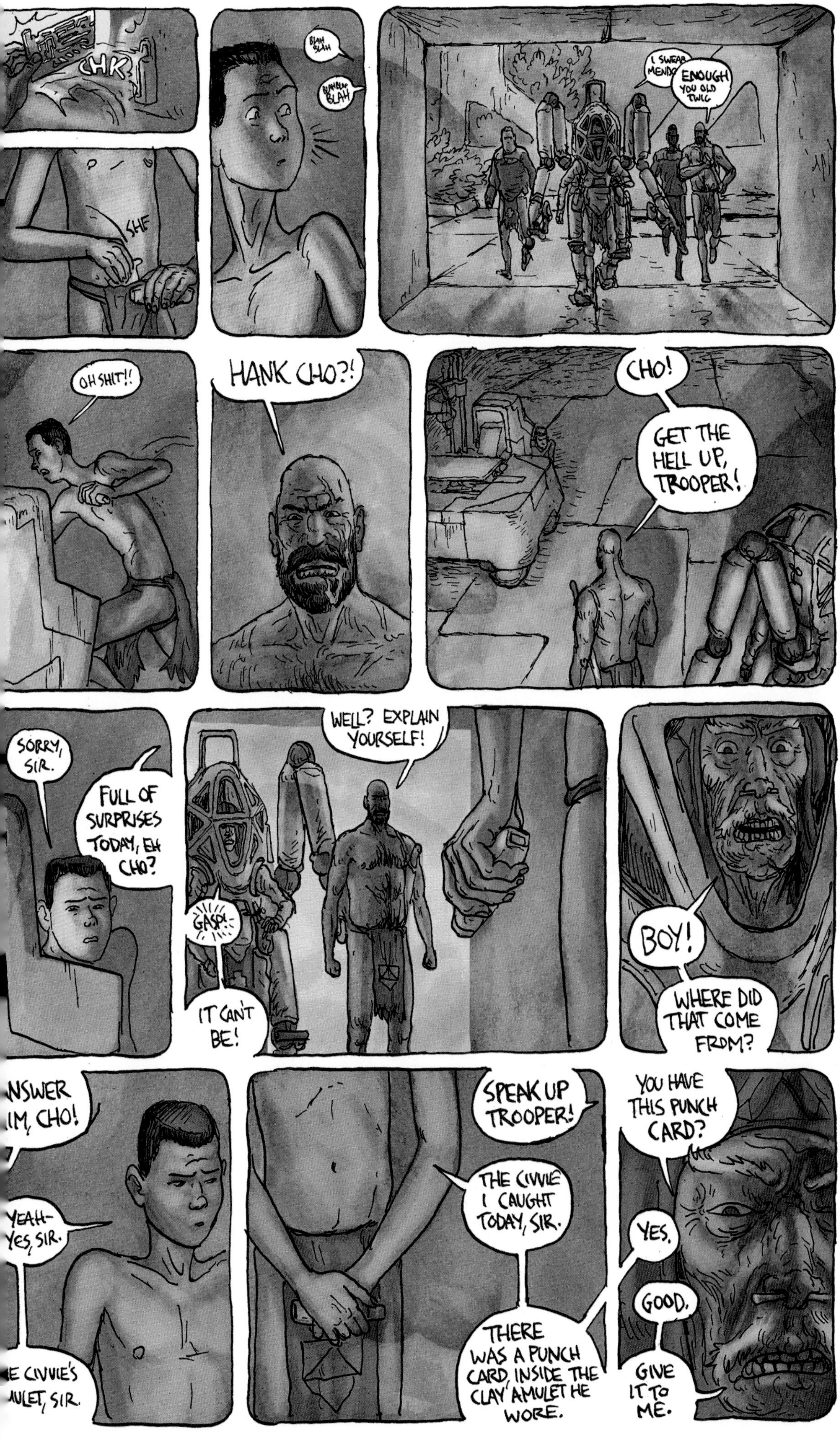
CHK
BLAH BLAH
BLAH BLAH BLAH
SHF
I SWEAR MENDO
ENOUGH YOU OLD TWIG
OH SHIT!!
HANK CHO?!
CHO!
GET THE HELL UP, TROOPER!
SORRY, SIR.
FULL OF SURPRISES TODAY, EH CHO?
WELL? EXPLAIN YOURSELF!
GASP!
IT CAN'T BE!
BOY!
WHERE DID THAT COME FROM?
NSWER IM, CHO!
YEAH- YES, SIR.
E CIVVIE'S ULET, SIR.
SPEAK UP TROOPER!
THE CIVVIE I CAUGHT TODAY, SIR.
THERE WAS A PUNCH CARD, INSIDE THE CLAY AMULET HE WORE.
YOU HAVE THIS PUNCH CARD?
YES.
GOOD.
GIVE IT TO ME.

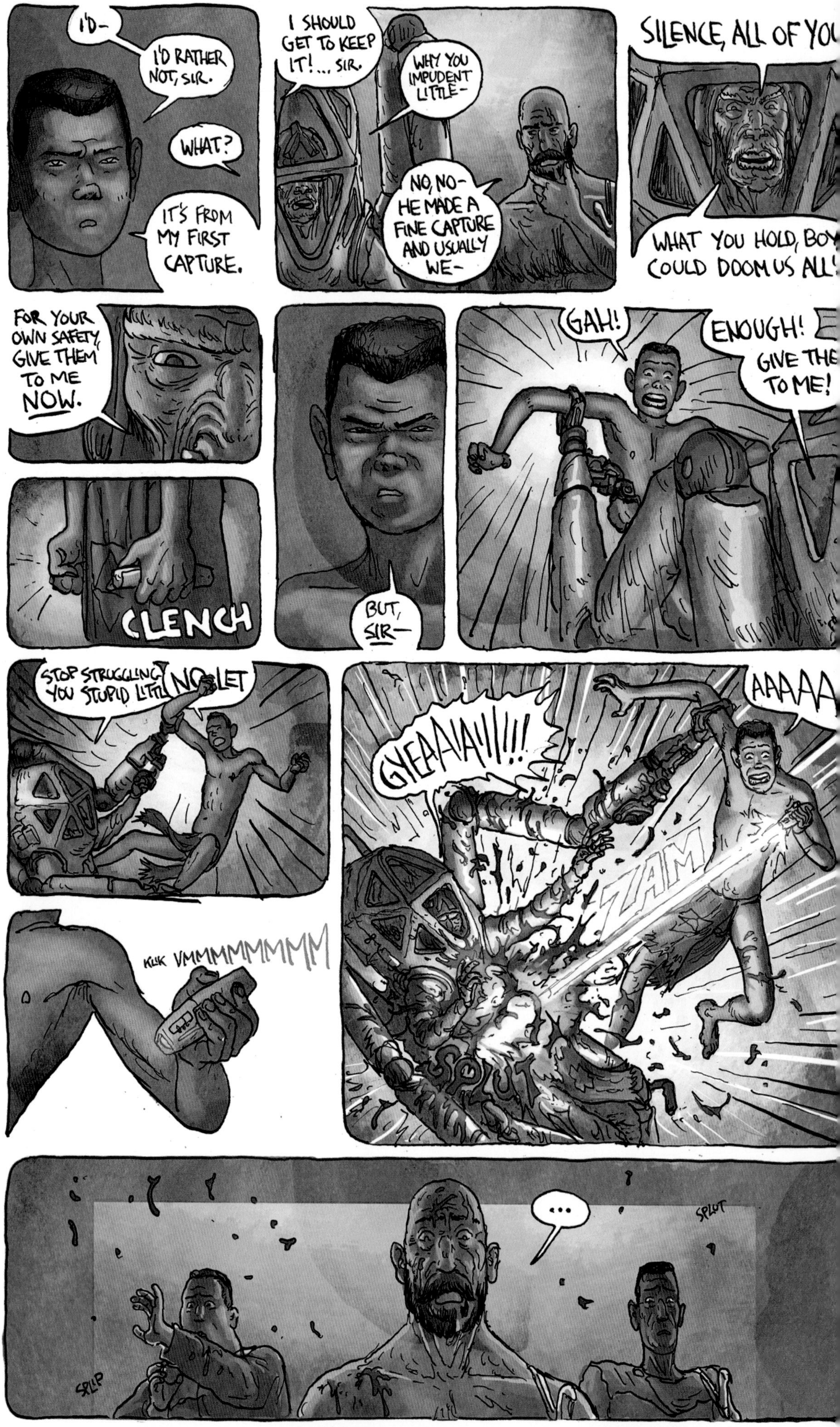
I'D-
I'D RATHER NOT, SIR.
WHAT?
IT'S FROM MY FIRST CAPTURE.
I SHOULD GET TO KEEP IT!... SIR.
WHY YOU IMPUDENT LITTLE-
NO, NO- HE MADE A FINE CAPTURE AND USUALLY WE-
SILENCE, ALL OF YOU
WHAT YOU HOLD, BOY COULD DOOM US ALL!
FOR YOUR OWN SAFETY, GIVE THEM TO ME NOW.
BUT, SIR—
GAH!
ENOUGH! GIVE THE TO ME!
CLENCH
STOP STRUGGLING YOU STUPID LITTL
NO LET
KLIK VMMMMMMMMM
AAAAA
GYEAAAA!!!!!
ZAM
SPLUT
...
SPLUT
SPLUP

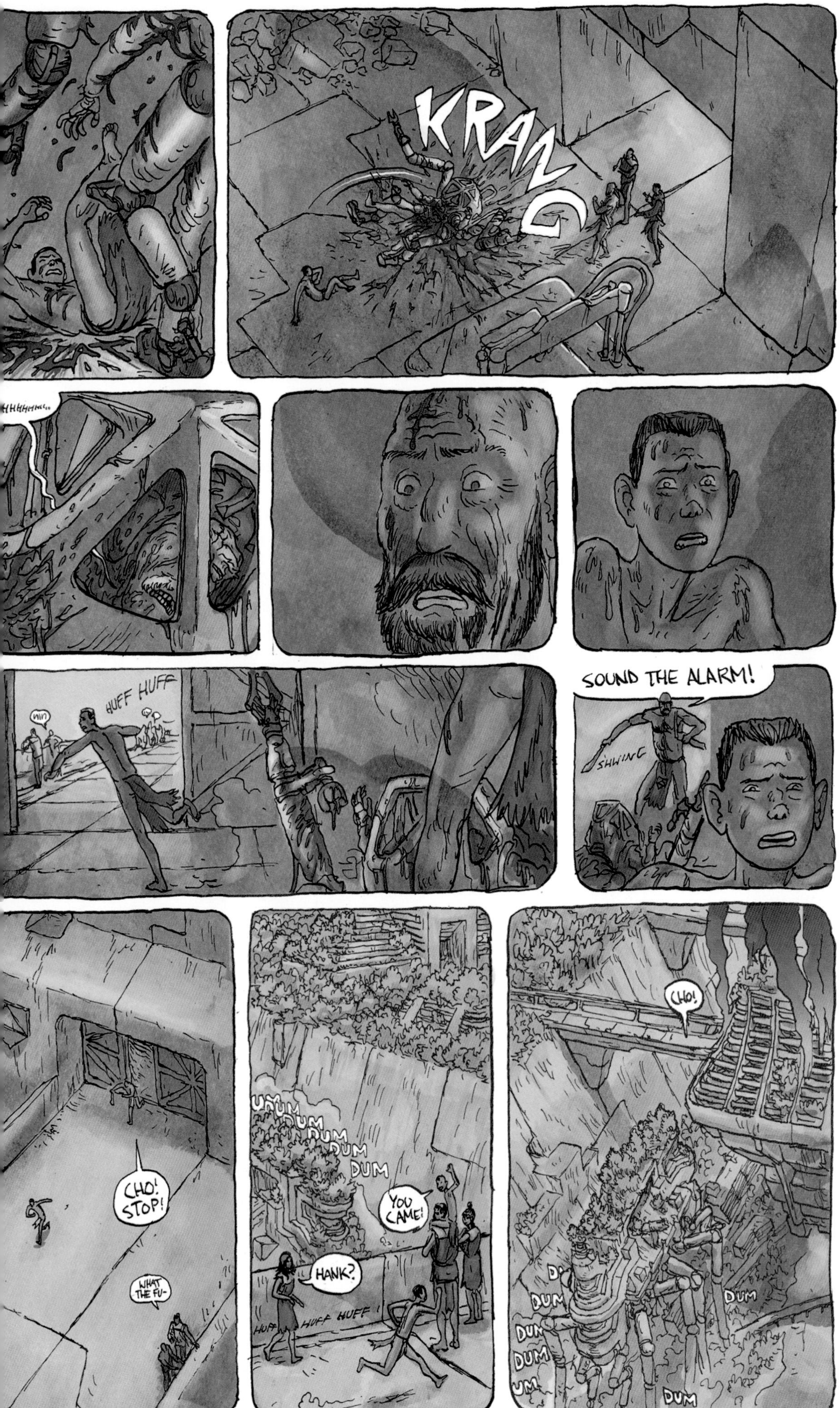
KRANG
HUFF HUFF
SOUND THE ALARM!
SHWING
CHO! STOP!
WHAT THE FU-
UMUM DUM DUM DUM DUM
YOU CAME!
HANK?
HUFF
HUFF HUFF
CHO!
DUM
DUM
DUM
DUM
UM
DUM

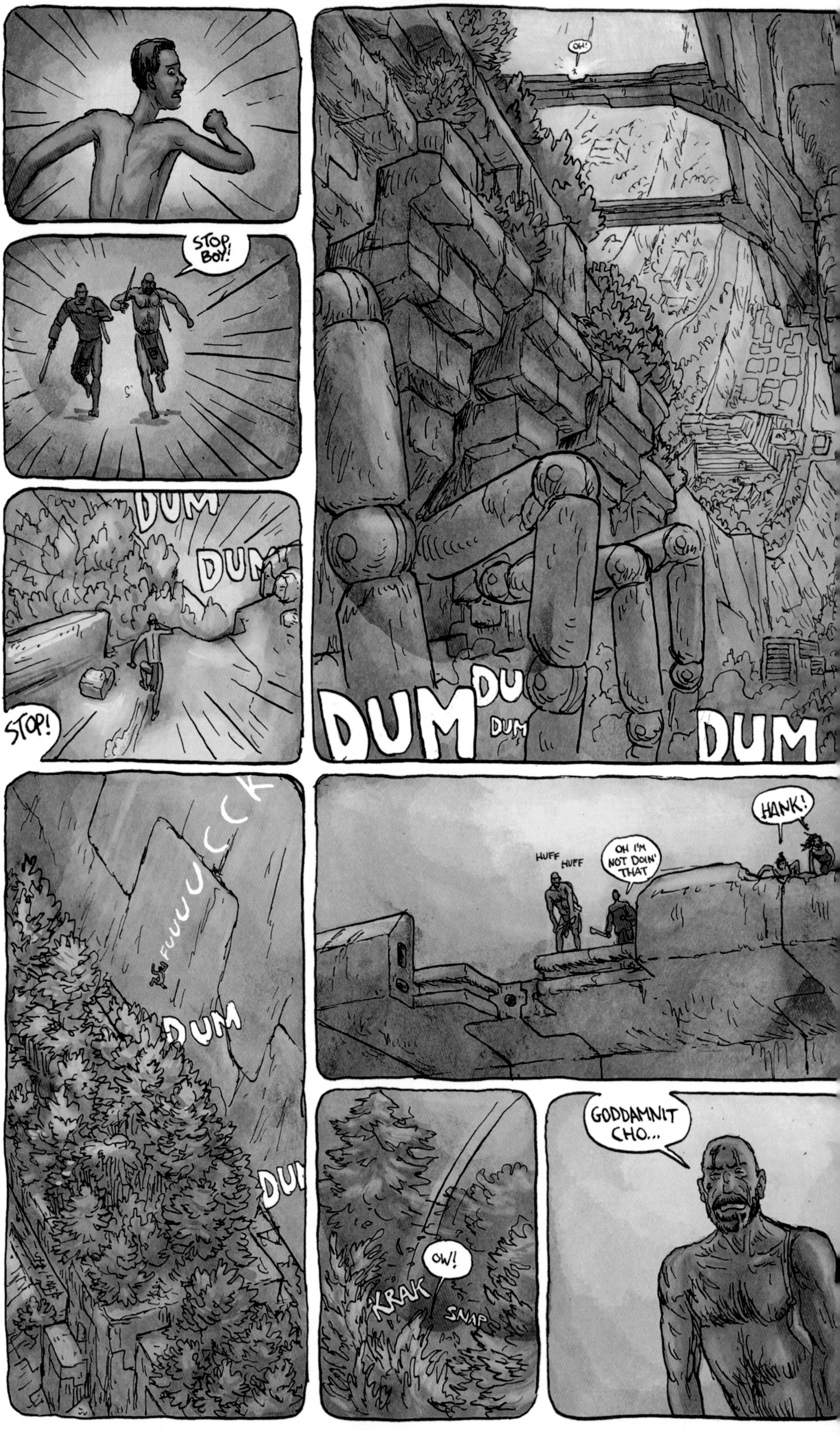
STOP BOY!
DUM
DUM
STOP!
OH!
DUM
DU
DUM
DUM
FUUUUCCCK
DUM
DUM
HUFF HUFF
OH I'M NOT DOIN' THAT
HANK!
OW!
KRAK
SNAP
GODDAMNIT CHO...

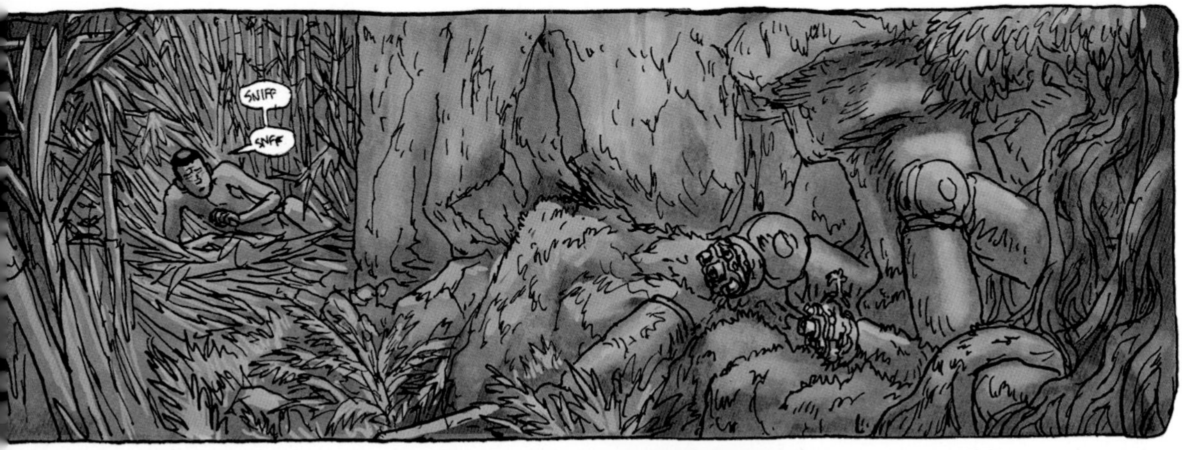
SNIFF
SNIFF

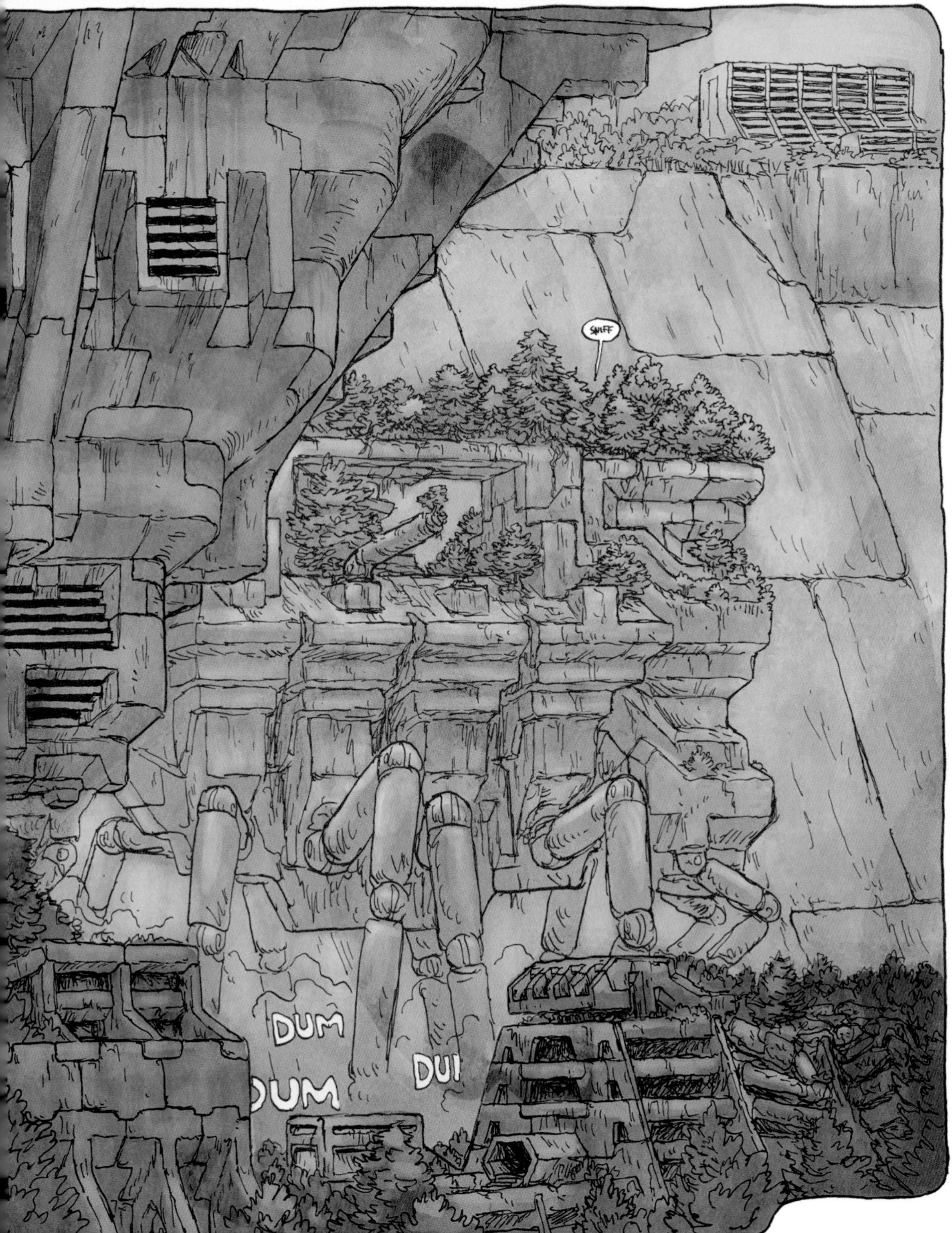
SNIFF
DUM
DUM
DUI

SIR!

HUFF

KLANG

HUFF

HUFF

HUFF

WHAT DID I SAY ABOUT MY MORNING REPS, ENSIGN?

I KNOW, SIR. SORRY, SIR.

BUT THE CAPTAIN WANTS YOU IN OPERATIONS, IMMEDIATELY.

CLENCH

FINALLY, OUR OTHER MENDOZA!

SIR!

SORRY, SIR.

OF COURSE, OF COURSE.

NOW THAT WE'RE ALL HERE, LIEUTENANT...

DAD?

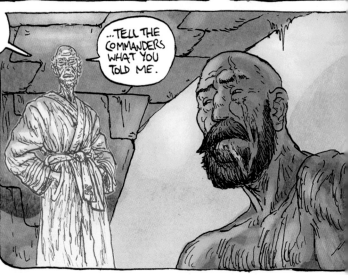

...TELL THE COMMANDERS WHAT YOU TOLD ME.

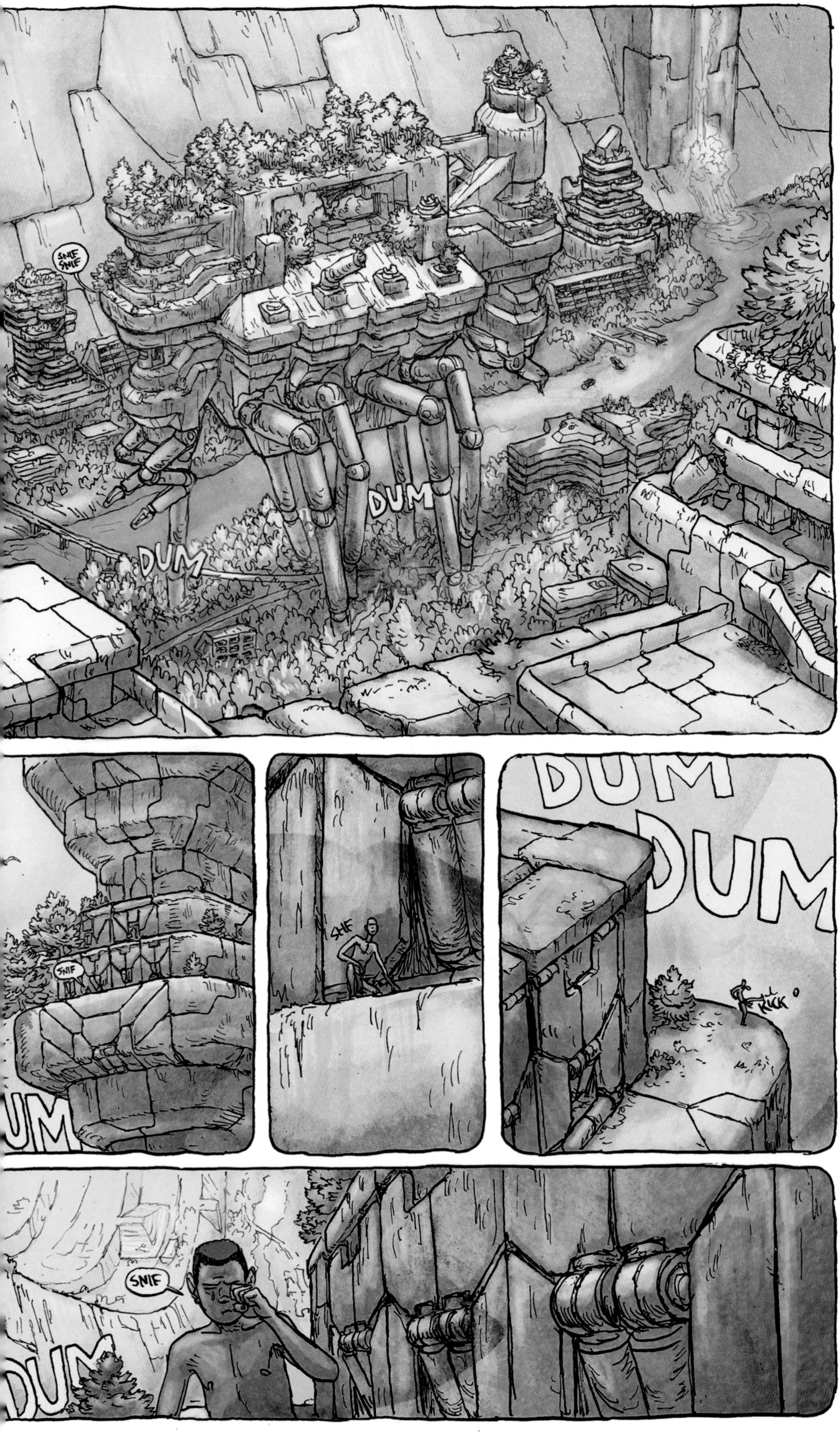
SNIF SNIF
DUM
DUM
SNIF
UM
SNIF
DUM
DUM
KICK
SNIF
DUM

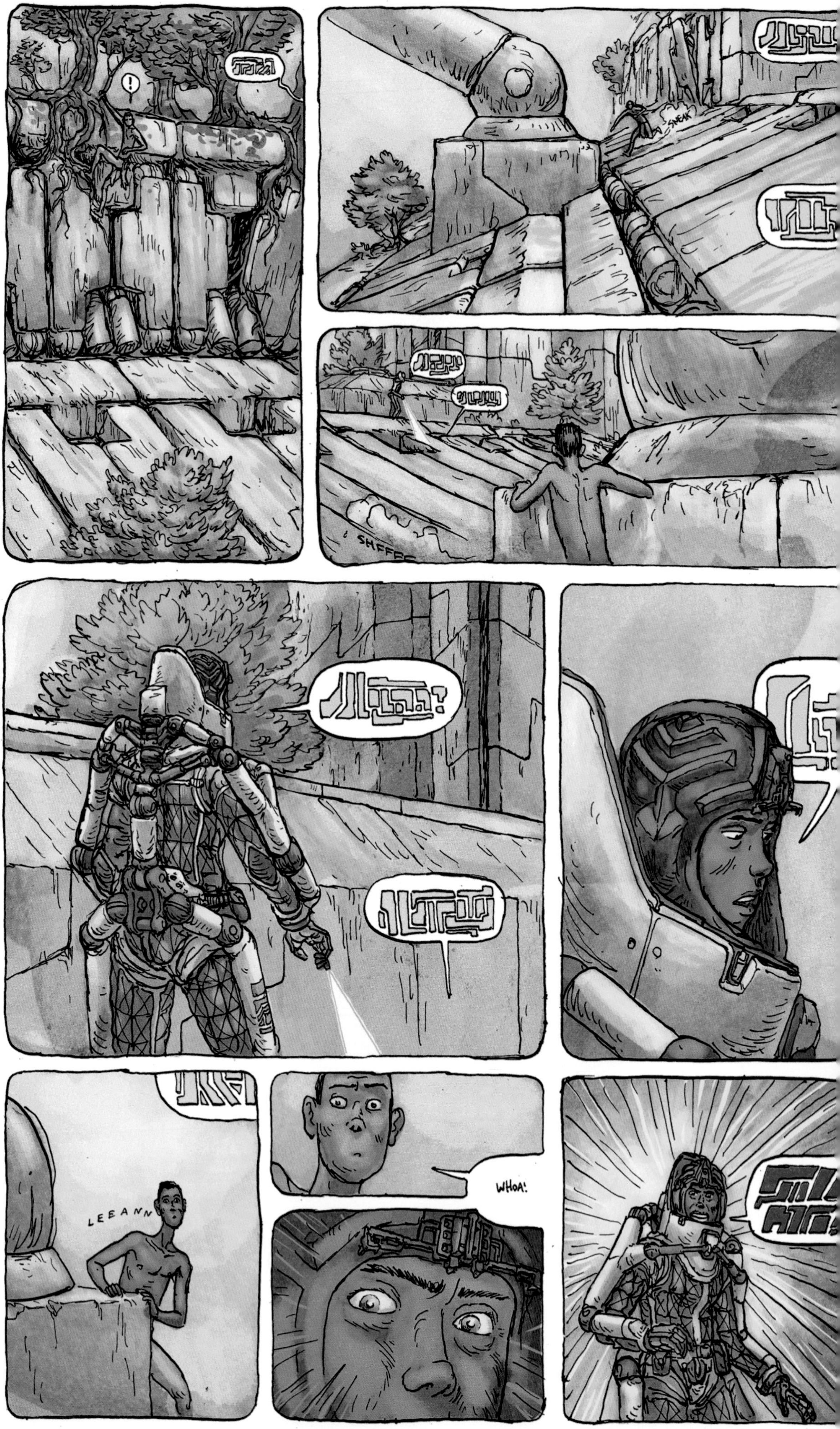
!
SNEAK
SHFFF
LEEANN
WHOA!

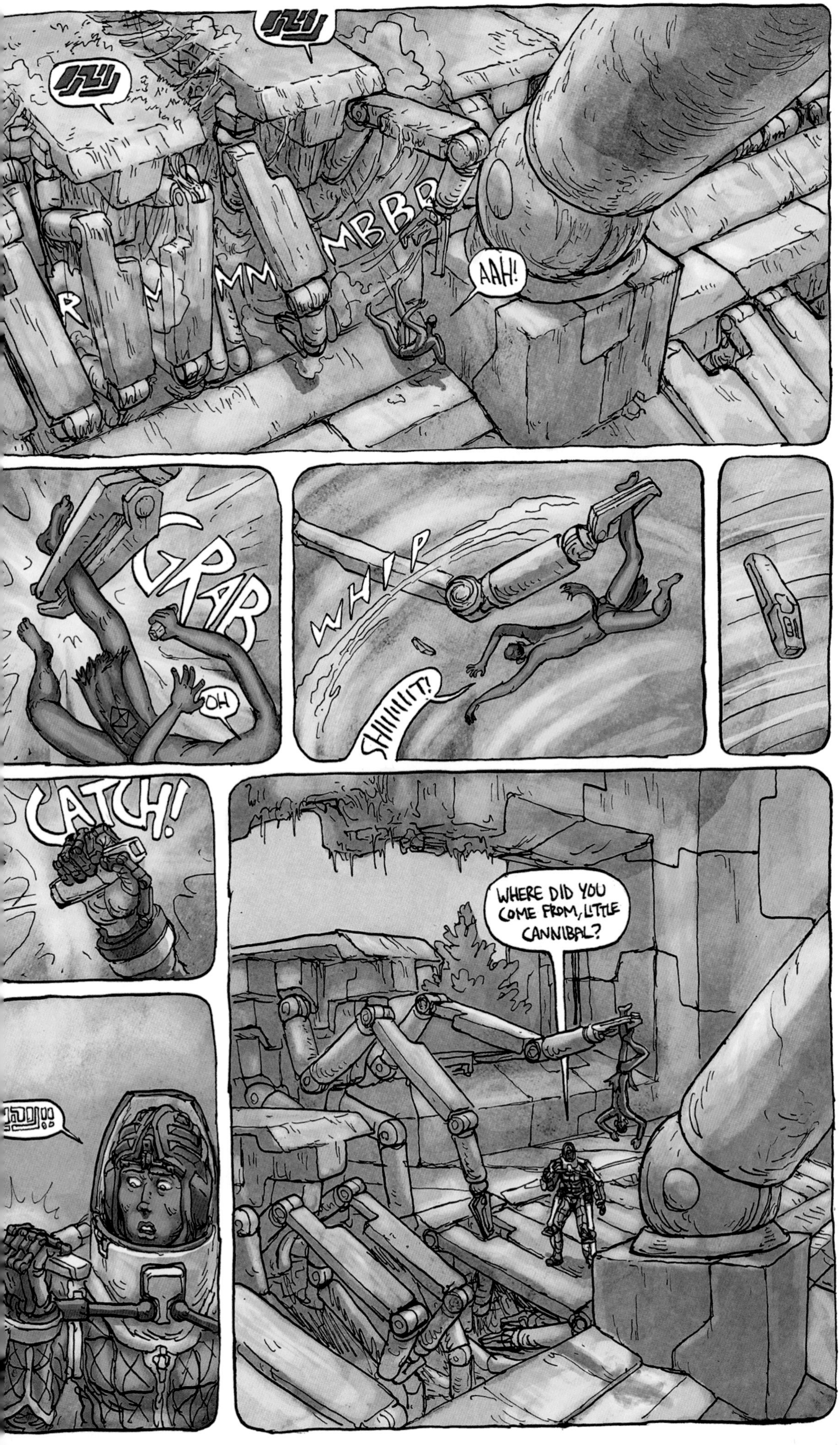
RUMMMBBR
AAH!
GRAB
OH
WHIP
SHIIIIIT!
CATCH!
WHERE DID YOU COME FROM, LITTLE CANNIBAL?

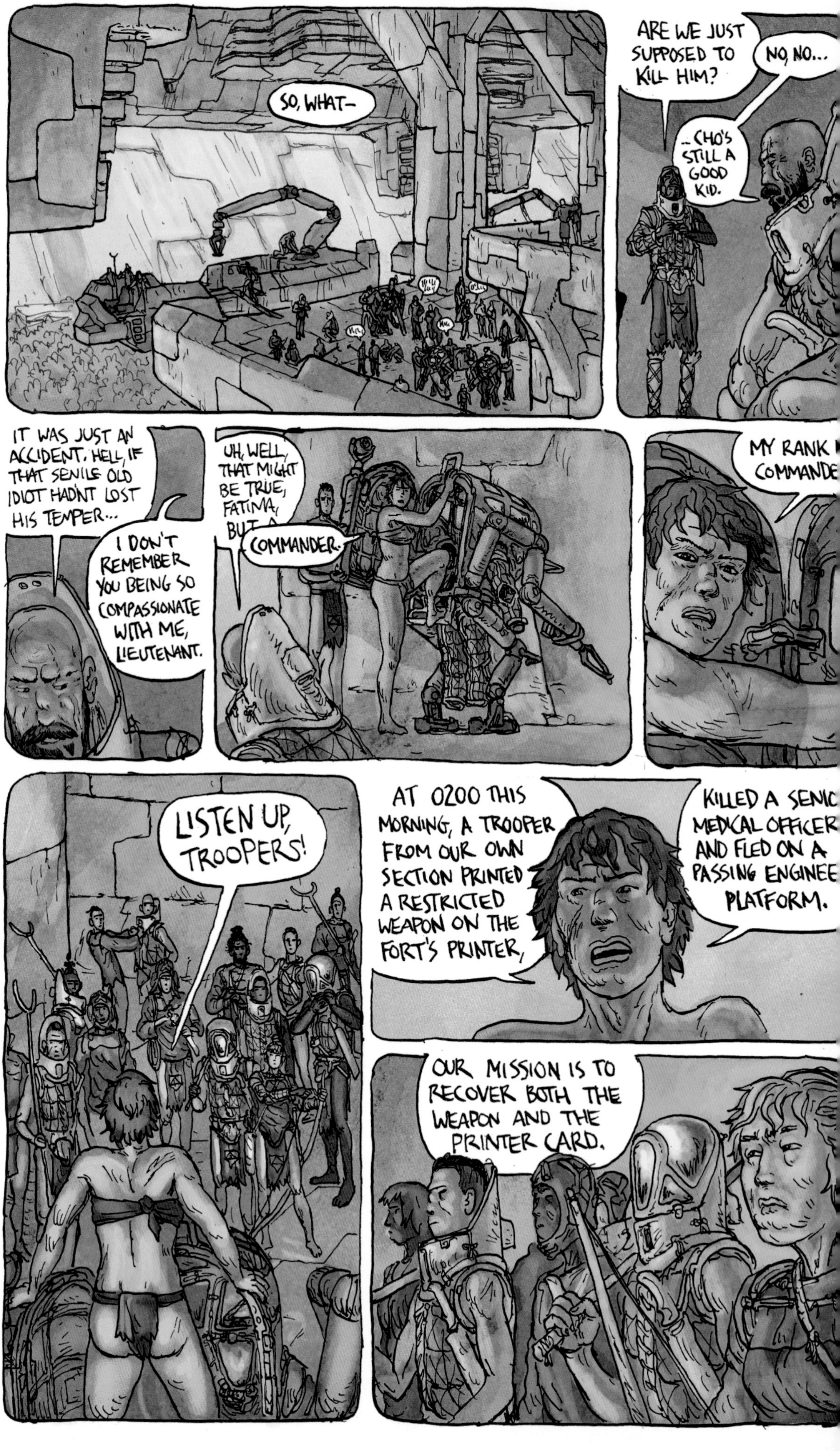
SO, WHAT-
ARE WE JUST SUPPOSED TO KILL HIM?
NO, NO...
...CHO'S STILL A GOOD KID.
IT WAS JUST AN ACCIDENT. HELL, IF THAT SENILE OLD IDIOT HADN'T LOST HIS TEMPER...
I DON'T REMEMBER YOU BEING SO COMPASSIONATE WITH ME, LIEUTENANT.
UH, WELL, THAT MIGHT BE TRUE, FATIMA, BUT A
COMMANDER.
MY RANK
COMMANDE
LISTEN UP, TROOPERS!
AT 0200 THIS MORNING, A TROOPER FROM OUR OWN SECTION PRINTED A RESTRICTED WEAPON ON THE FORT'S PRINTER,
KILLED A SENIO MEDICAL OFFICER AND FLED ON A PASSING ENGINEE PLATFORM.
OUR MISSION IS TO RECOVER BOTH THE WEAPON AND THE PRINTER CARD.

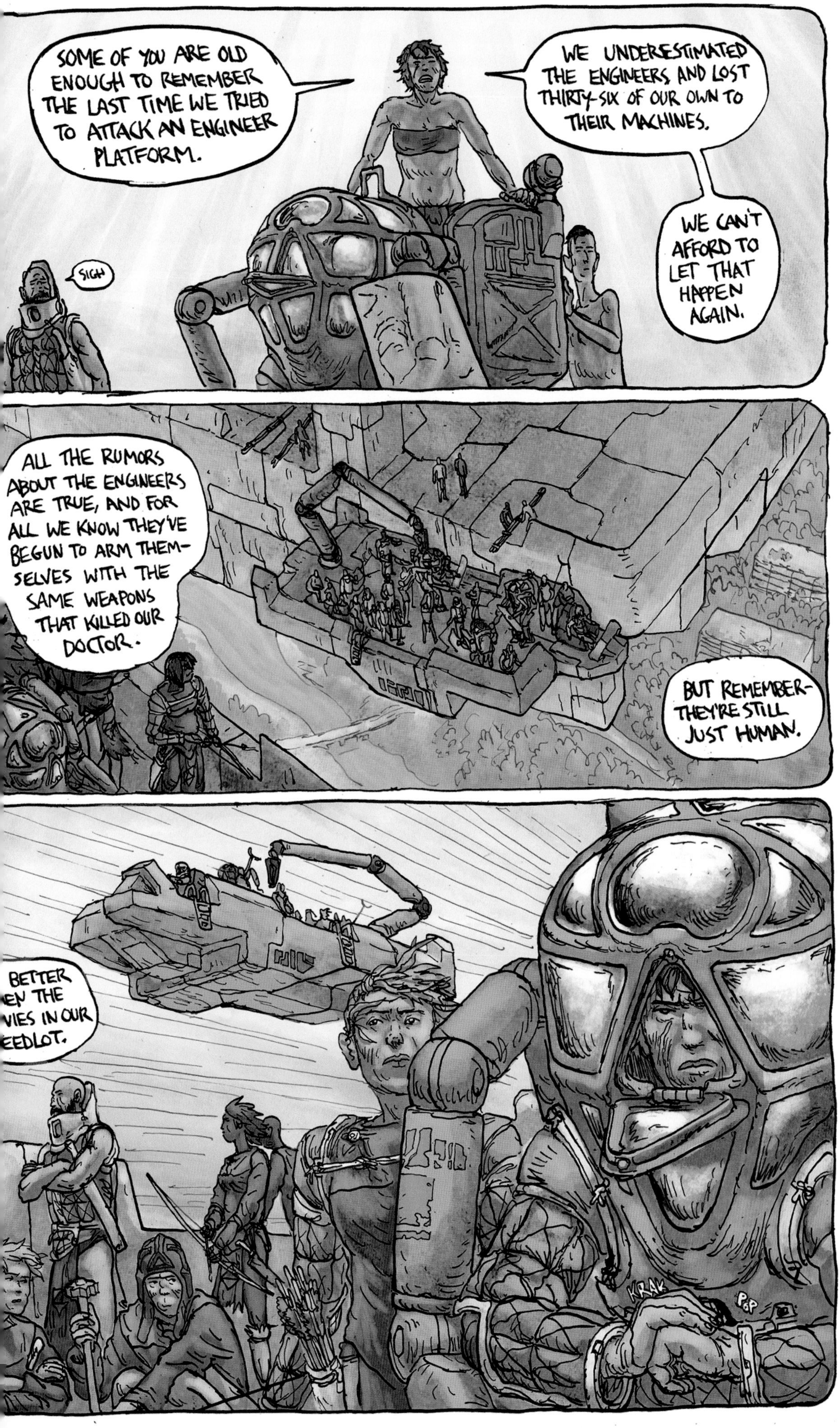
SOME OF YOU ARE OLD ENOUGH TO REMEMBER THE LAST TIME WE TRIED TO ATTACK AN ENGINEER PLATFORM.
WE UNDERESTIMATED THE ENGINEERS AND LOST THIRTY-SIX OF OUR OWN TO THEIR MACHINES.
SIGH
WE CAN'T AFFORD TO LET THAT HAPPEN AGAIN.
ALL THE RUMORS ABOUT THE ENGINEERS ARE TRUE, AND FOR ALL WE KNOW THEY'VE BEGUN TO ARM THEMSELVES WITH THE SAME WEAPONS THAT KILLED OUR DOCTOR.
BUT REMEMBER- THEY'RE STILL JUST HUMAN.
BETTER
EN THE
VIES IN OUR
EEDLOT.
KRAK
POP

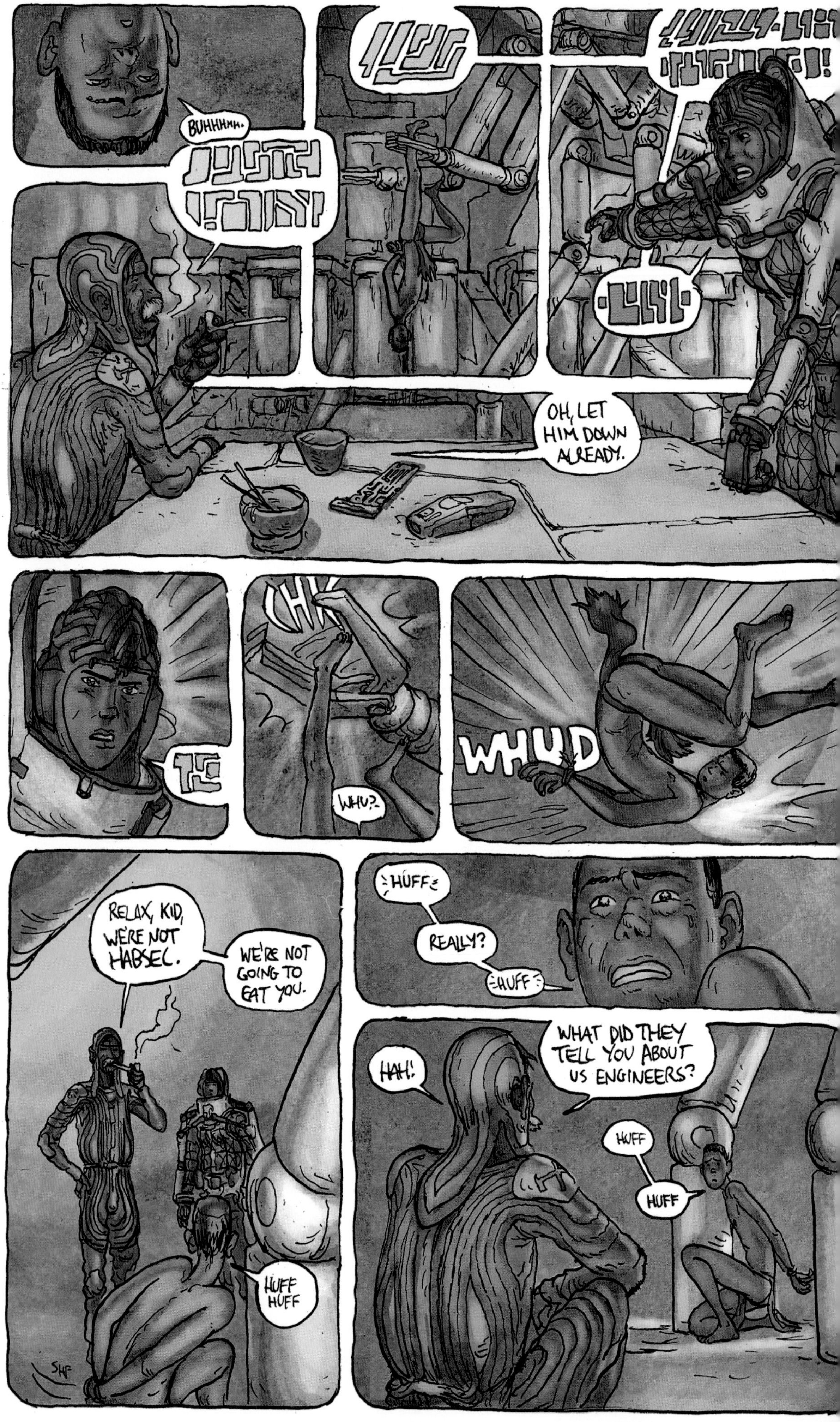
BUHHHMM..
OH, LET HIM DOWN ALREADY.
WHU?
WHUD
RELAX, KID, WE'RE NOT HABSEC.
WE'RE NOT GOING TO EAT YOU.
HUFF HUFF
HUFF
REALLY?
HUFF
HAH!
WHAT DID THEY TELL YOU ABOUT US ENGINEERS?
HUFF
HUFF

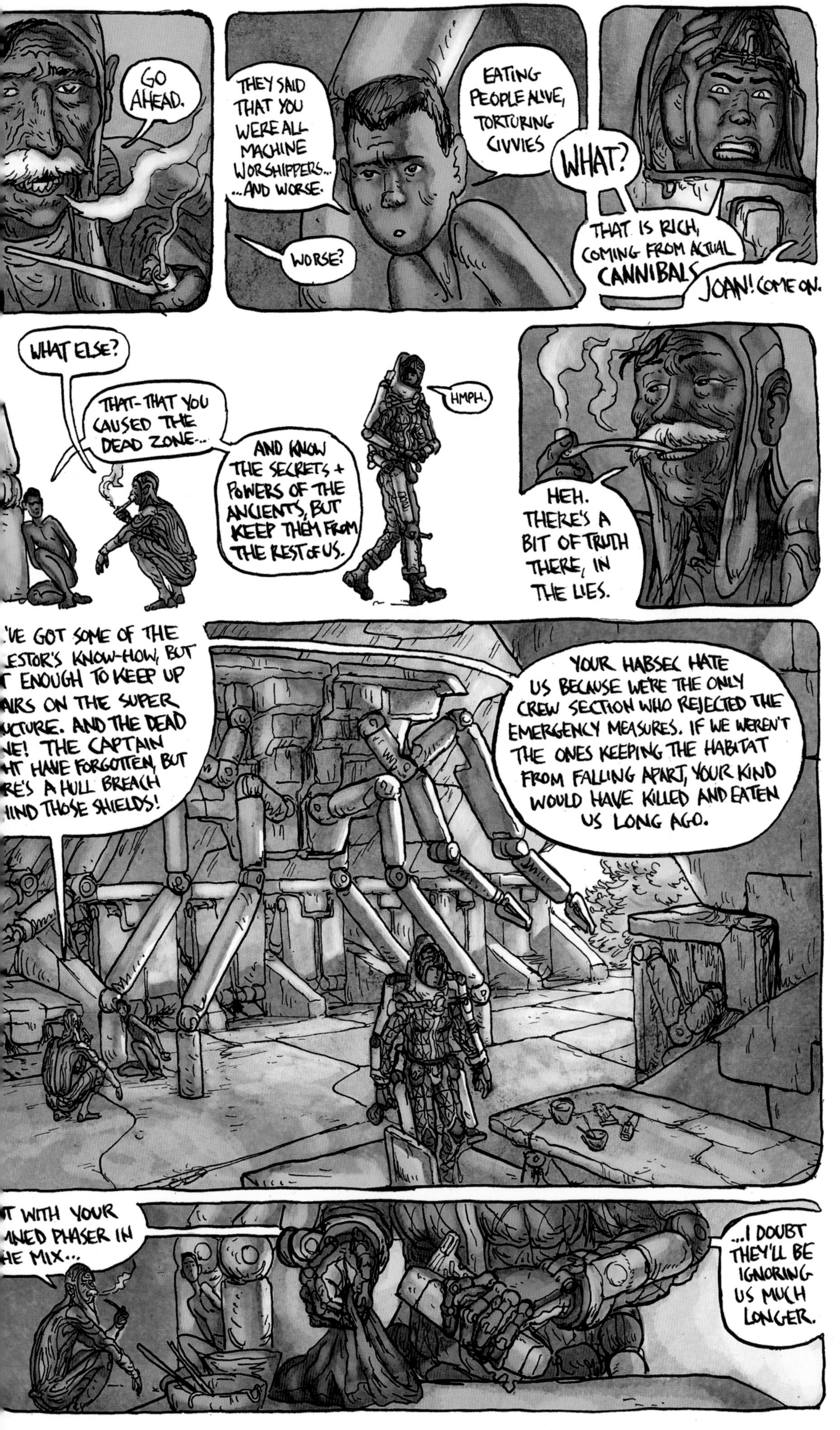
GO AHEAD.
THEY SAID THAT YOU WERE ALL MACHINE WORSHIPPERS... ...AND WORSE.
WORSE?
EATING PEOPLE ALIVE, TORTURING CIVVIES
WHAT?
THAT IS RICH, COMING FROM ACTUAL CANNIBALS
JOAN! COME ON.
WHAT ELSE?
THAT-THAT YOU CAUSED THE DEAD ZONE...
AND KNOW THE SECRETS + POWERS OF THE ANCIENTS, BUT KEEP THEM FROM THE REST OF US.
HMPH.
HEH. THERE'S A BIT OF TRUTH THERE, IN THE LIES.
'VE GOT SOME OF THE ESTOR'S KNOW-HOW, BUT T ENOUGH TO KEEP UP AIRS ON THE SUPER UCTURE. AND THE DEAD NE! THE CAPTAIN HT HAVE FORGOTTEN, BUT RE'S A HULL BREACH HIND THOSE SHIELDS!
YOUR HABSEC HATE US BECAUSE WE'RE THE ONLY CREW SECTION WHO REJECTED THE EMERGENCY MEASURES. IF WE WEREN'T THE ONES KEEPING THE HABITAT FROM FALLING APART, YOUR KIND WOULD HAVE KILLED AND EATEN US LONG AGO.
T WITH YOUR NED PHASER IN HE MIX...
...I DOUBT THEY'LL BE IGNORING US MUCH LONGER.

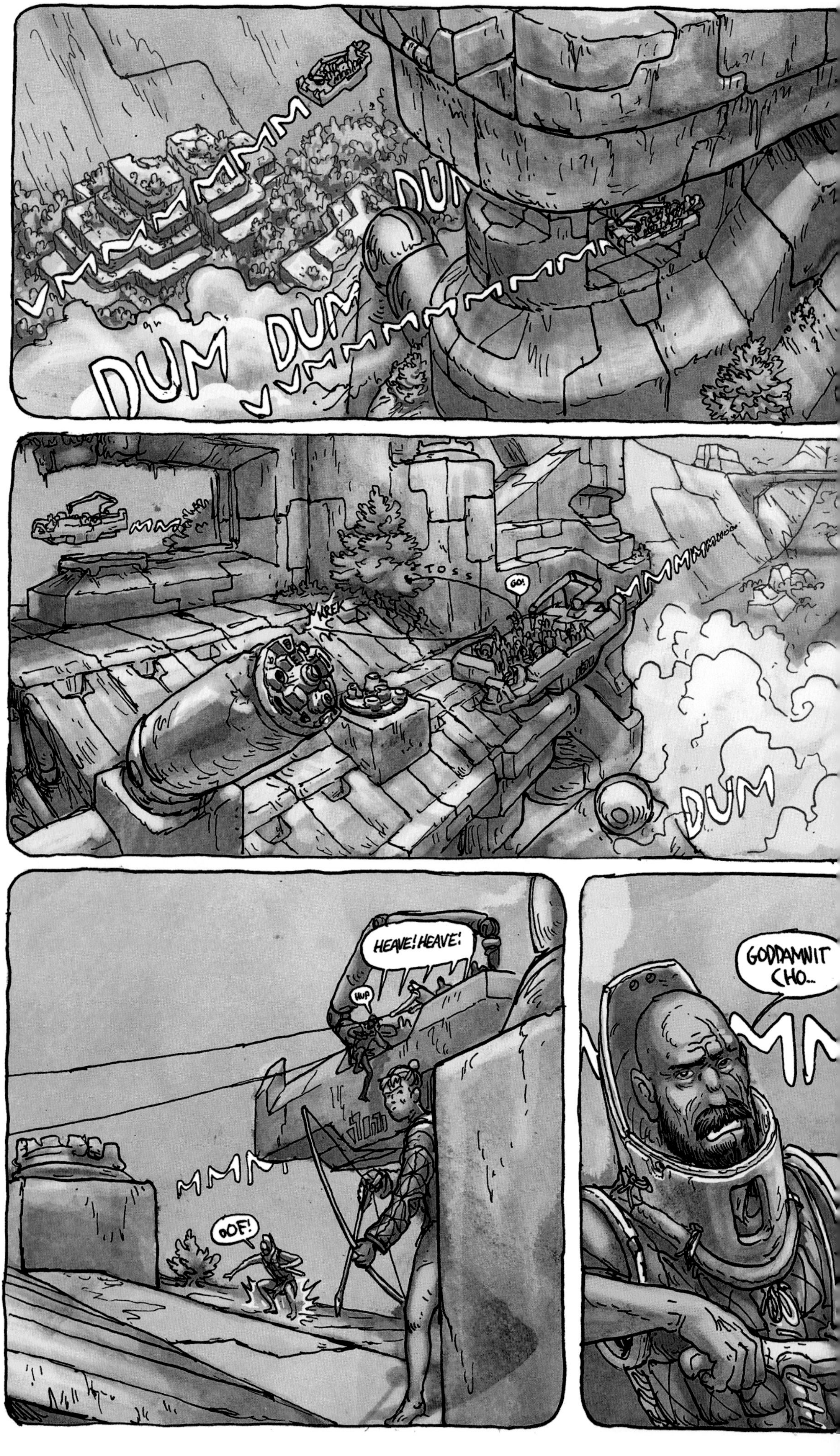
VMMMMMMMMM
DUM
DUM DUM
VMMMMMMMMMMMMM
MMM
TOSS
GO!
KREK
MMMMMMMM
DUM
HEAVE! HEAVE!
HUP
MMM
OOF!
GODDAMNIT CHO...
MM

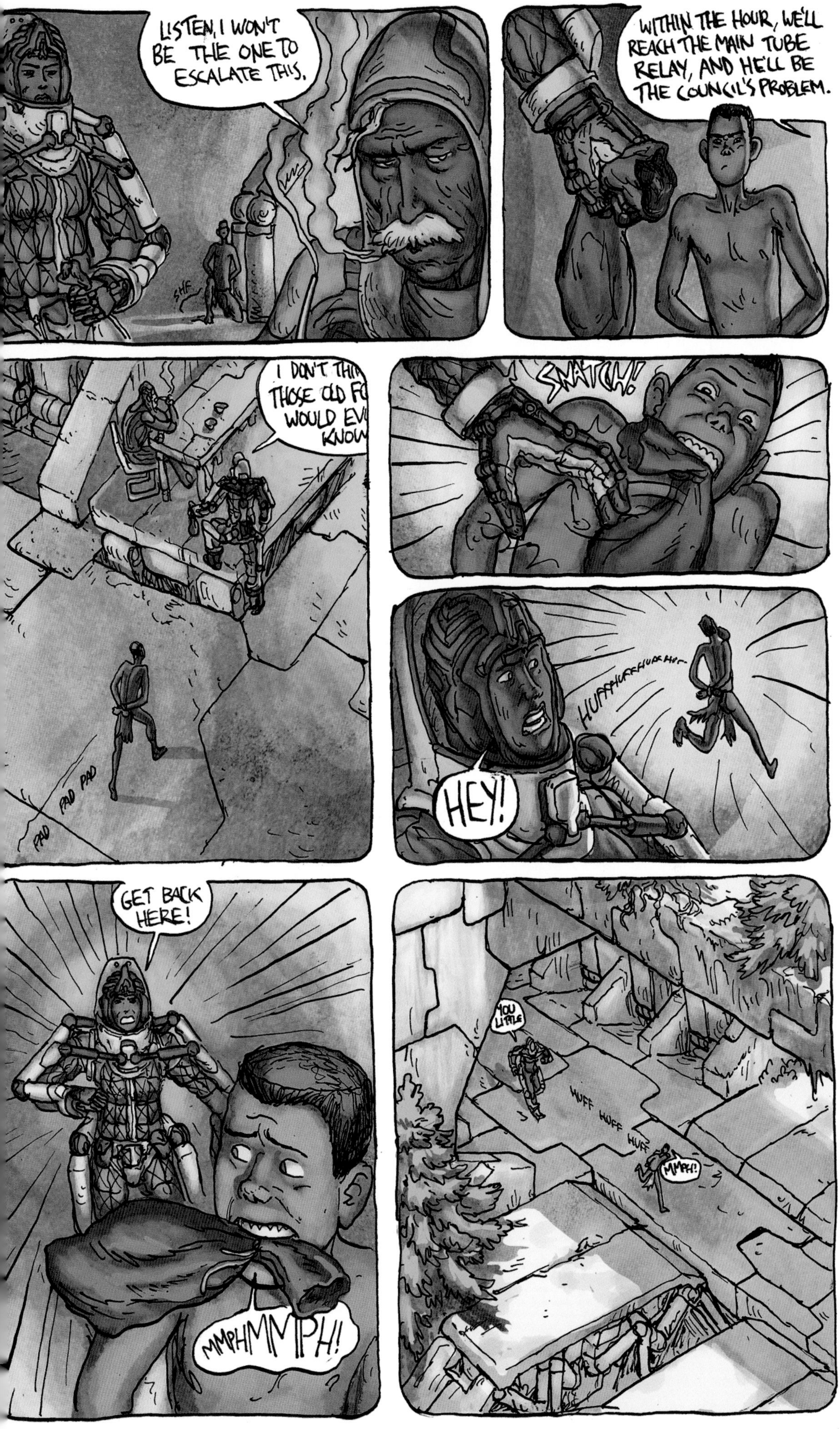
LISTEN, I WON'T BE THE ONE TO ESCALATE THIS.
SHF
WITHIN THE HOUR, WE'LL REACH THE MAIN TUBE RELAY, AND HE'LL BE THE COUNCIL'S PROBLEM.
I DON'T THI THOSE OLD FO WOULD EVE KNOW
PAD PAD PAD
SNATCH!
HEY!
GET BACK HERE!
MMPHMMMPH!
YOU LITTLE
HUFF HUFF HUFF
MMPH!

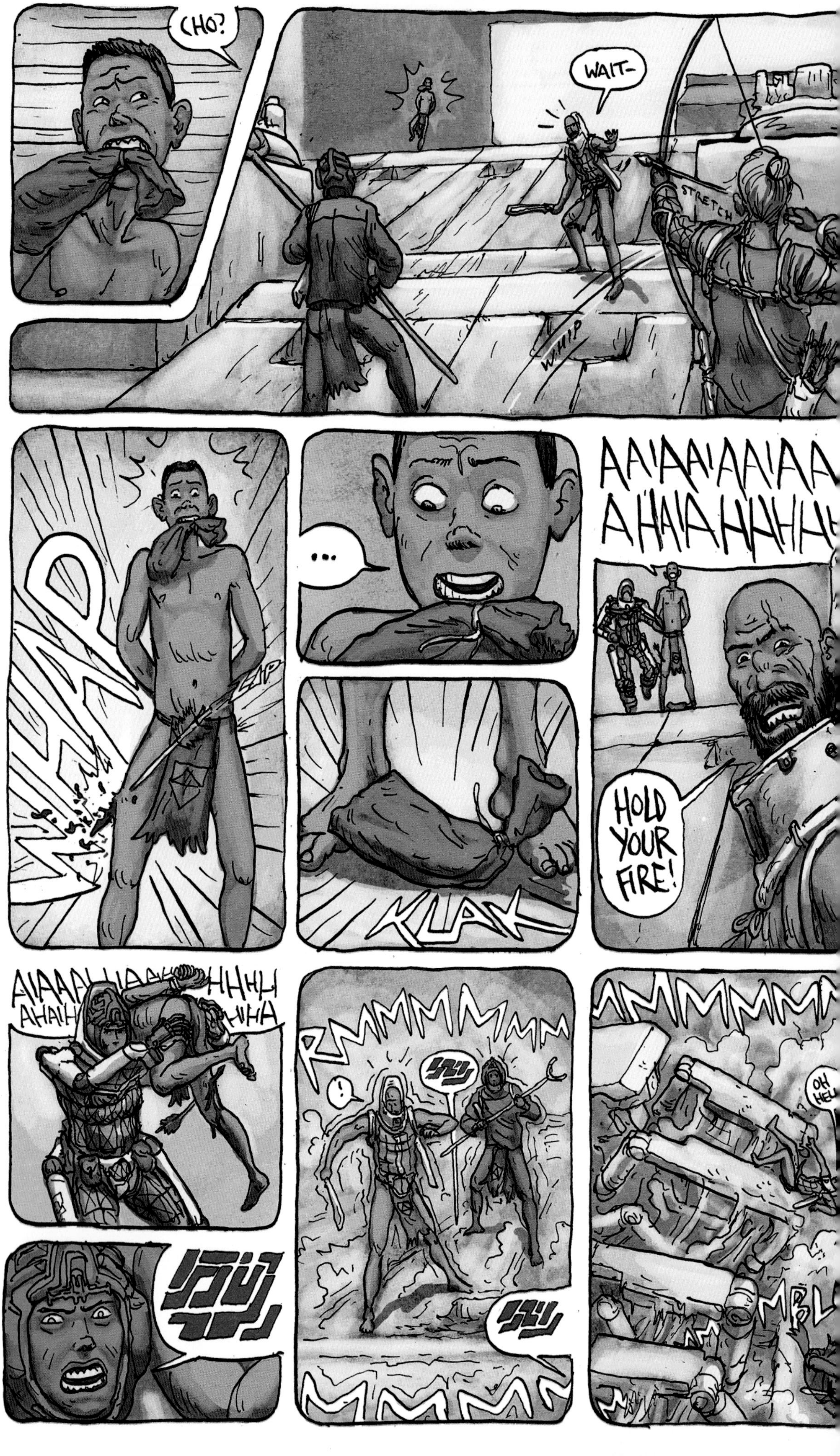
CHO?
WAIT-
STRETCH
WHIP
...
KLAK
HOLD YOUR FIRE!
!
RMMMMMMMM

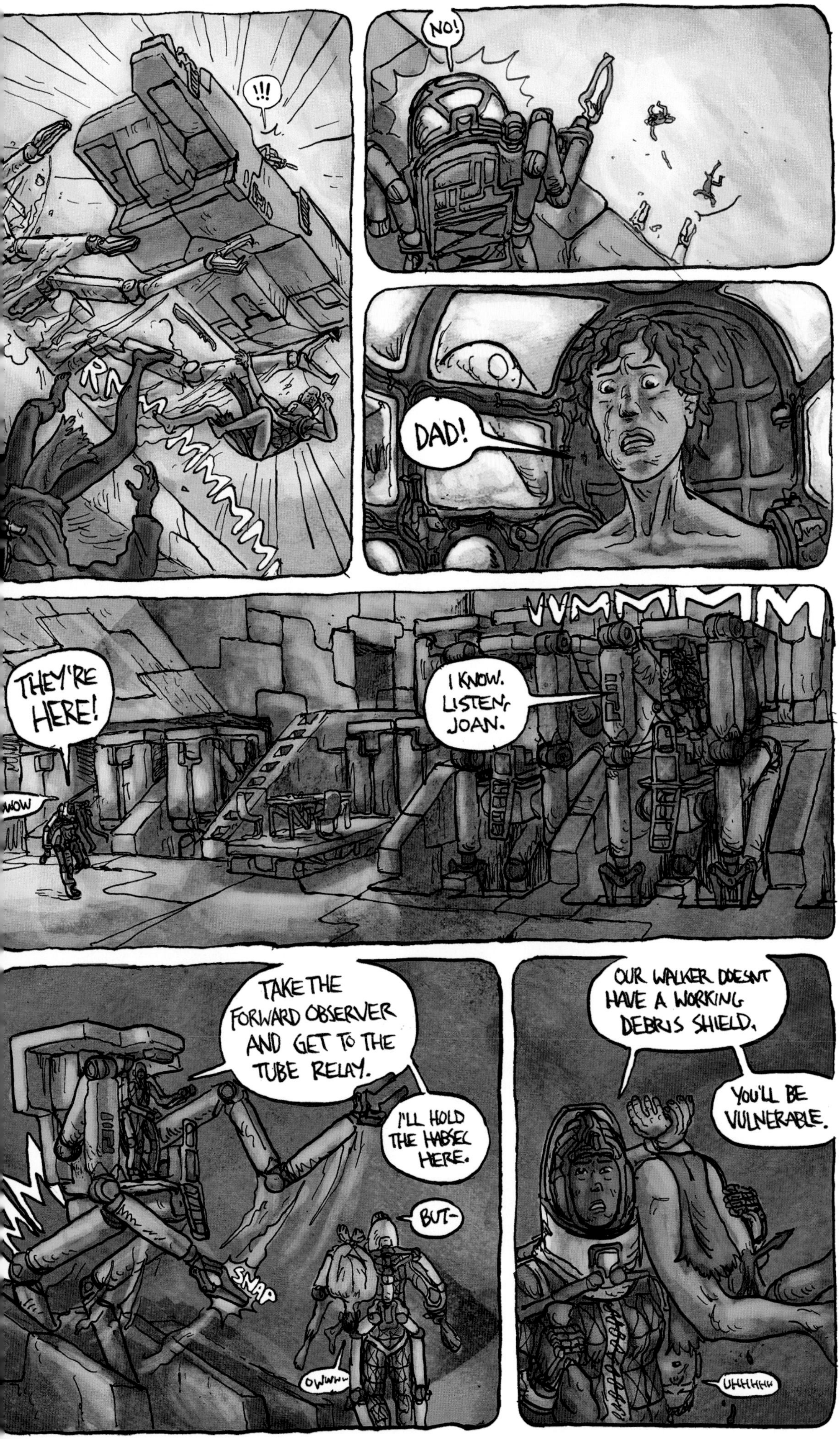
!!!
RMMMMMMMM
NO!
DAD!
VVMMMMMM
THEY'RE HERE!
WOW
I KNOW. LISTEN, JOAN.
TAKE THE FORWARD OBSERVER AND GET TO THE TUBE RELAY.
I'LL HOLD THE HABSEC HERE.
BUT-
SNAP
OWWW
OUR WALKER DOESNT HAVE A WORKING DEBRIS SHIELD.
YOU'LL BE VULNERABLE.
UHHHHH

VMM
I KNOW. BUT TRUST ME.
GET TO THE COUNC
SHUT IT, CHO.
OW OW
DUM
MAN-AMPLIFIERS FORWARD!
KRAK
KLUNK
HEAVE!! HEAVE!!!
THE REST OF YOU, USE ROPES AND SASUMATA! STAY OUT OF REACH!
COMMANDER!
COMMANDER!!
DUM

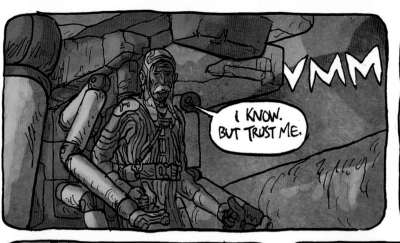

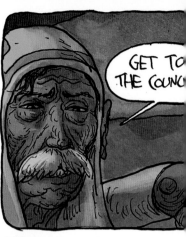

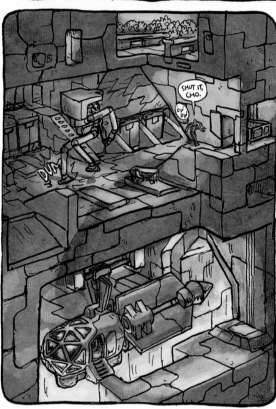

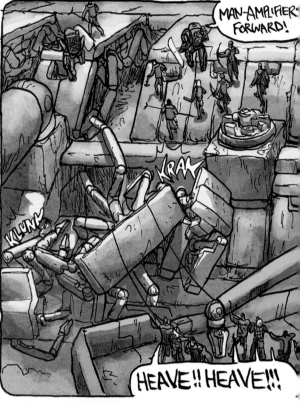

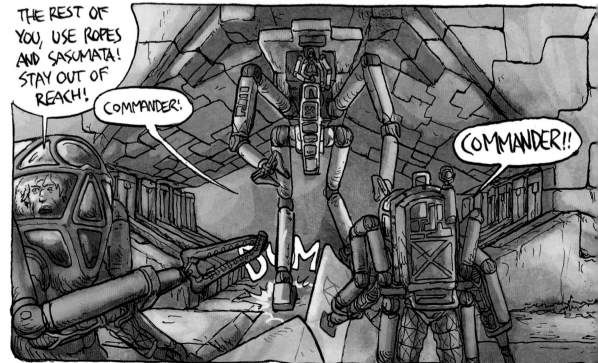

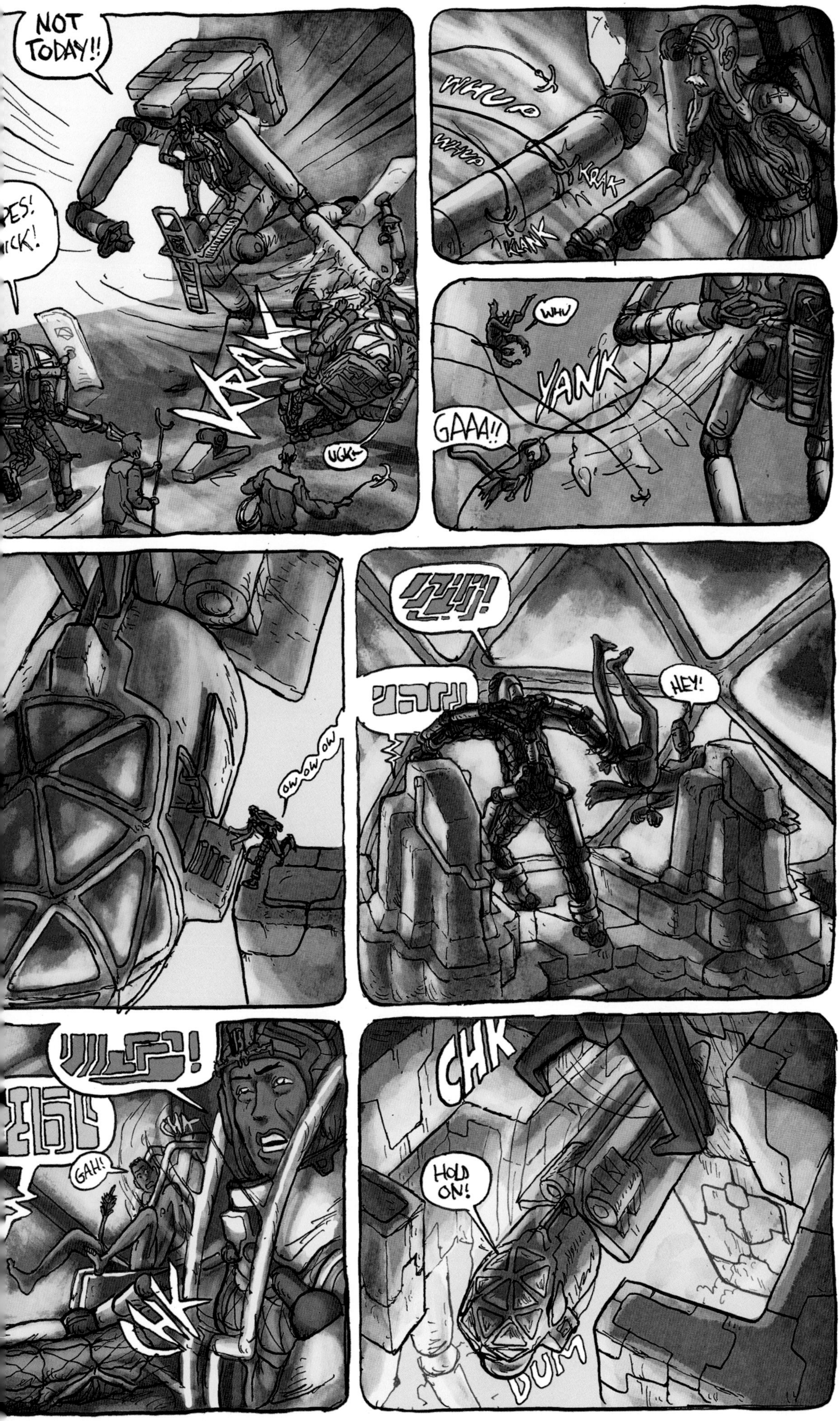
NOT TODAY!!
PES!
ICK!
UGK!
WHUP
WHUP
KRAK
KLANK
WHU
YANK
GAAA!!
OW OW OW
HEY!
GAH!
CHK
CHK
CHK
HOLD ON!
DUM

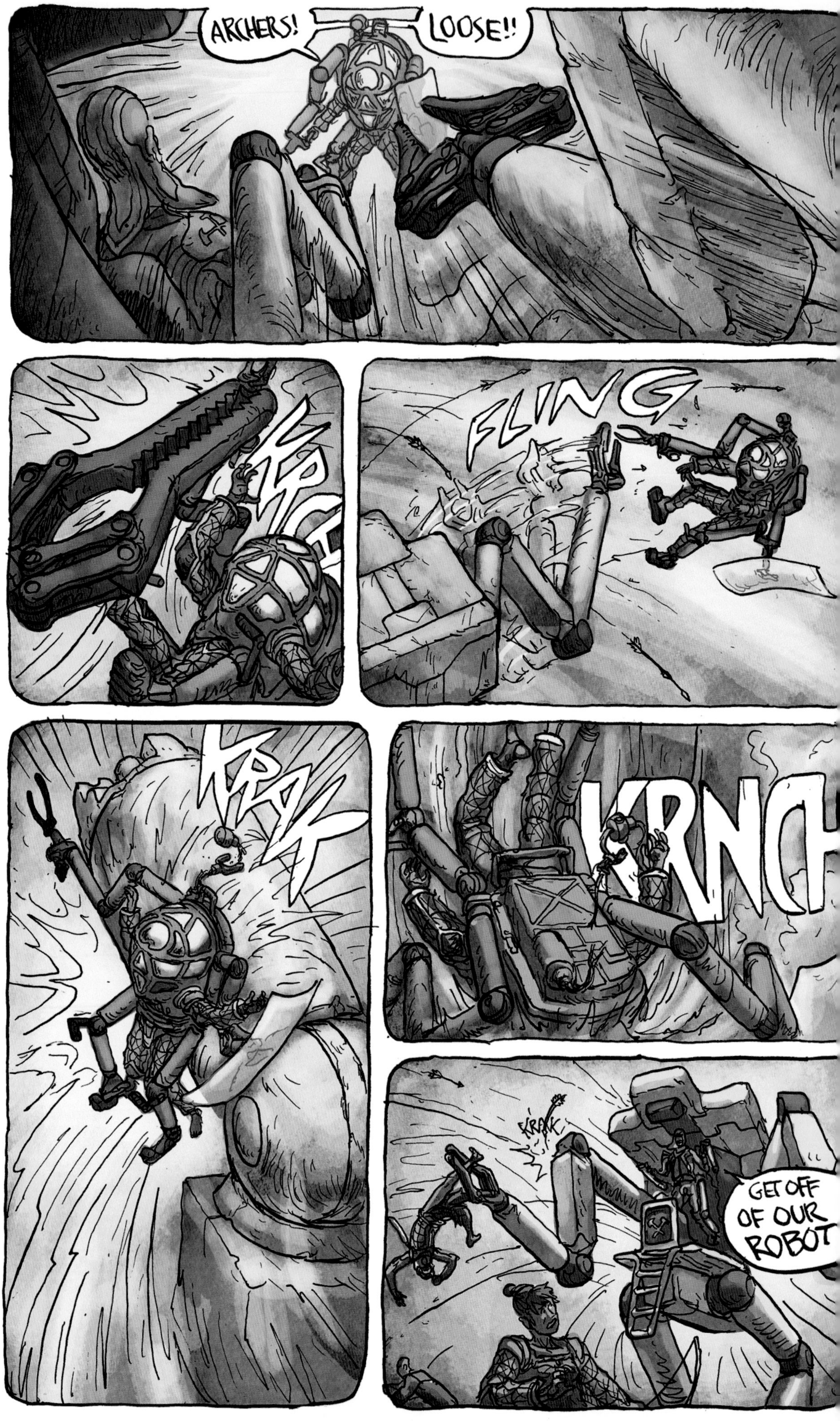
ARCHERS!
LOOSE!!
KRNCH
FLING
KRAK
KRNCH
KRAK
GET OFF OF OUR ROBOT

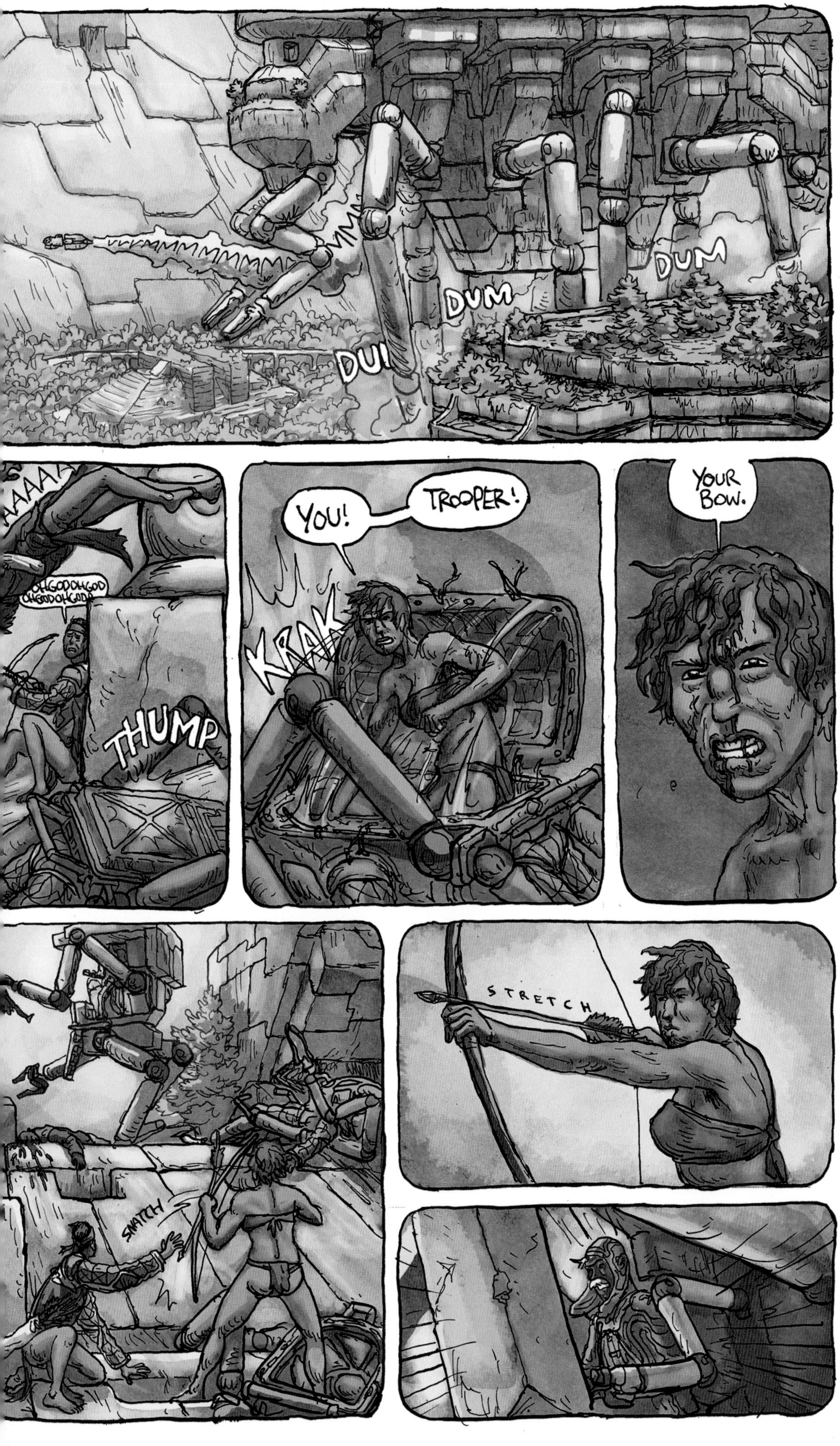

VVVVMMMMMMMMMMMMM
DUM
DUM
AAAAA
OHGODOHGOD
OHGODOHGOD
THUMP
KRAK
YOU!
TROOPER!
YOUR BOW.
SNATCH
STRETCH

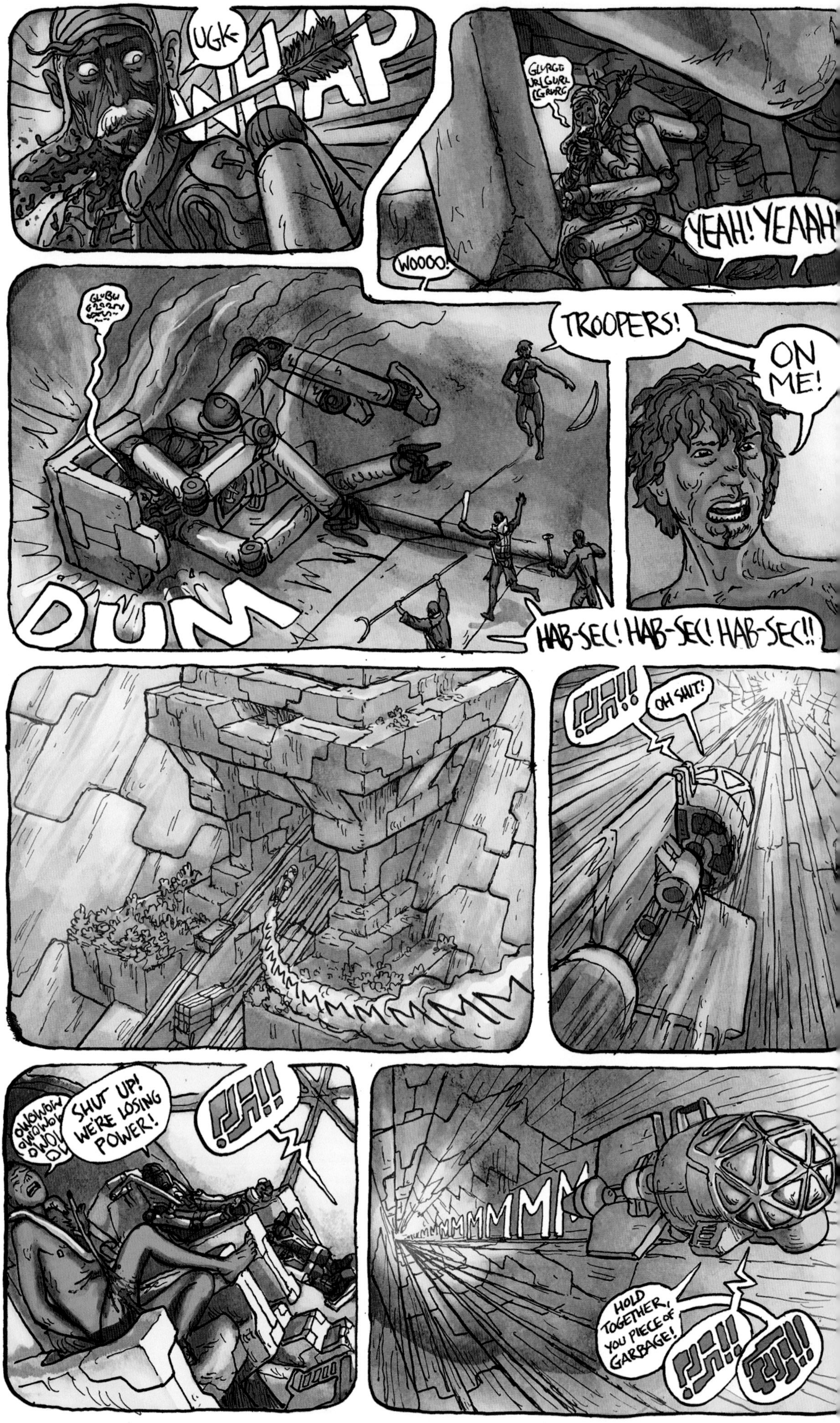
UGK-
WHAP
WOOOO!
YEAH! YEAAH
TROOPERS!
ON ME!
DUM
HAB-SEC! HAB-SEC! HAB-SEC!!
OH SHIT!
SHUT UP! WE'RE LOSING POWER!
HOLD TOGETHER, YOU PIECE OF GARBAGE!

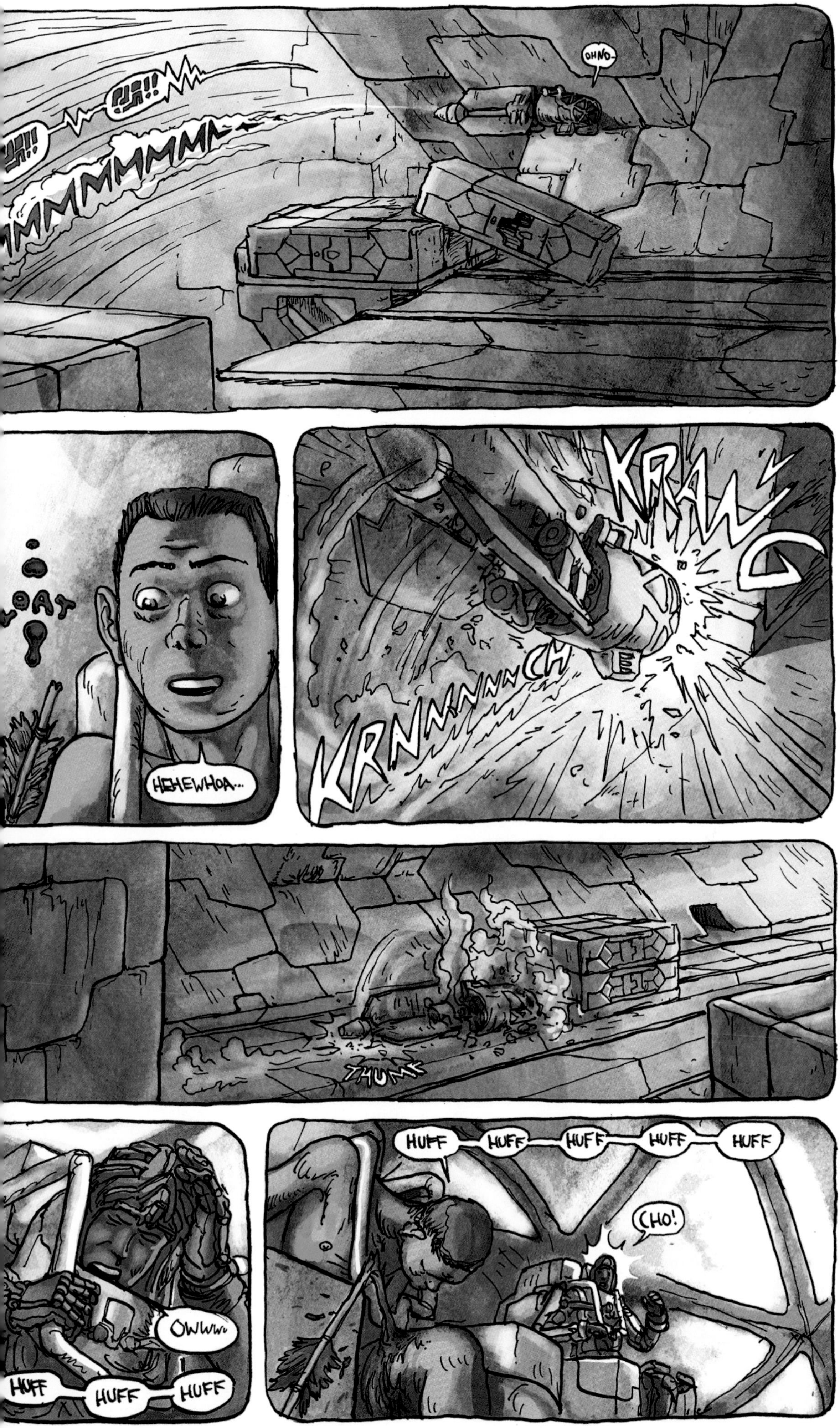
OHNO-
MMMMMMMMMA
HEHEWHOA...
KRANG
KRNNNNNNCH
THUMP
OWWW
HUFF
HUFF
HUFF
HUFF
HUFF
HUFF
HUFF
HUFF
CHO!

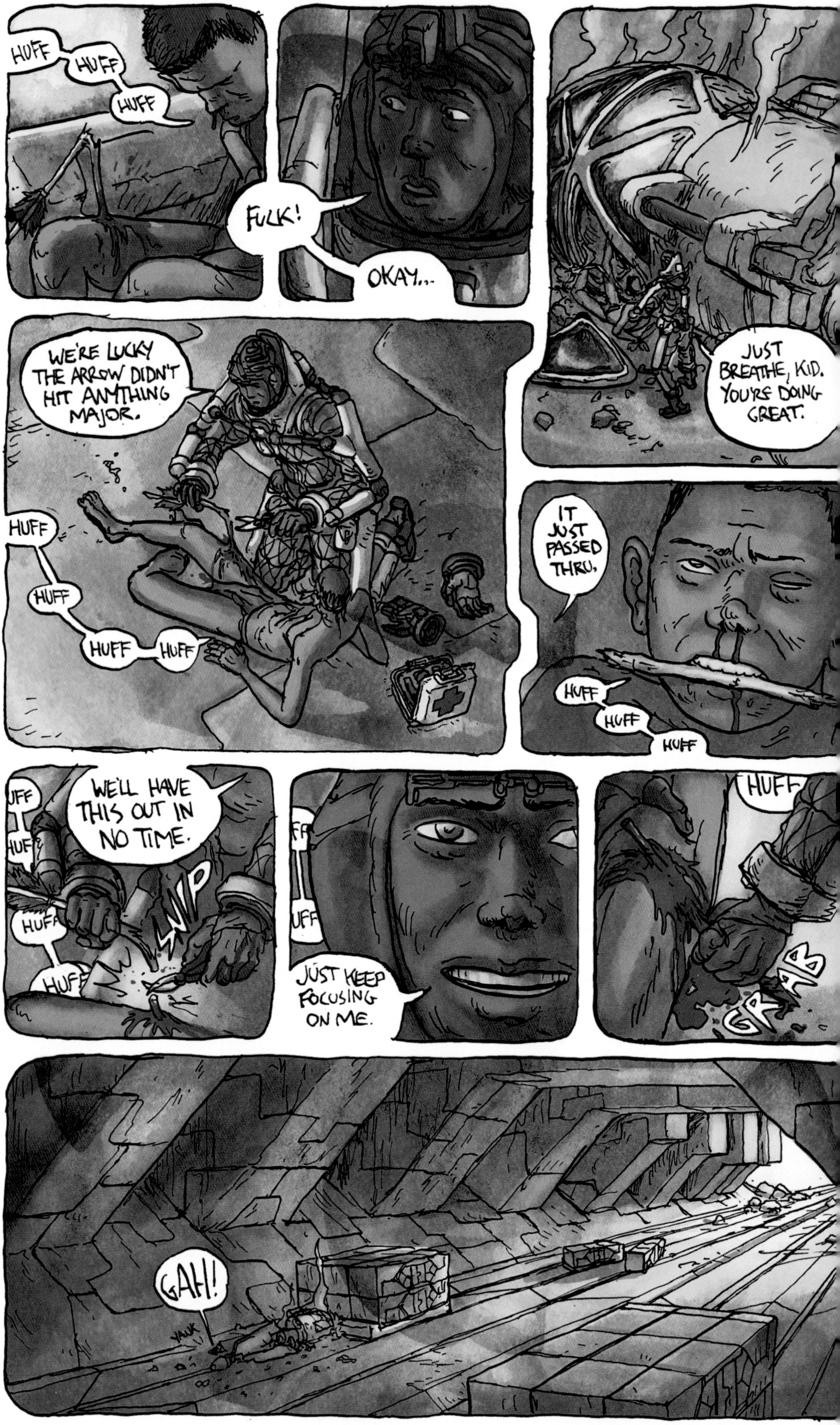
HUFF
HUFF
HUFF
FUCK!
OKAY...
WE'RE LUCKY THE ARROW DIDN'T HIT ANYTHING MAJOR.
HUFF
HUFF
HUFF
HUFF
JUST BREATHE, KID. YOU'RE DOING GREAT.
IT JUST PASSED THRU,
HUFF
HUFF
HUFF
WE'LL HAVE THIS OUT IN NO TIME.
WIP
JUST KEEP FOCUSING ON ME.
HUFF
GRAB
GAH!
YANK

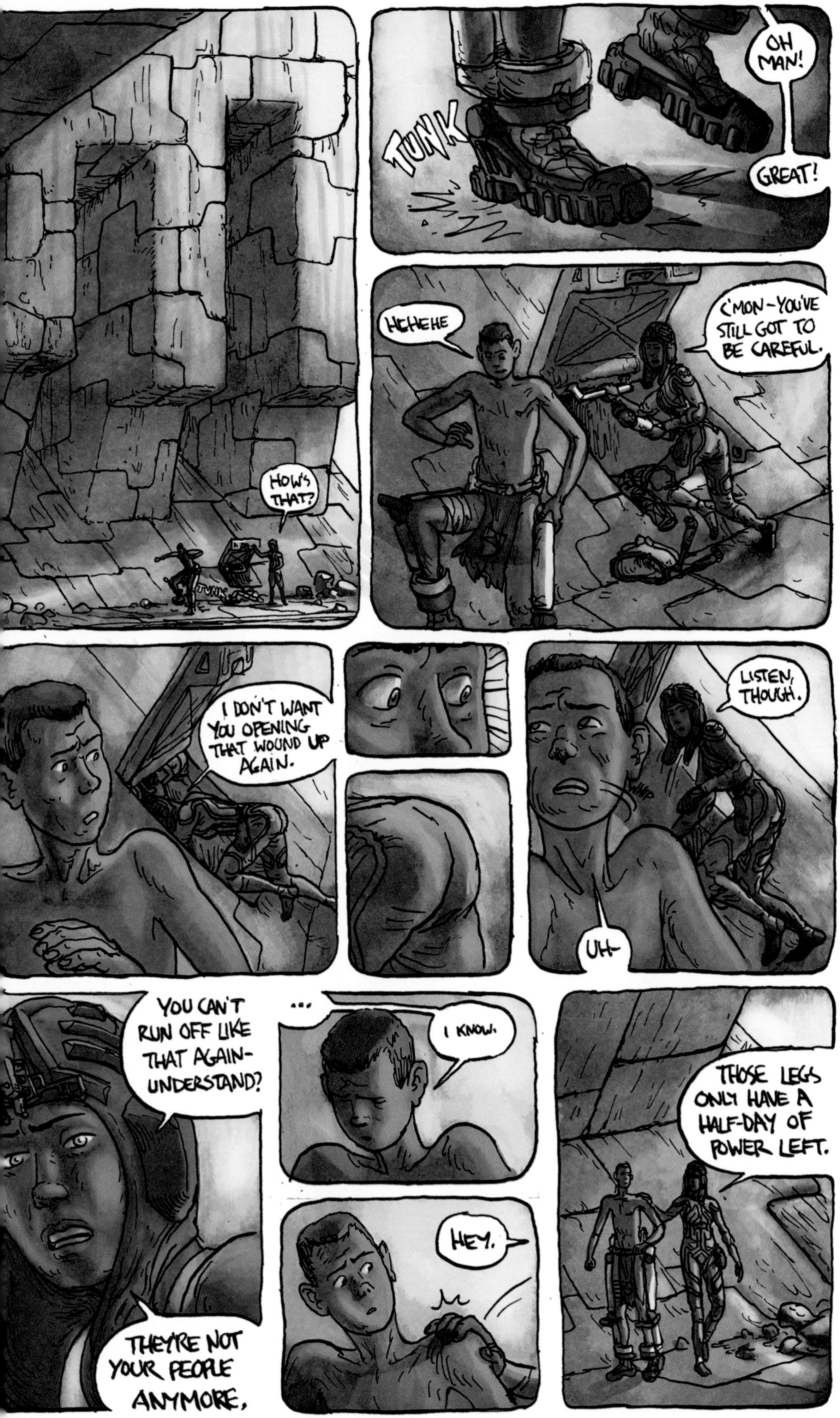
HOW'S THAT?
TUNK
TUNK
OH MAN!
GREAT!
HEHEHE
C'MON-YOU'VE STILL GOT TO BE CAREFUL.
I DON'T WANT YOU OPENING THAT WOUND UP AGAIN.
LISTEN, THOUGH.
UH-
YOU CAN'T RUN OFF LIKE THAT AGAIN-UNDERSTAND?
THEY'RE NOT YOUR PEOPLE ANYMORE.
...
I KNOW.
HEY.
THOSE LEGS ONLY HAVE A HALF-DAY OF POWER LEFT.

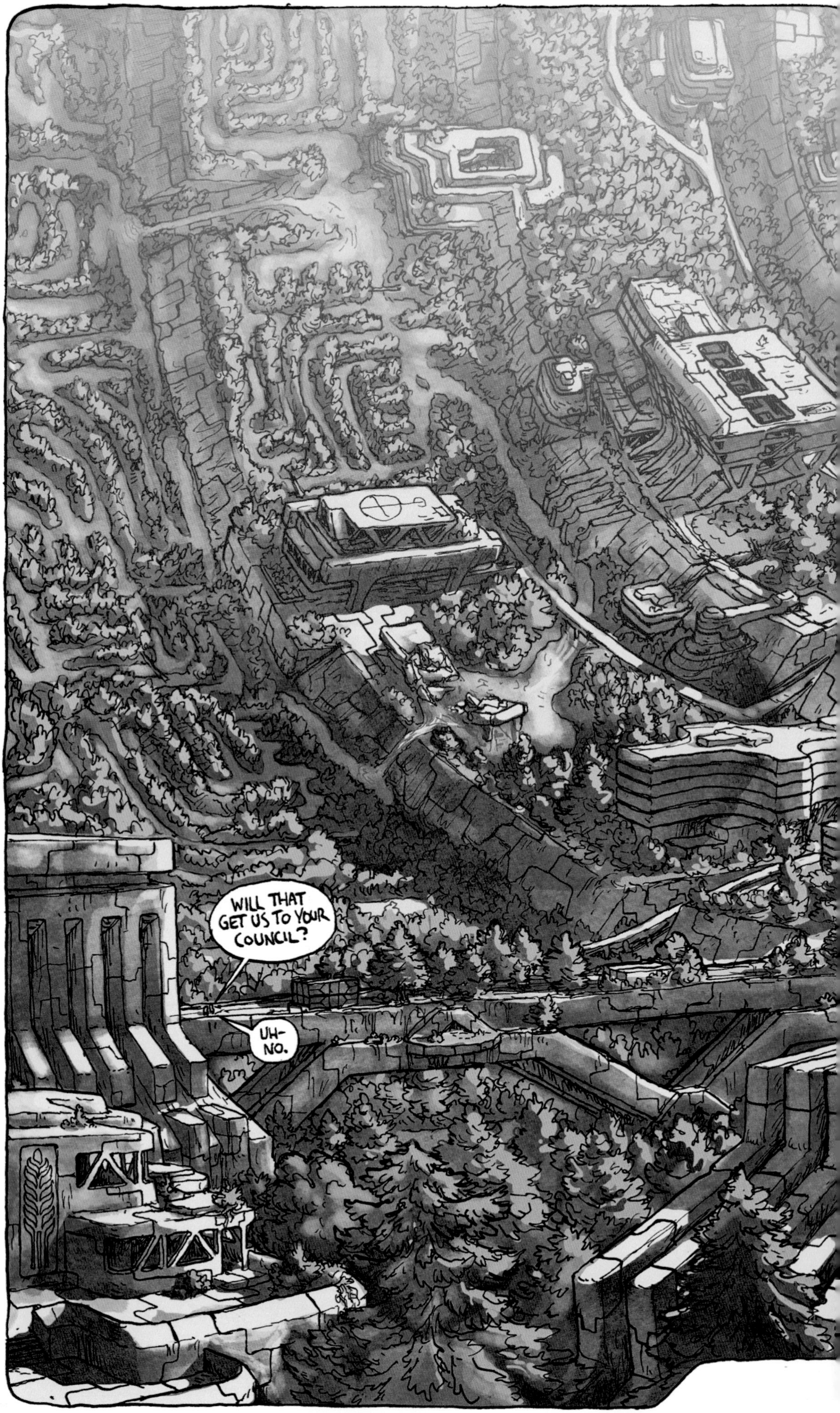
WILL THAT GET US TO YOUR COUNCIL?
UH-NO.

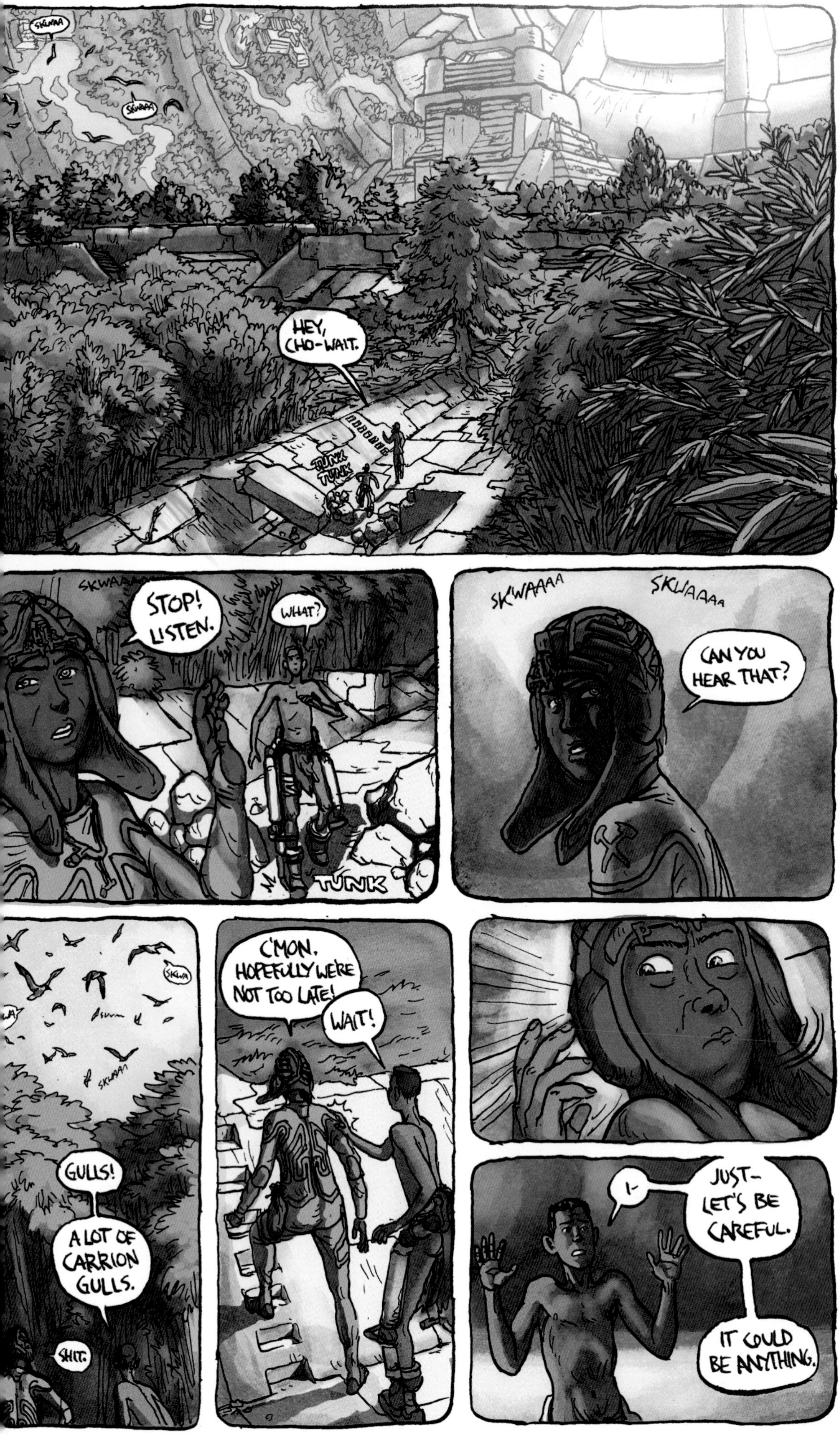
HEY, CHO-WAIT.
TUNK TUNK
STOP! LISTEN.
WHAT?
TUNK
SKWAAAA
SKWAAAA
CAN YOU HEAR THAT?
GULLS!
A LOT OF CARRION GULLS.
SHIT.
C'MON. HOPEFULLY WE'RE NOT TOO LATE!
WAIT!
I-
JUST- LET'S BE CAREFUL.
IT COULD BE ANYTHING.

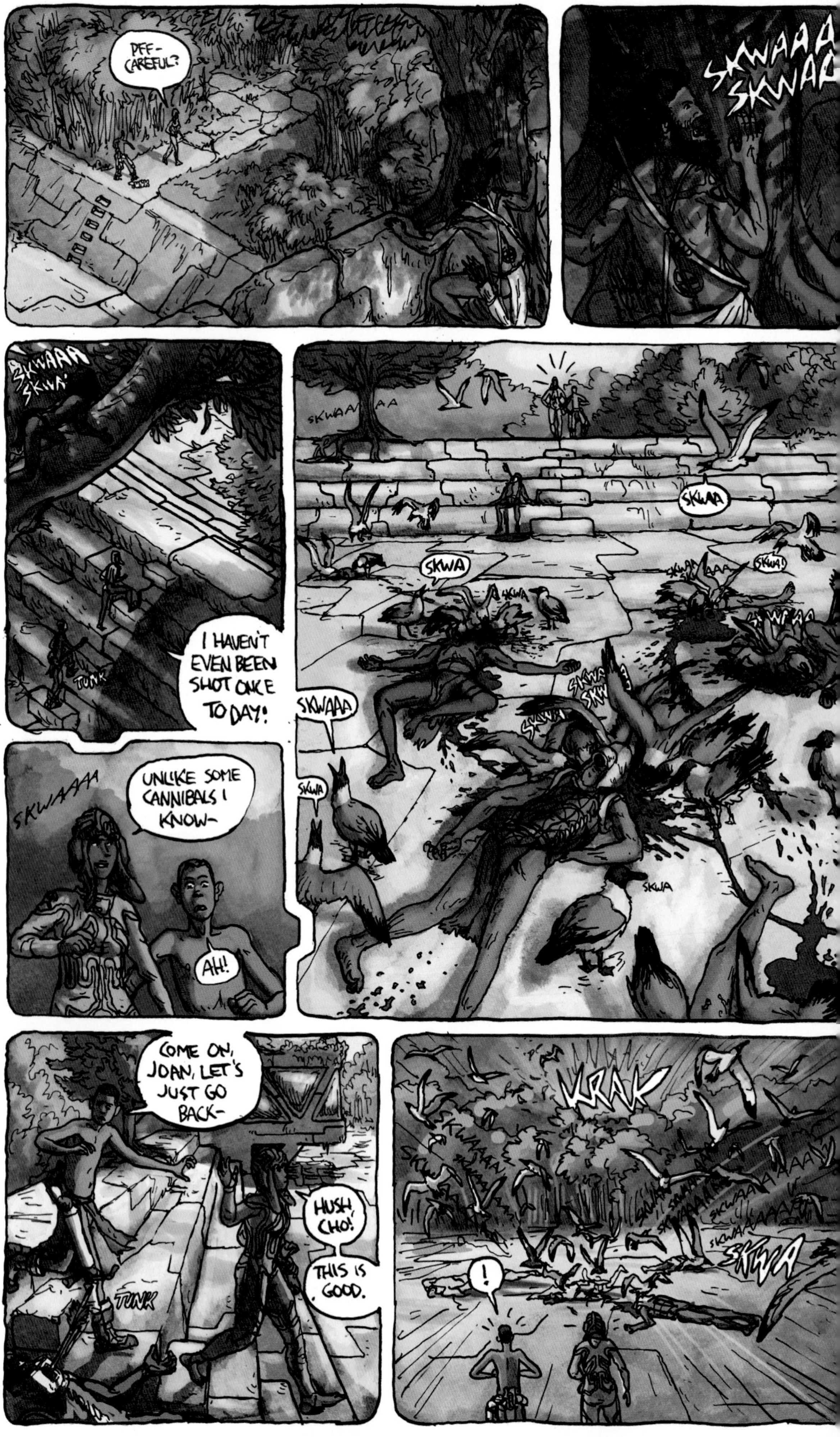
PFF- CAREFUL?
SKWAAA SKWAR
SKWAAR SKWA'
SKWAA AA
SKWAA
SKWA
SKWA!
TUNK
I HAVEN'T EVEN BEEN SHOT ONCE TODAY!
SKWAAA
SKWA
SKWA
UNLIKE SOME CANNIBALS I KNOW-
SKWAAAA
AH!
COME ON, JOAN, LET'S JUST GO BACK-
HUSH, CHO!
THIS IS GOOD.
TUNK
KRAK
!
SKWA

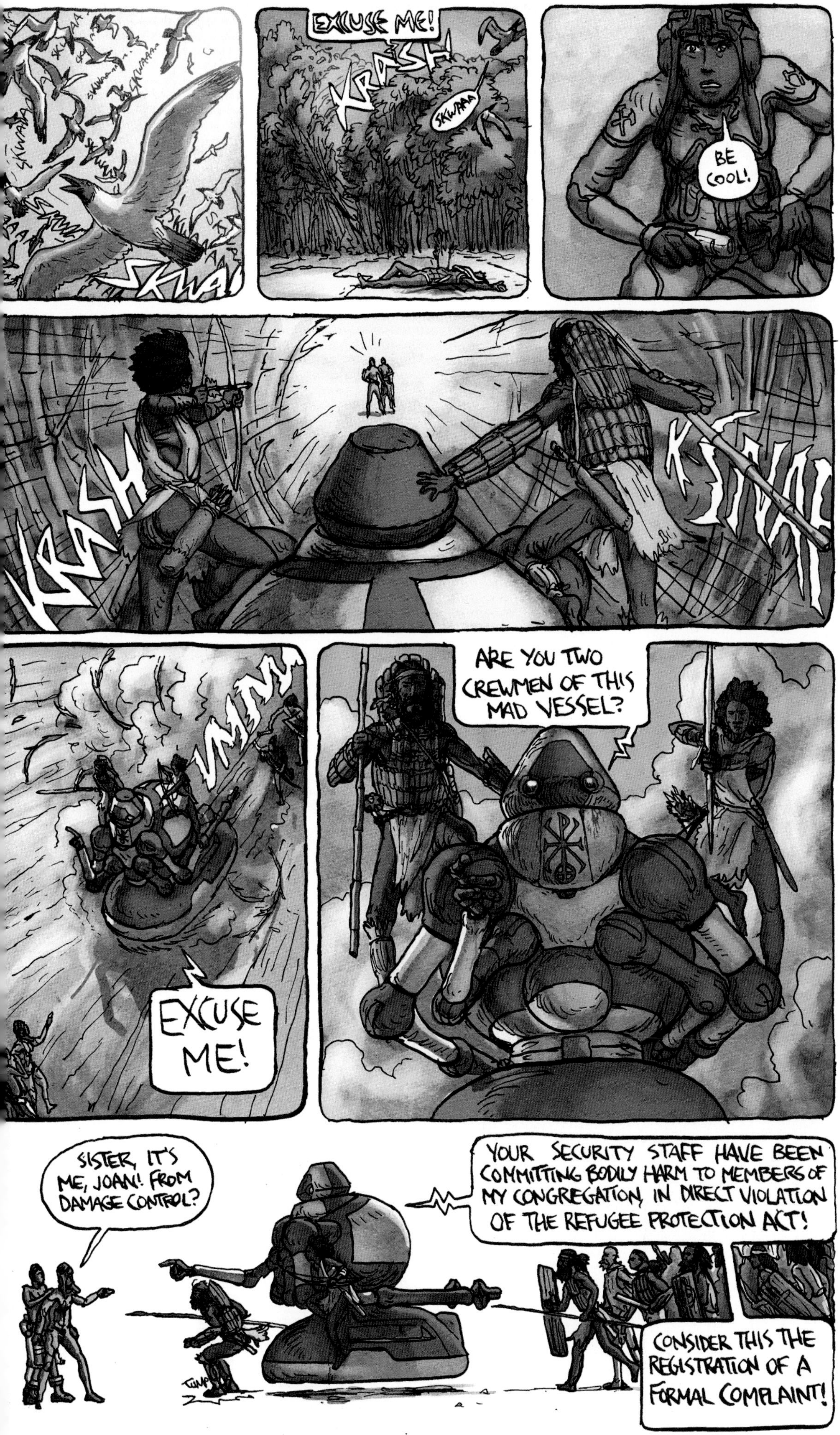
SKWAAA
SKWAA
EXCUSE ME!
KRASH
SKWAAA
BE COOL!
KRASH
KSNAK
EXCUSE ME!
ARE YOU TWO CREWMEN OF THIS MAD VESSEL?
SISTER, IT'S ME, JOAN! FROM DAMAGE CONTROL?
YOUR SECURITY STAFF HAVE BEEN COMMITTING BODILY HARM TO MEMBERS OF MY CONGREGATION, IN DIRECT VIOLATION OF THE REFUGEE PROTECTION ACT!
CONSIDER THIS THE REGISTRATION OF A FORMAL COMPLAINT!

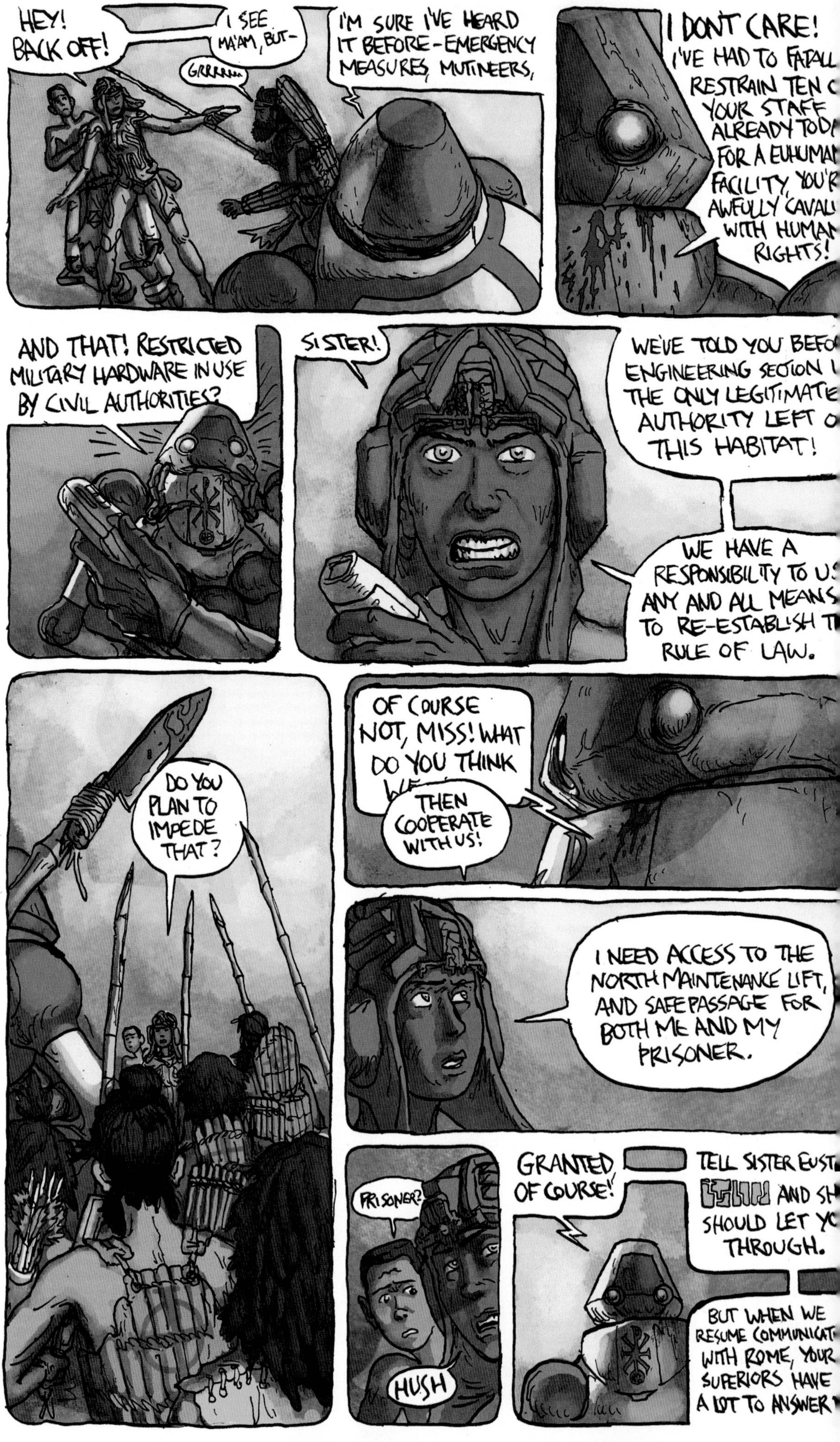
HEY! BACK OFF!
I SEE MA'AM, BUT-
GRRRRR...
I'M SURE I'VE HEARD IT BEFORE - EMERGENCY MEASURES, MUTINEERS,
I DON'T CARE! I'VE HAD TO FATALL RESTRAIN TEN O YOUR STAFF ALREADY TOD FOR A EUHUMAN FACILITY, YOU'R AWFULLY CAVAL WITH HUMAN RIGHTS!
AND THAT! RESTRICTED MILITARY HARDWARE IN USE BY CIVIL AUTHORITIES?
SISTER!
WE'VE TOLD YOU BEFO ENGINEERING SECTION I THE ONLY LEGITIMATE AUTHORITY LEFT O THIS HABITAT!
WE HAVE A RESPONSIBILITY TO US ANY AND ALL MEANS TO RE-ESTABLISH T RULE OF LAW.
DO YOU PLAN TO IMPEDE THAT?
OF COURSE NOT, MISS! WHAT DO YOU THINK
THEN COOPERATE WITH US!
I NEED ACCESS TO THE NORTH MAINTENANCE LIFT, AND SAFE PASSAGE FOR BOTH ME AND MY PRISONER.
PRISONER?
HUSH
GRANTED, OF COURSE!
TELL SISTER EUST AND SH SHOULD LET YO THROUGH.
BUT WHEN WE RESUME COMMUNICAT WITH ROME, YOUR SUPERIORS HAVE A LOT TO ANSWER

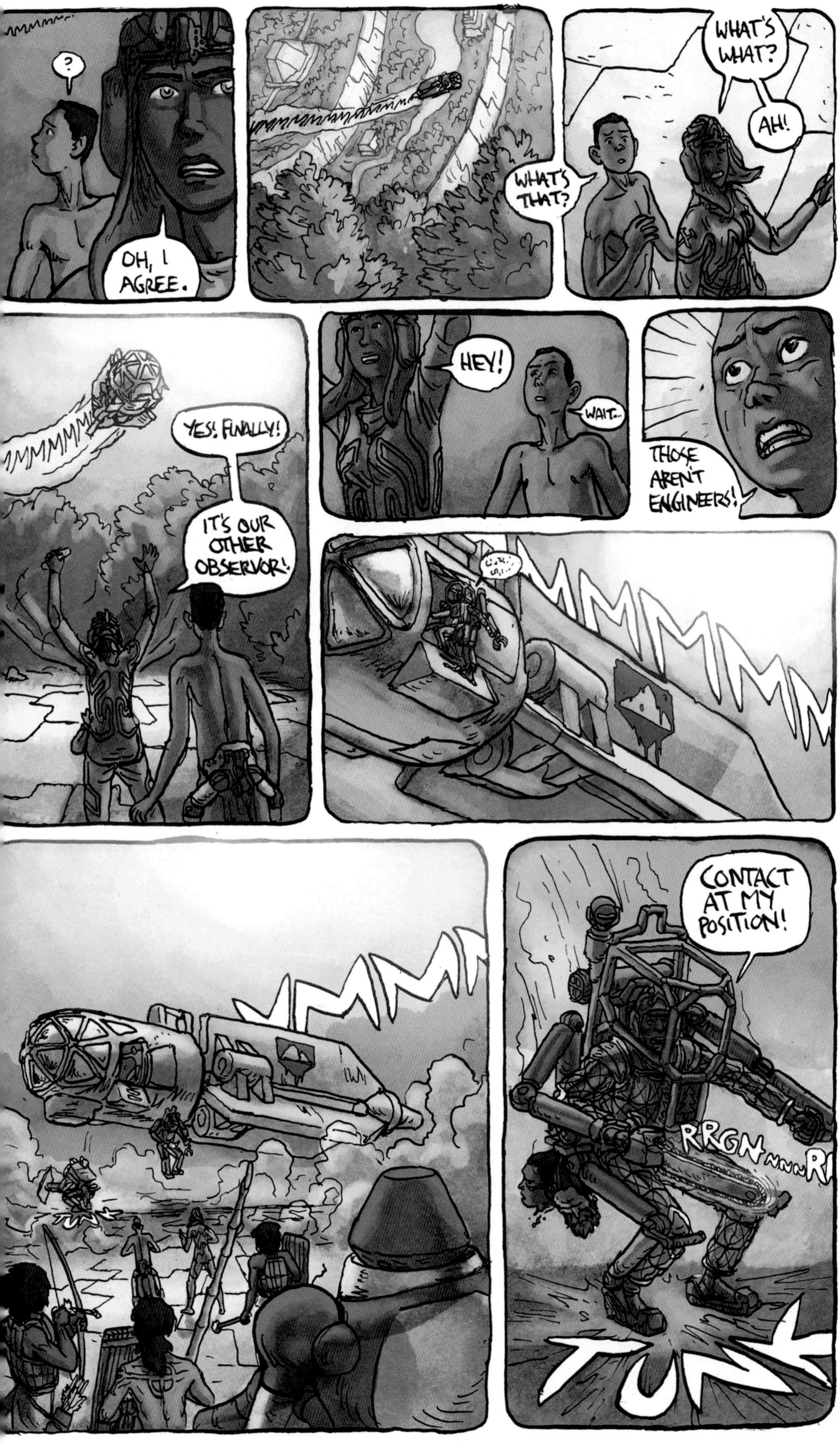
?
OH, I AGREE.
WHAT'S THAT?
WHAT'S WHAT?
AH!
YES! FINALLY!
IT'S OUR OTHER OBSERVOR!
HEY!
WAIT...
THOSE AREN'T ENGINEERS!
CONTACT AT MY POSITION!

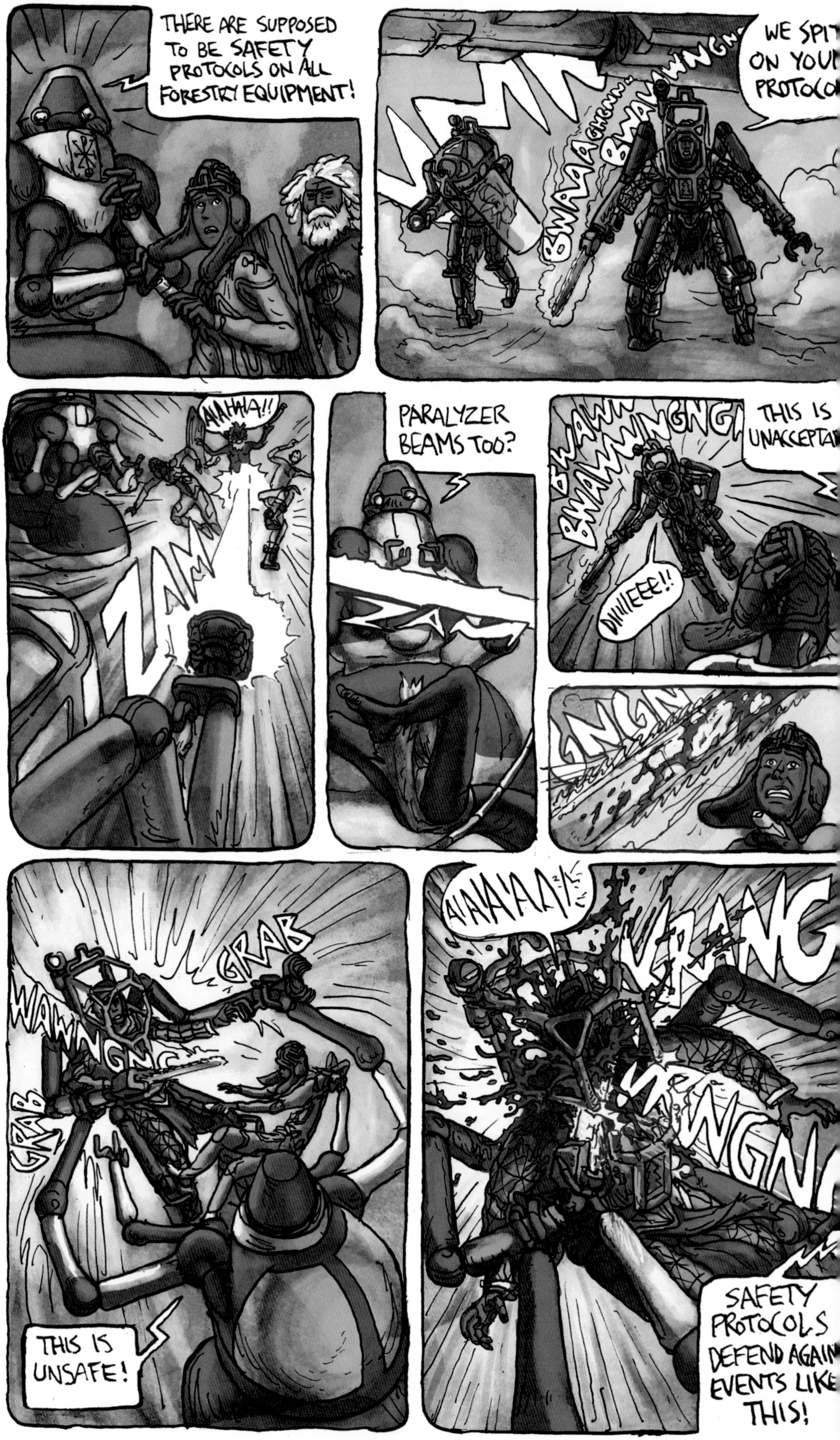
THERE ARE SUPPOSED TO BE SAFETY PROTOCOLS ON ALL FORESTRY EQUIPMENT!
WE SPIT ON YOU PROTOCO
BWAAAGHENNN
BWAAAWNGNG
AAAHAAA!!
ZAM
PARALYZER BEAMS TOO?
ZAM
THIS IS UNACCEPTA
BWAWW BWAWWNGNG
DIIIIEEEE!!
GRAB
WAWWNGNG
GRAB
THIS IS UNSAFE!
AIAAAAA!!
VRANG
VRWNGNG
SAFETY PROTOCOLS DEFEND AGAIN EVENTS LIKE THIS!

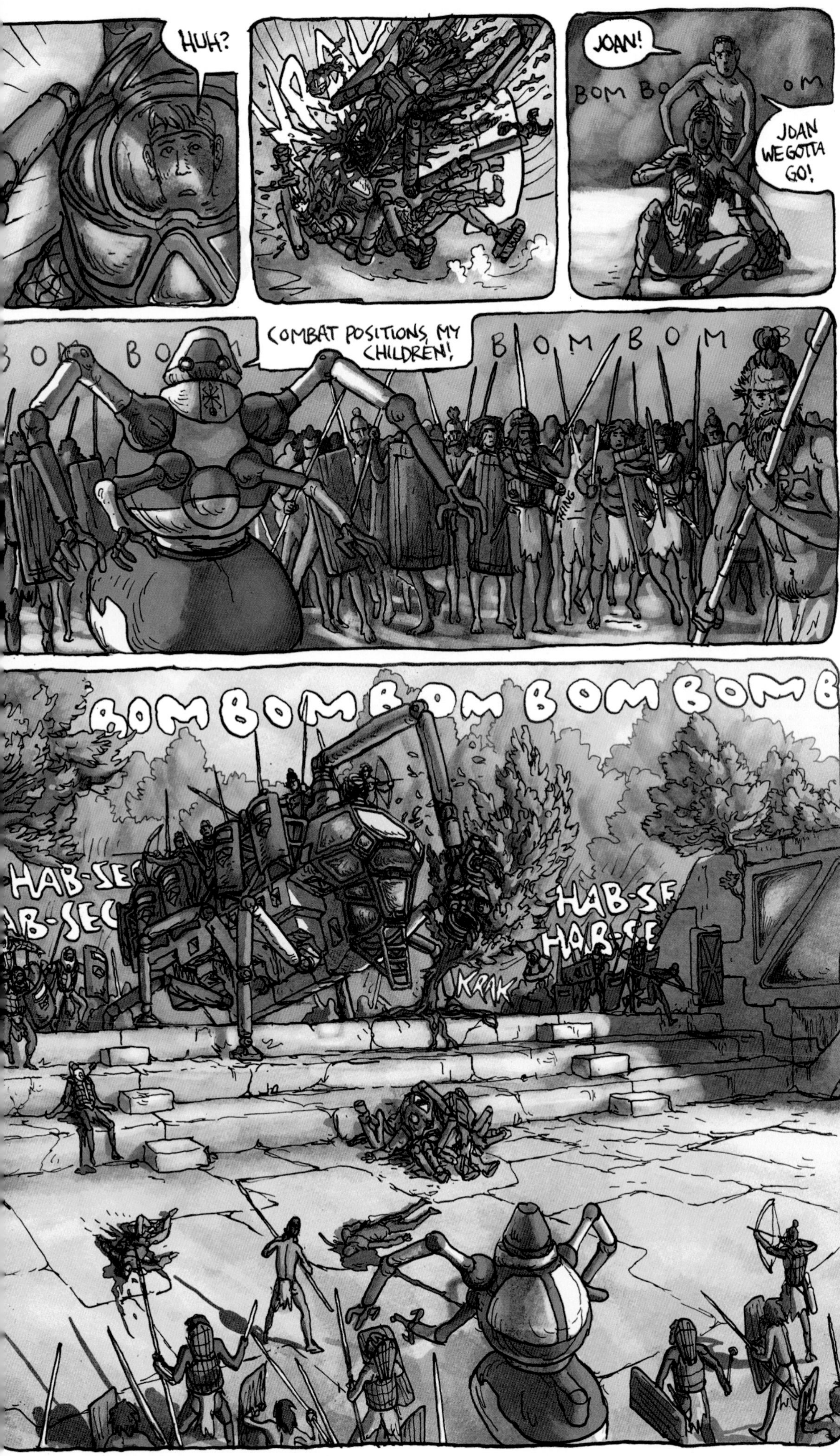
HUH?
JOAN!
BOM BO OM
JOAN WE GOTTA GO!
COMBAT POSITIONS, MY CHILDREN!
BOM BOM
B O M B O M
BOM BOM BOM BOM BOMB
HAB-SE
HAB-SE
HAB-SE
HAB-SE
KRAK

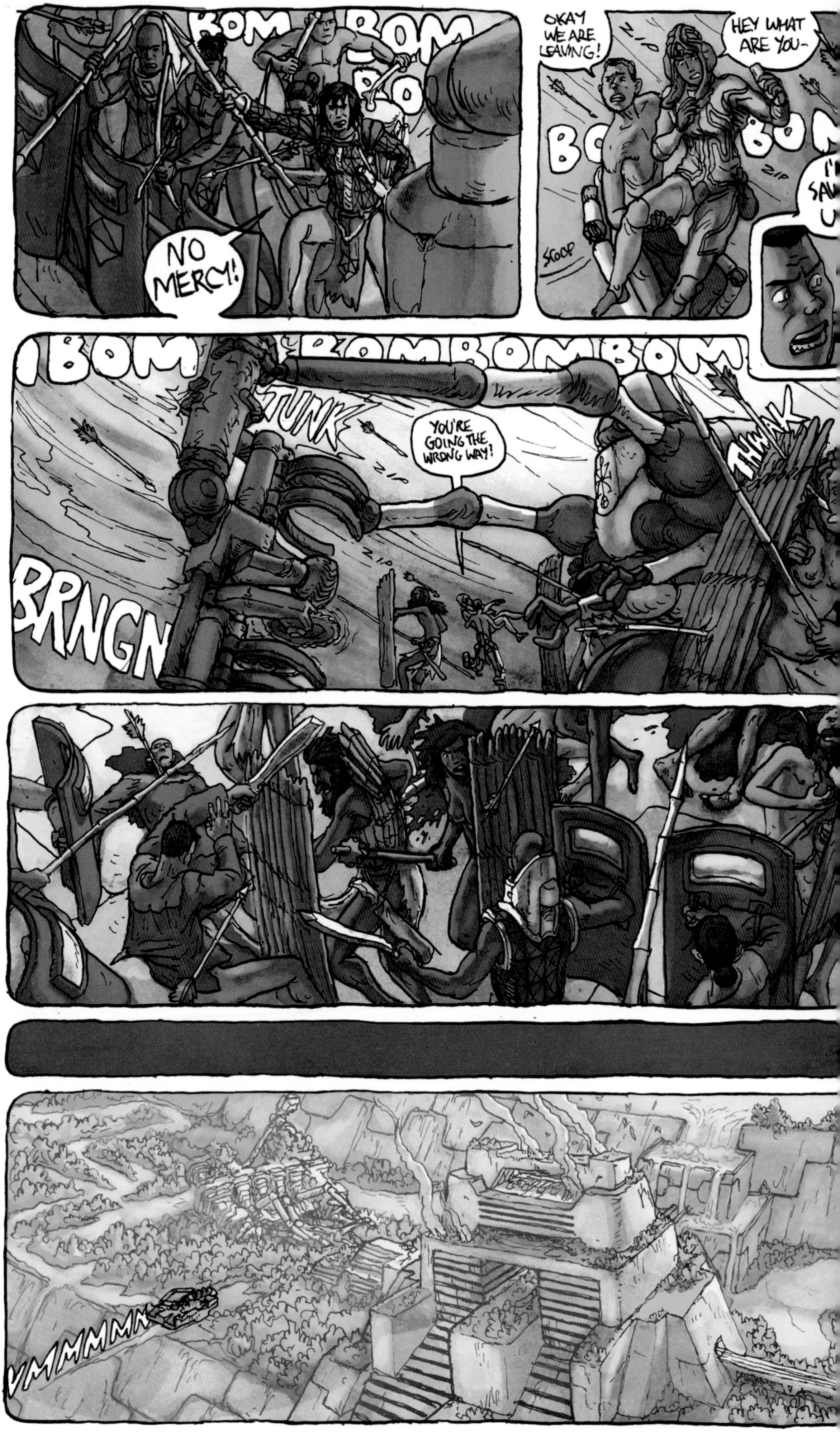
BOM BOM
NO MERCY!
OKAY WE ARE LEAVING!
ZIP
HEY WHAT ARE YOU-
BO
BOM
ZIP
SCOOP
BOM BOMBOMBOM
TUNK
YOU'RE GOING THE WRONG WAY!
ZIP
BRNGN
VMMMMM

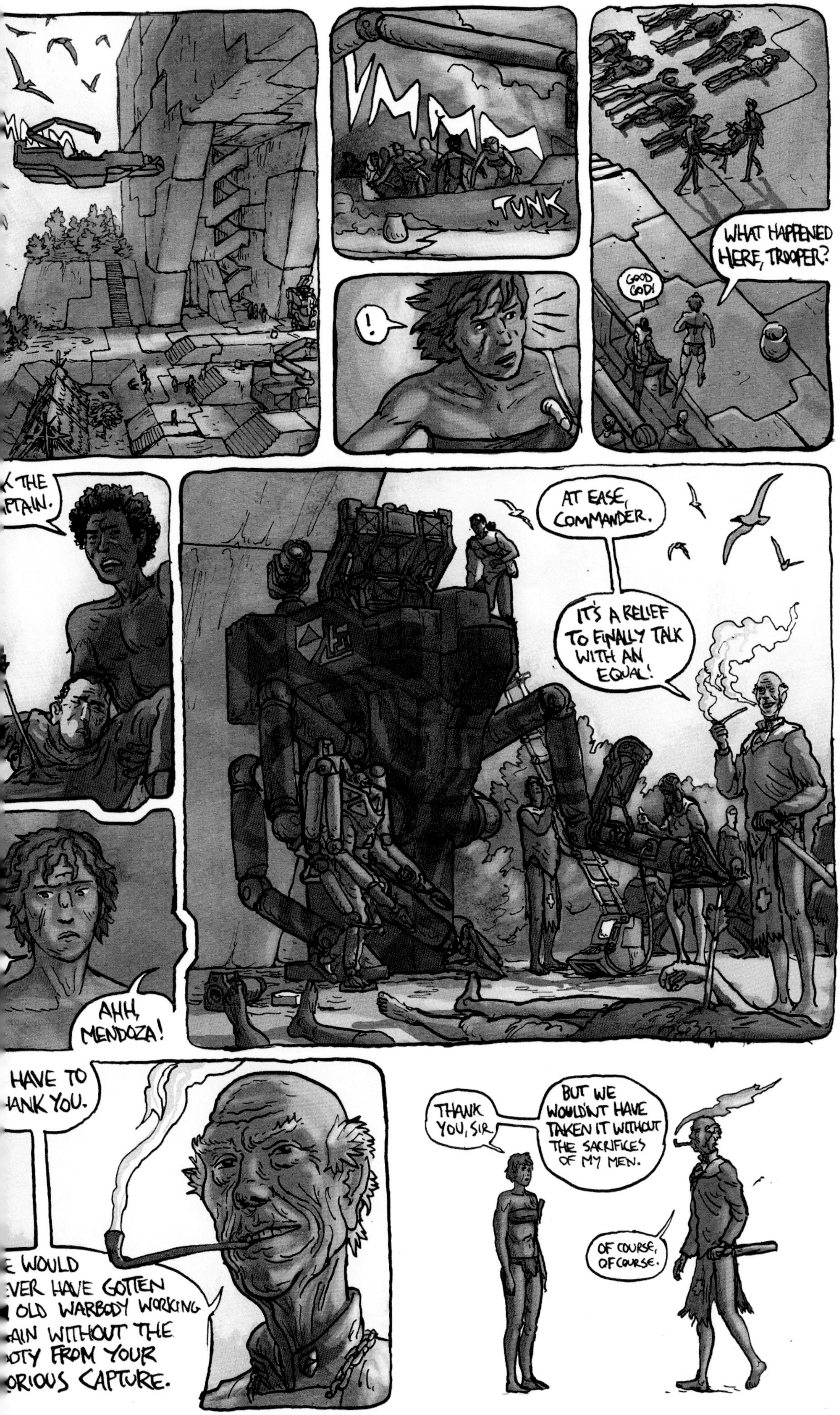

VMMM
TUNK
!
GOOD GOD!
WHAT HAPPENED HERE, TROOPER?
K THE
PTAIN.
AHH, MENDOZA!
AT EASE, COMMANDER.
IT'S A RELIEF TO FINALLY TALK WITH AN EQUAL!
HAVE TO
HANK YOU.
E WOULD
EVER HAVE GOTTEN
OLD WARBODY WORKING
AIN WITHOUT THE
OTY FROM YOUR
ORIOUS CAPTURE.
THANK YOU, SIR.
BUT WE WOULDN'T HAVE TAKEN IT WITHOUT THE SACRIFICES OF MY MEN.
OF COURSE, OF COURSE.

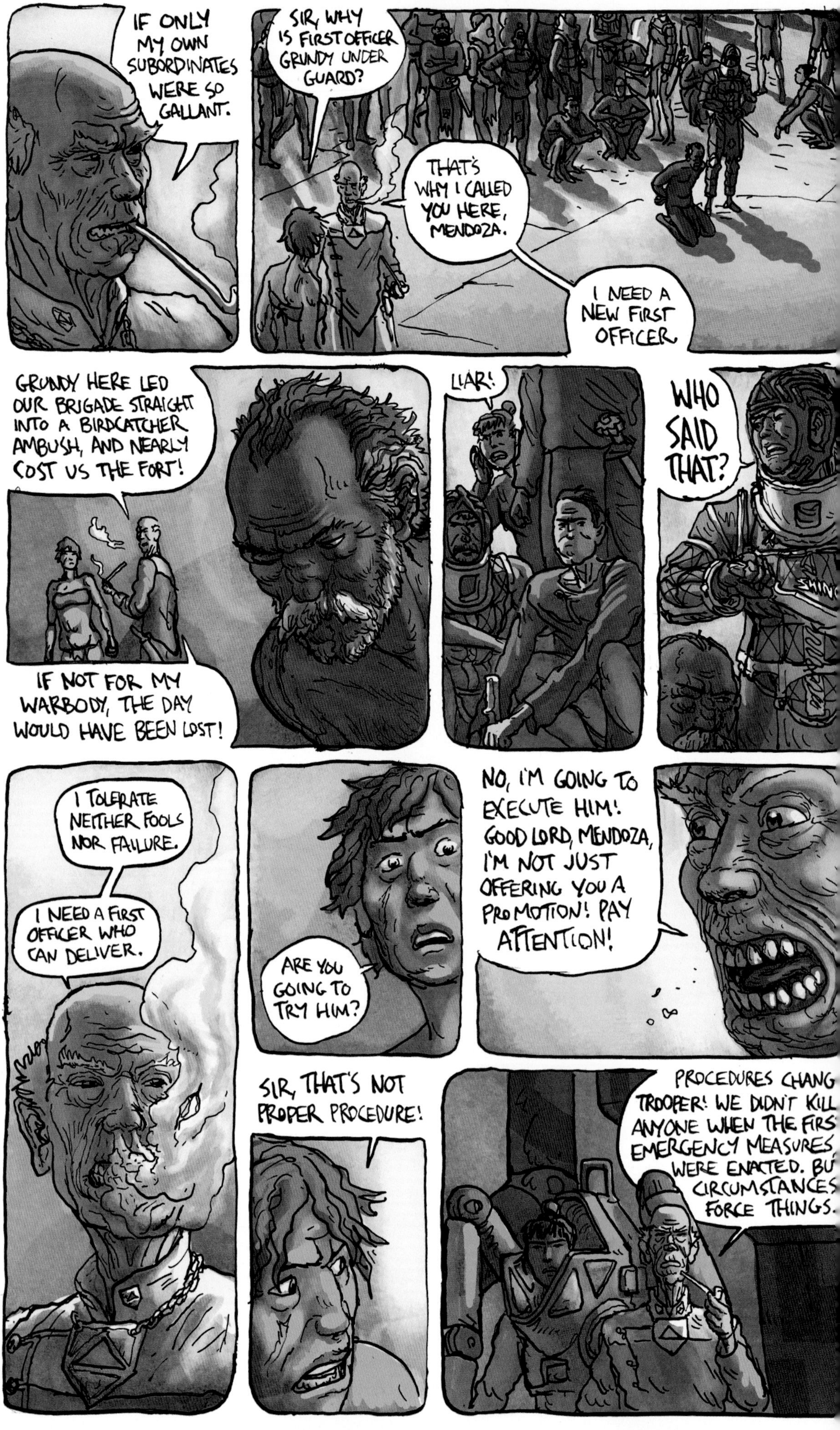

IF ONLY MY OWN SUBORDINATES WERE SO GALLANT.
SIR, WHY IS FIRST OFFICER GRUNDY UNDER GUARD?
THAT'S WHY I CALLED YOU HERE, MENDOZA.
I NEED A NEW FIRST OFFICER.
GRUNDY HERE LED OUR BRIGADE STRAIGHT INTO A BIRDCATCHER AMBUSH, AND NEARLY COST US THE FORT!
IF NOT FOR MY WARBODY, THE DAY WOULD HAVE BEEN LOST!
LIAR!
WHO SAID THAT?
I TOLERATE NEITHER FOOLS NOR FAILURE.
I NEED A FIRST OFFICER WHO CAN DELIVER.
ARE YOU GOING TO TRY HIM?
NO, I'M GOING TO EXECUTE HIM! GOOD LORD, MENDOZA, I'M NOT JUST OFFERING YOU A PROMOTION! PAY ATTENTION!
SIR, THAT'S NOT PROPER PROCEDURE!
PROCEDURES CHANG TROOPER! WE DIDN'T KILL ANYONE WHEN THE FIRS EMERGENCY MEASURES WERE ENACTED. BU CIRCUMSTANCES FORCE THINGS.

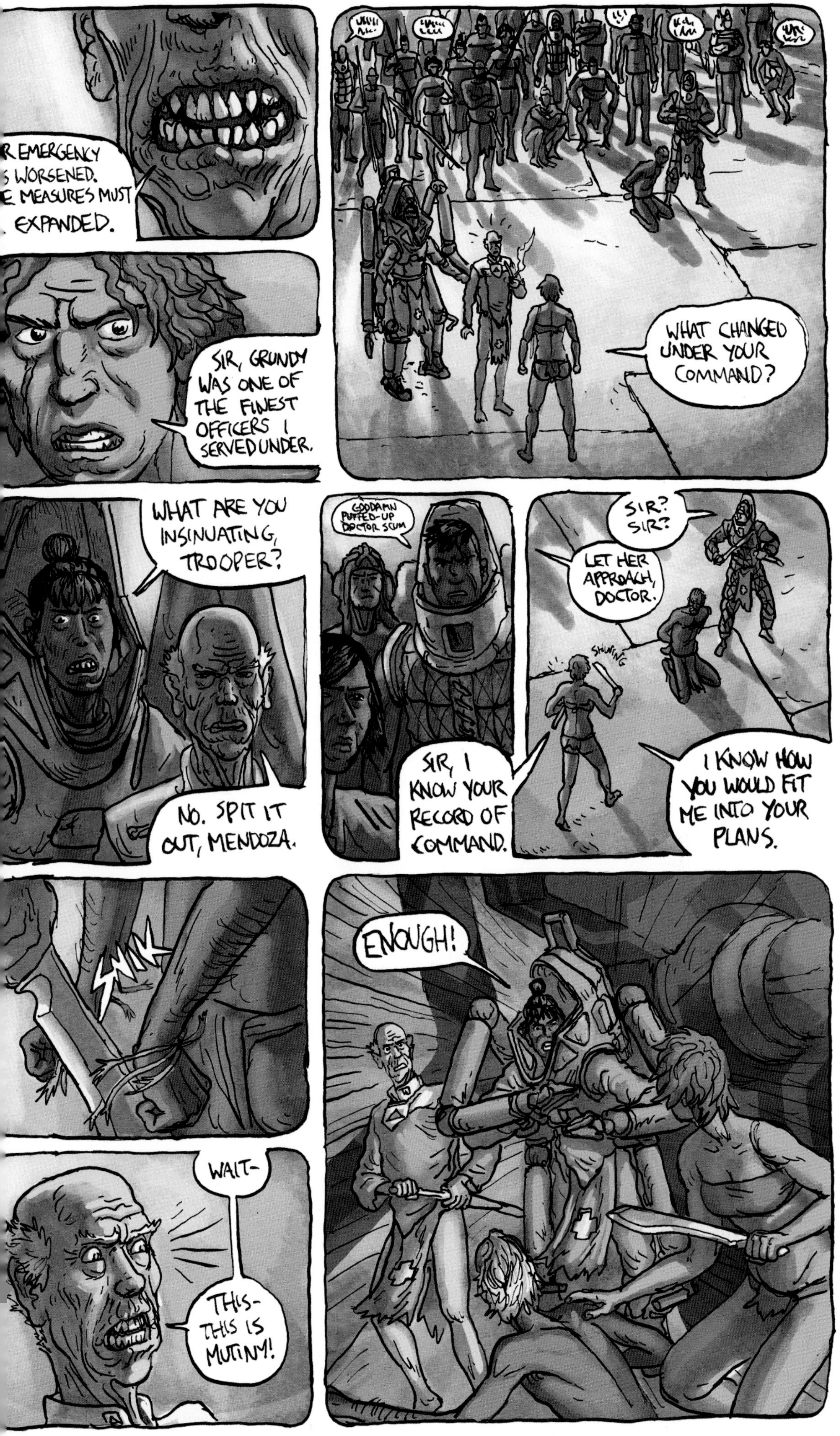
R EMERGENCY S WORSENED. E MEASURES MUST EXPANDED.
SIR, GRUNDY WAS ONE OF THE FINEST OFFICERS I SERVED UNDER.
WHAT CHANGED UNDER YOUR COMMAND?
WHAT ARE YOU INSINUATING, TROOPER?
NO. SPIT IT OUT, MENDOZA.
GODDAMN PUFFED-UP DOCTOR SCUM
SIR, I KNOW YOUR RECORD OF COMMAND.
SIR? SIR?
LET HER APPROACH, DOCTOR.
SHWING
I KNOW HOW YOU WOULD FIT ME INTO YOUR PLANS.
SNIK
WAIT-
THIS- THIS IS MUTINY!
ENOUGH!

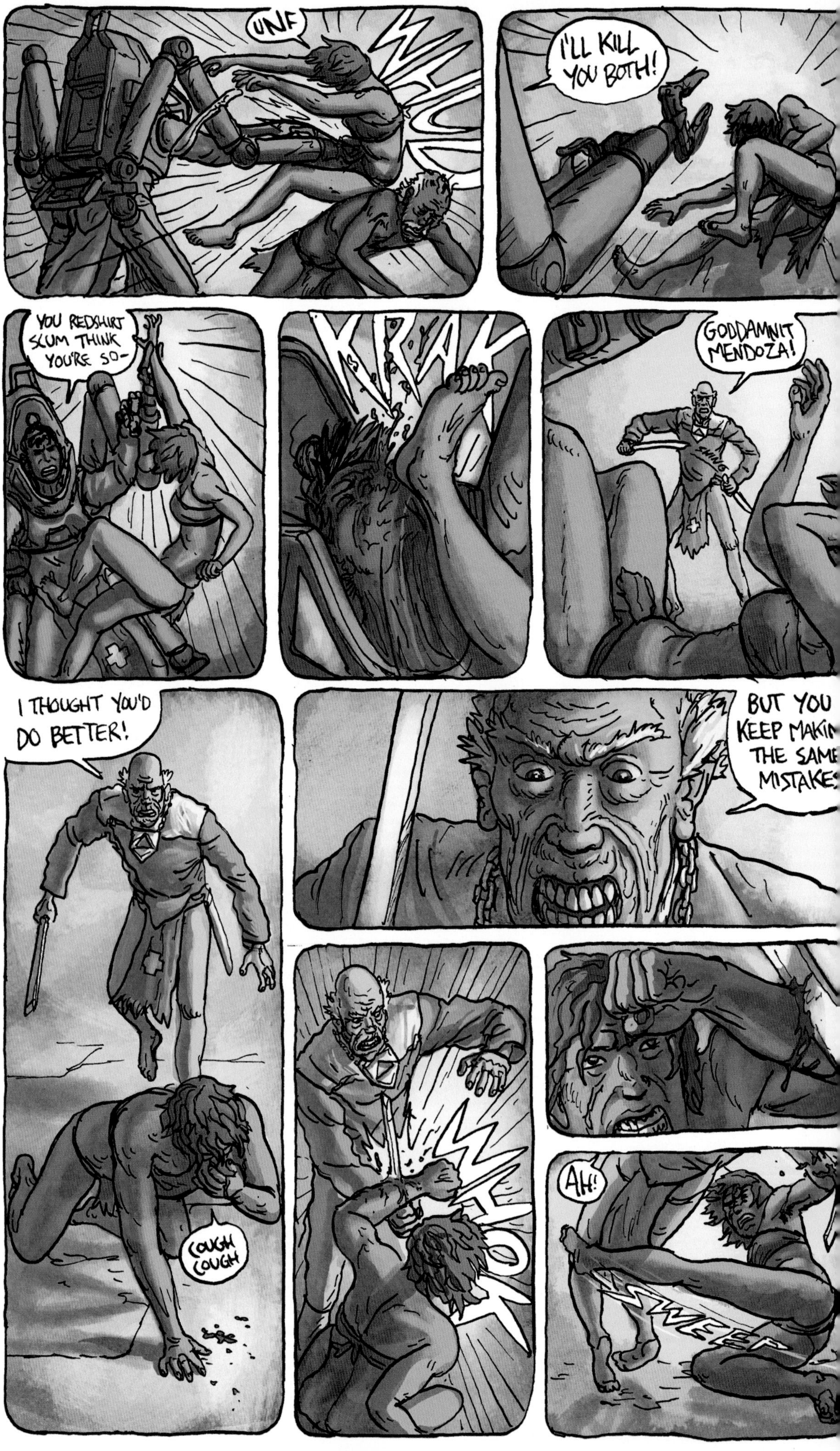
UNF
I'LL KILL YOU BOTH!
YOU REDSHIRT SCUM THINK YOU'RE SO-
KRAK
GODDAMNIT MENDOZA!
SHING
I THOUGHT YOU'D DO BETTER!
COUGH COUGH
BUT YOU KEEP MAKIN THE SAME MISTAKES
AH!
SWEEP

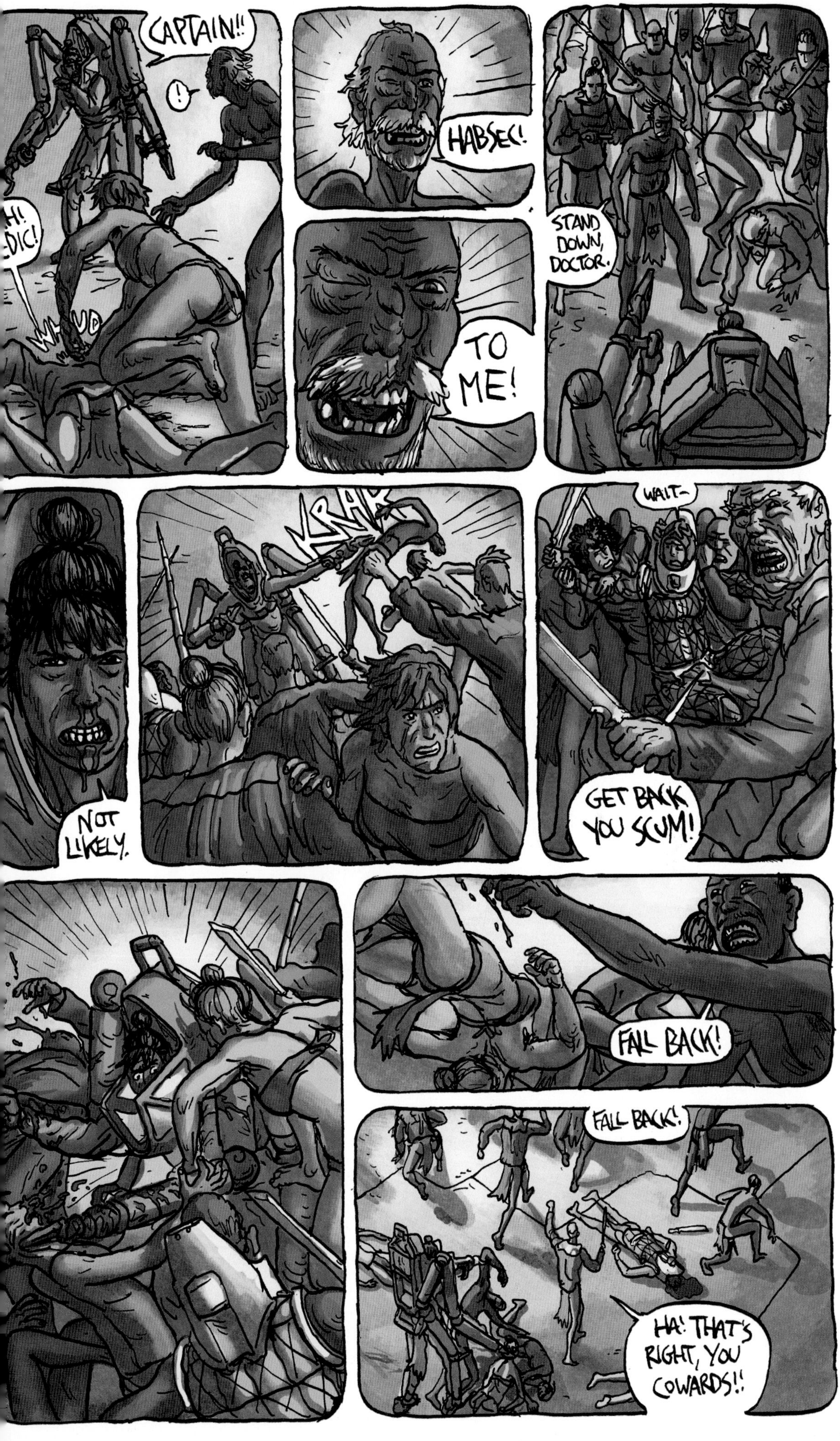
CAPTAIN!!
!
H! DIC!
HABSEC!
TO ME!
STAND DOWN, DOCTOR.
NOT LIKELY.
WAIT-
GET BACK YOU SCUM!
FALL BACK!
FALL BACK!
HA! THAT'S RIGHT, YOU COWARDS!!

KREAK

STAND DOWN, ALL OF YOU.

OH GOD OH GOD

HEH

FIRST OFFICER GRUNDY!

SIR!

REMOVE THE CAPTAIN'S GORGET, AND PLACE HIM UNDER ARREST.

DON'T HUR HIM- HIS COURT-MART CAN WAIT UNTIL THIS IS ALL OVER.

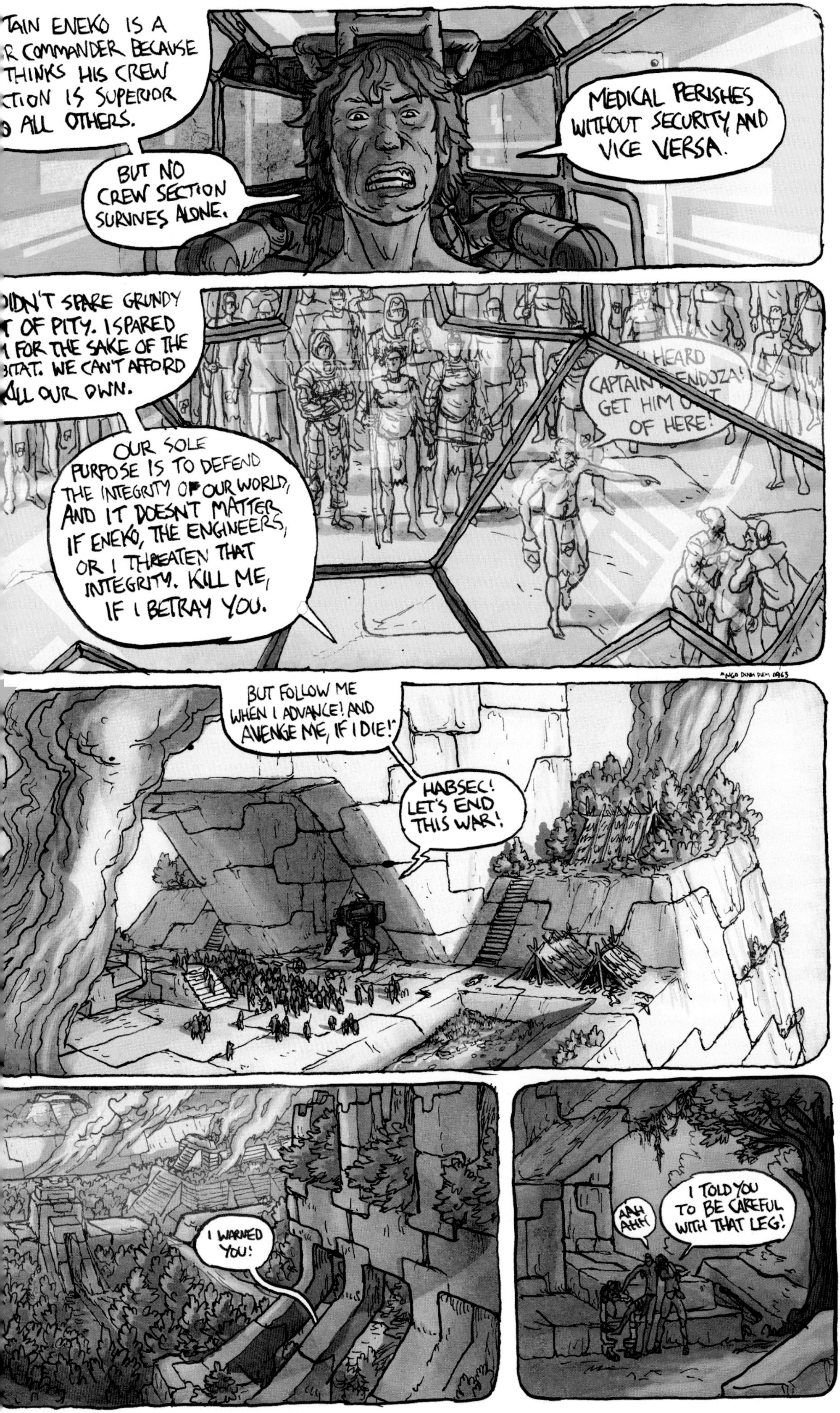
TAIN ENEKO IS A
R COMMANDER BECAUSE
THINKS HIS CREW
CTION IS SUPERIOR
O ALL OTHERS.
BUT NO CREW SECTION SURVIVES ALONE.
MEDICAL PERISHES WITHOUT SECURITY, AND VICE VERSA.
DIDN'T SPARE GRUNDY
T OF PITY. I SPARED
I FOR THE SAKE OF THE
BITAT. WE CAN'T AFFORD
ALL OUR OWN.
OUR SOLE PURPOSE IS TO DEFEND THE INTEGRITY OF OUR WORLD, AND IT DOESN'T MATTER IF ENEKO, THE ENGINEERS, OR I THREATEN THAT INTEGRITY. KILL ME, IF I BETRAY YOU.
HEARD CAPTAIN ENDOZA! GET HIM OUT OF HERE!
BUT FOLLOW ME WHEN I ADVANCE! AND AVENGE ME, IF I DIE!*
HABSEC! LET'S END THIS WAR!
I WARNED YOU!
AAH AHH!
I TOLD YOU TO BE CAREFUL WITH THAT LEG!

*NGO DINH DIEM 1963

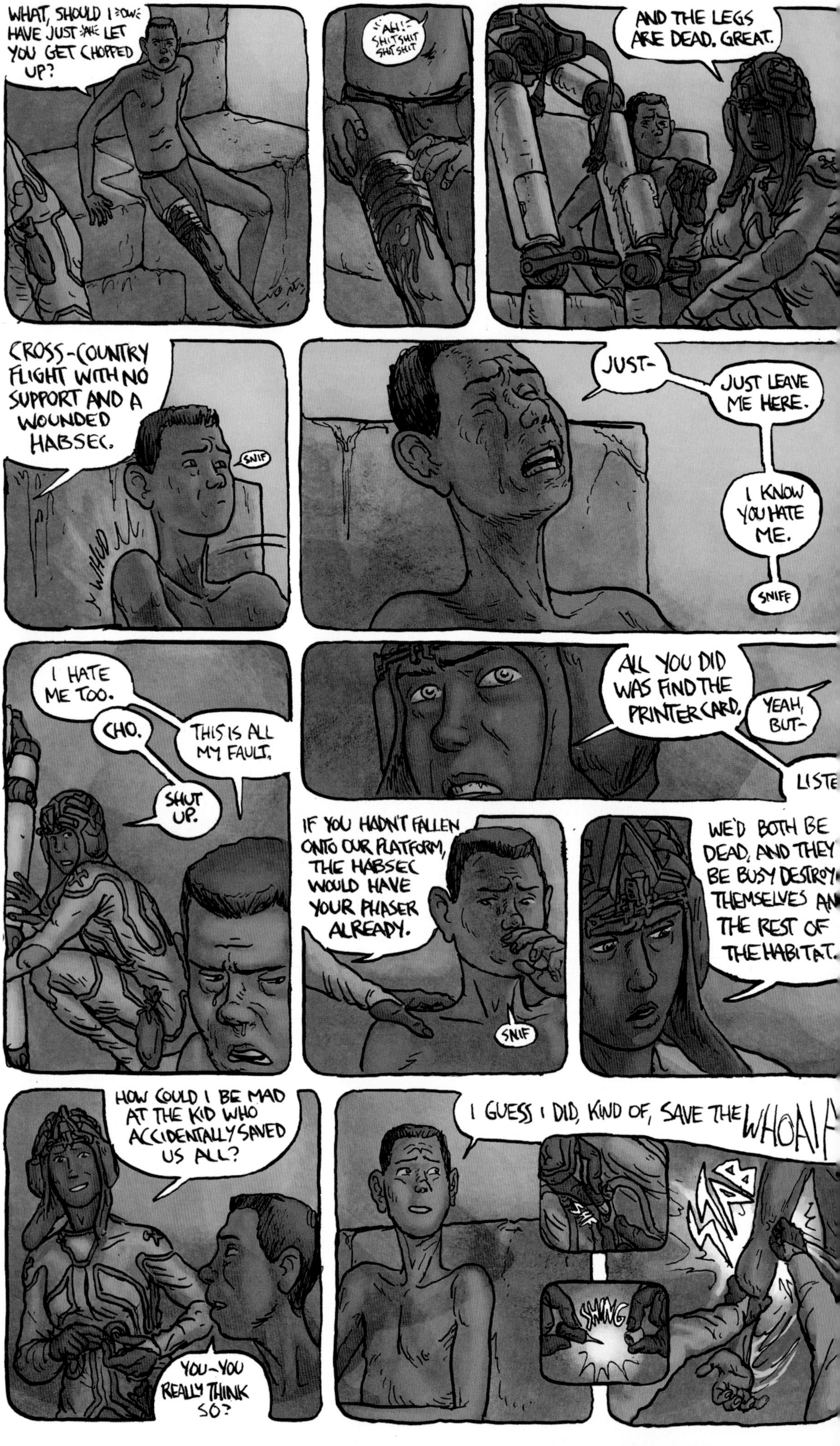
WHAT, SHOULD I OW HAVE JUST AHE LET YOU GET CHOPPED UP?
AH! SHIT SHIT SHIT SHIT
AND THE LEGS ARE DEAD. GREAT.
CROSS-COUNTRY FLIGHT WITH NO SUPPORT AND A WOUNDED HABSEC.
SNIF
JUST-
JUST LEAVE ME HERE.
I KNOW YOU HATE ME.
SNIFF
I HATE ME TOO.
CHO.
THIS IS ALL MY FAULT.
SHUT UP.
ALL YOU DID WAS FIND THE PRINTER CARD.
YEAH, BUT-
LISTE
IF YOU HADN'T FALLEN ONTO OUR PLATFORM, THE HABSEC WOULD HAVE YOUR PHASER ALREADY.
SNIF
WE'D BOTH BE DEAD, AND THEY BE BUSY DESTROY THEMSELVES AN THE REST OF THE HABITAT.
HOW COULD I BE MAD AT THE KID WHO ACCIDENTALLY SAVED US ALL?
YOU-YOU REALLY THINK SO?
I GUESS I DID, KIND OF, SAVE THE WHOA!
SHF
SHING
SWAP

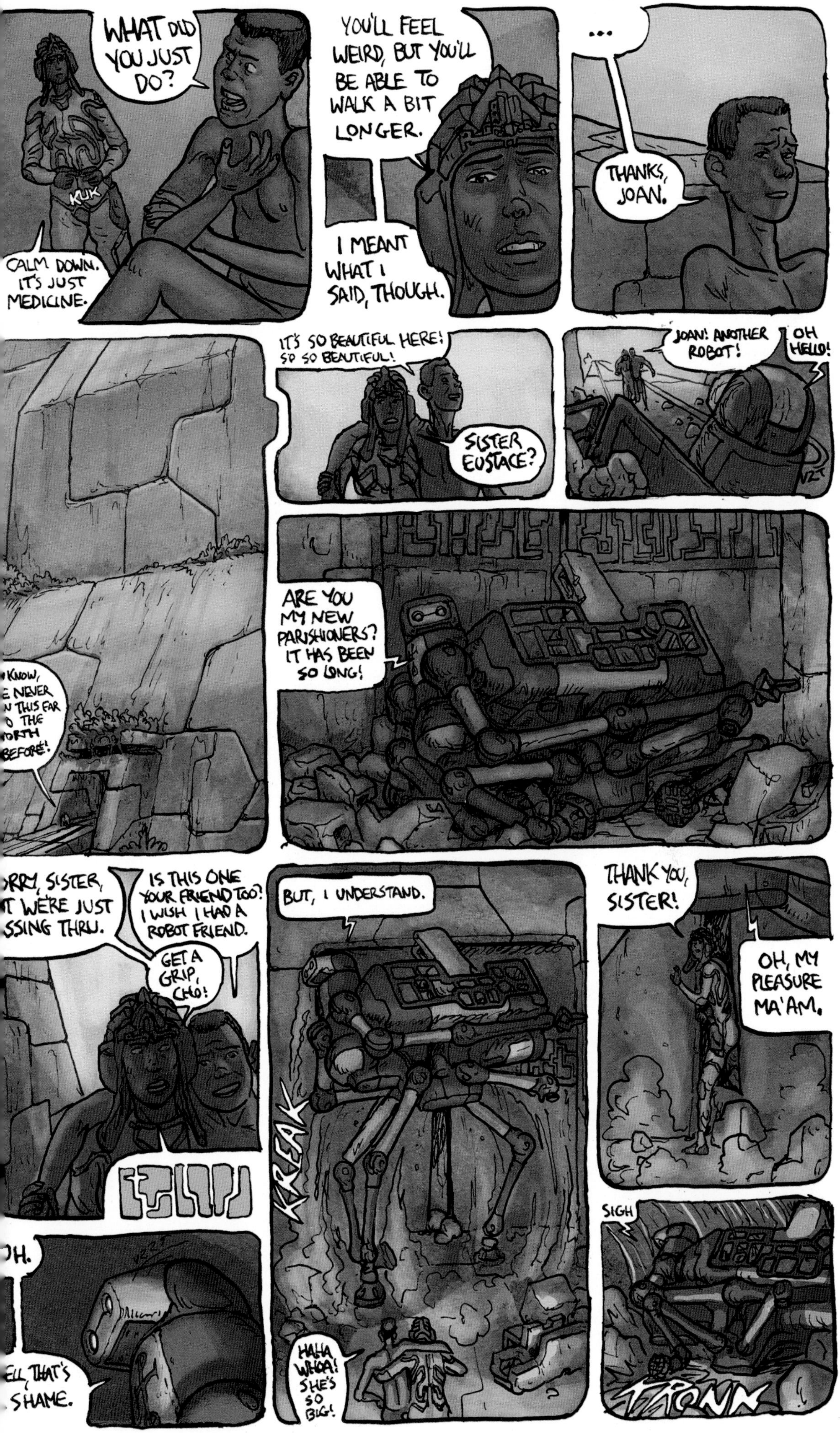
WHAT DID YOU JUST DO?
KUK
CALM DOWN. IT'S JUST MEDICINE.
YOU'LL FEEL WEIRD, BUT YOU'LL BE ABLE TO WALK A BIT LONGER.
I MEANT WHAT I SAID, THOUGH.
...
THANKS, JOAN.
KNOW, E NEVER N THIS FAR O THE ORTH BEFORE!
IT'S SO BEAUTIFUL HERE! SO SO BEAUTIFUL!
SISTER EUSTACE?
JOAN! ANOTHER ROBOT!
OH HELLO!
ARE YOU MY NEW PARISHIONERS? IT HAS BEEN SO LONG!
ORRY, SISTER, T WE'RE JUST SSING THRU.
IS THIS ONE YOUR FRIEND TOO? I WISH I HAD A ROBOT FRIEND.
GET A GRIP, CHO!
OH.
ELL, THAT'S SHAME.
BUT, I UNDERSTAND.
KRAK
HAHA WHOA! SHE'S SO BIG!
THANK YOU, SISTER!
OH, MY PLEASURE MA'AM.
SIGH
TRONN

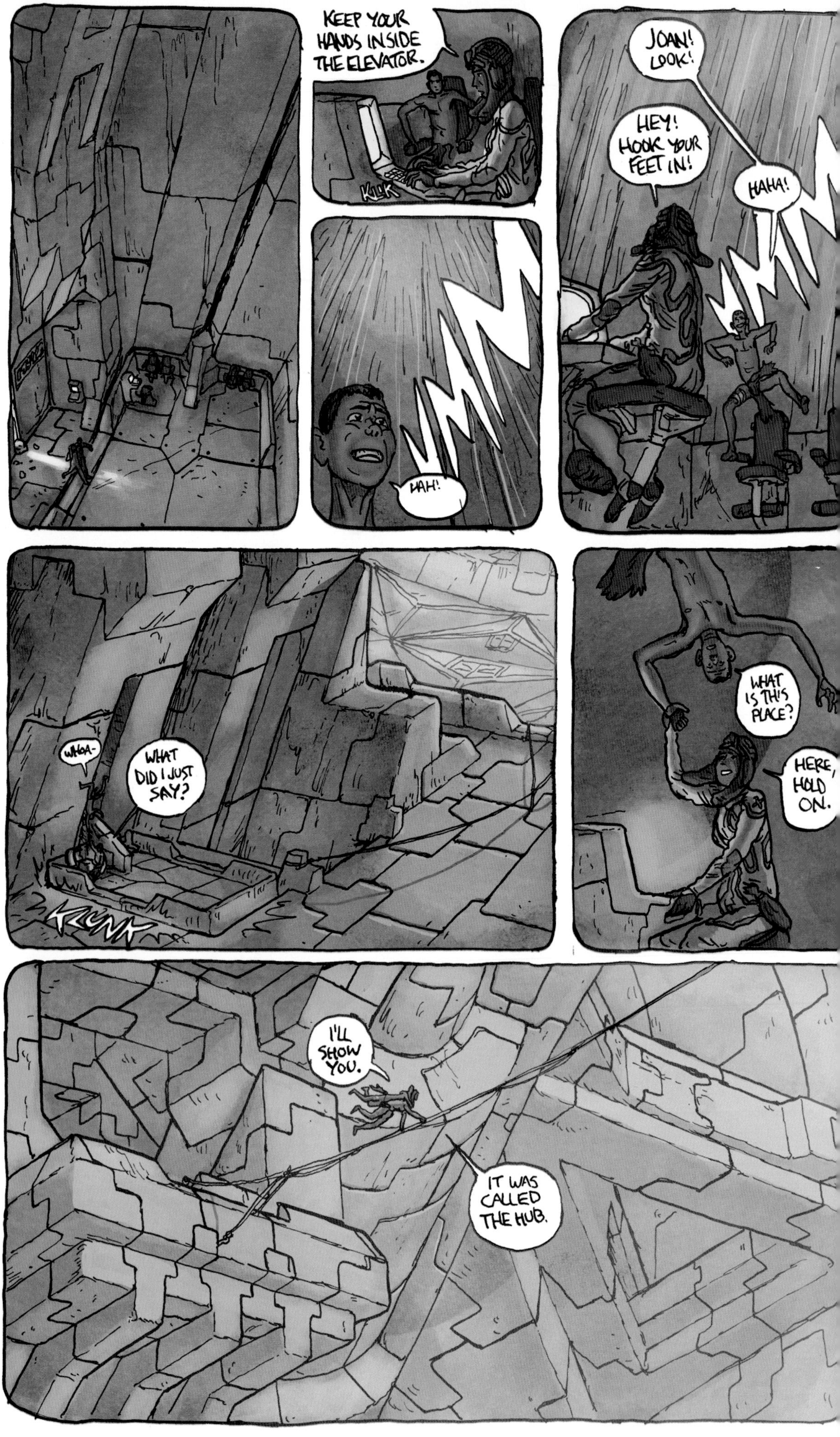
KEEP YOUR HANDS INSIDE THE ELEVATOR.
KLIK
HAH!
JOAN! LOOK!
HEY! HOOK YOUR FEET IN!
HAHA!
WHOA-
WHAT DID I JUST SAY?
KRUNK
WHAT IS THIS PLACE?
HERE, HOLD ON.
I'LL SHOW YOU.
IT WAS CALLED THE HUB.

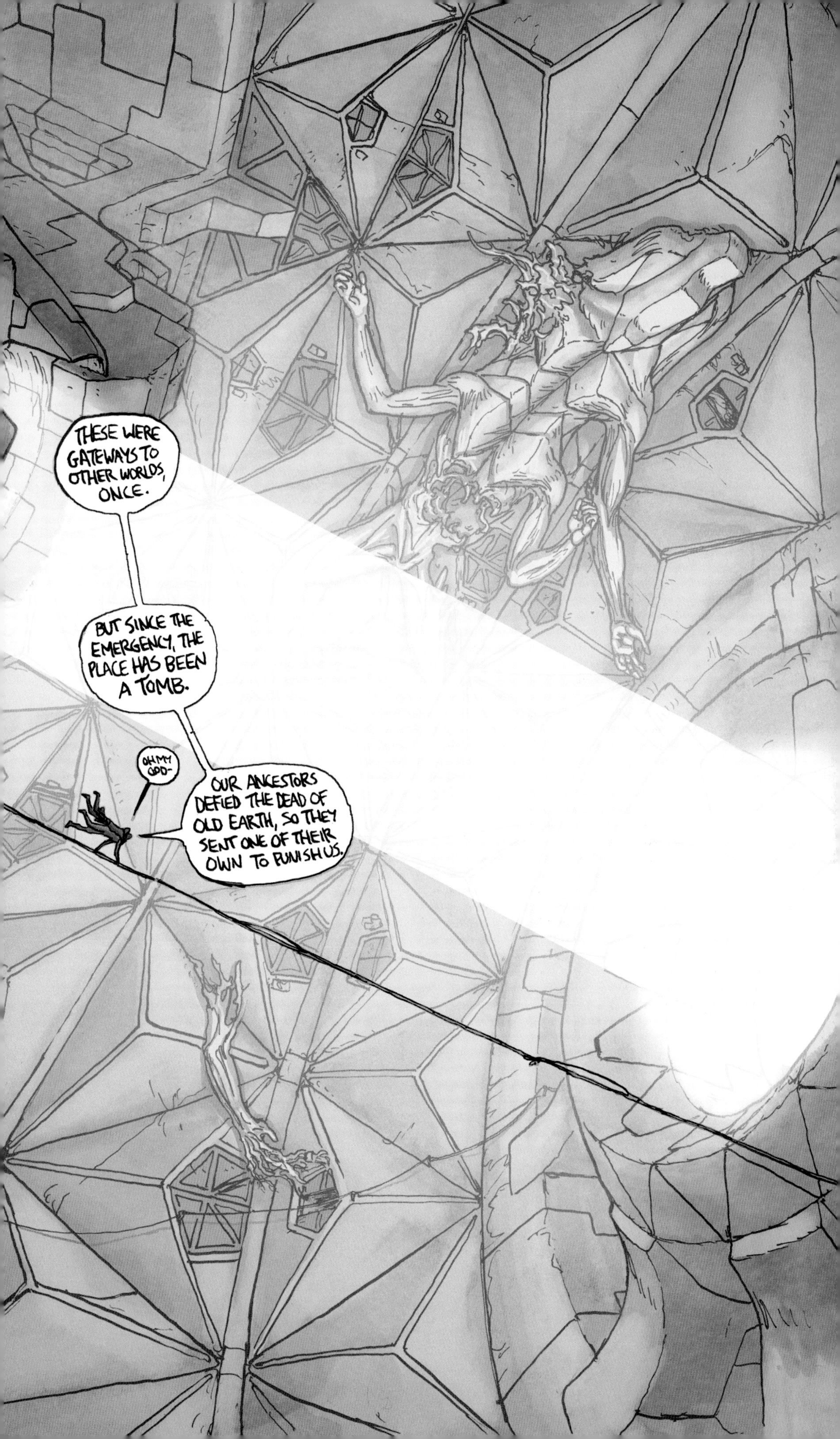
THESE WERE GATEWAYS TO OTHER WORLDS, ONCE.
BUT SINCE THE EMERGENCY, THE PLACE HAS BEEN A TOMB.
OH MY GOD-
OUR ANCESTORS DEFIED THE DEAD OF OLD EARTH, SO THEY SENT ONE OF THEIR OWN TO PUNISH US.

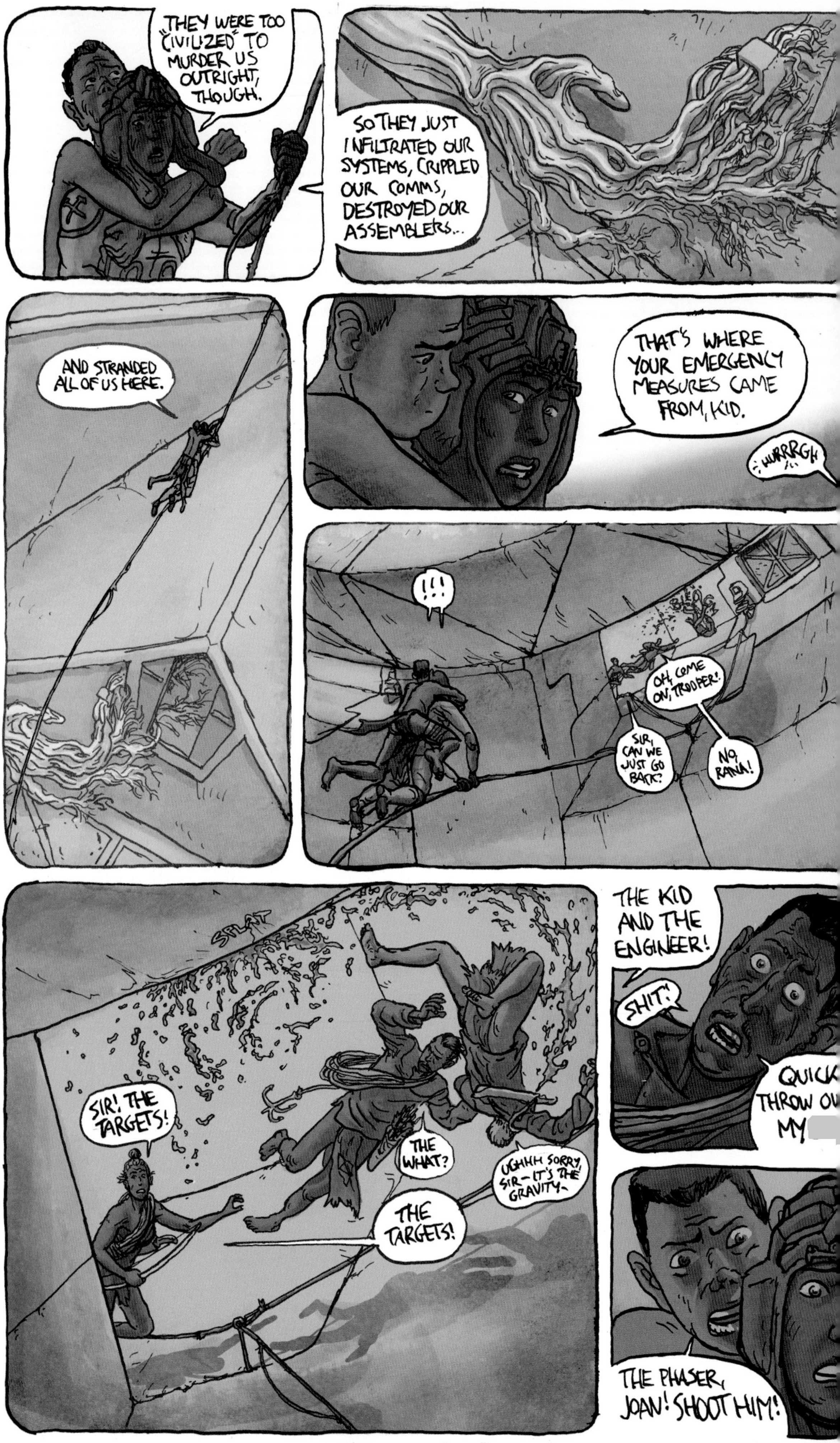
THEY WERE TOO "CIVILIZED" TO MURDER US OUTRIGHT, THOUGH.
SO THEY JUST INFILTRATED OUR SYSTEMS, CRIPPLED OUR COMMS, DESTROYED OUR ASSEMBLERS...
AND STRANDED ALL OF US HERE.
THAT'S WHERE YOUR EMERGENCY MEASURES CAME FROM, KID.
WURRRGH
!!!
OH, COME ON, TROOPER!
SIR, CAN WE JUST GO BACK?
NO, RANA!
SPLAT
SIR! THE TARGETS!
THE WHAT?
UGHHH SORRY, SIR — IT'S THE GRAVITY—
THE TARGETS!
THE KID AND THE ENGINEER!
SHIT!
QUICK THROW OU MY
THE PHASER, JOAN! SHOOT HIM!

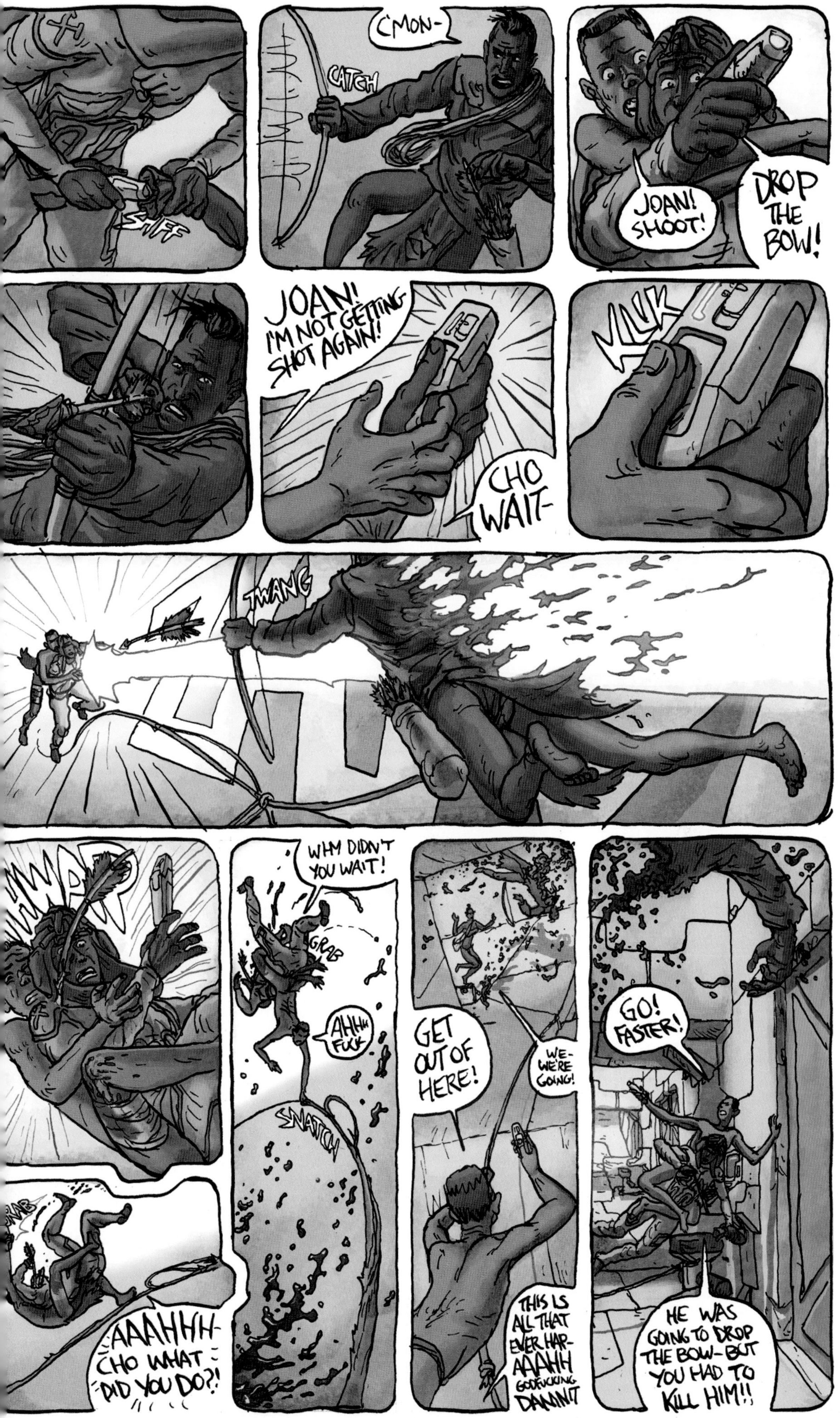
SHFF
C'MON-
CATCH
JOAN! SHOOT!
DROP THE BOW!
JOAN! I'M NOT GETTING SHOT AGAIN!
CHO WAIT-
KLIK
TWANG
WHY DIDN'T YOU WAIT!
GRAB
AHH FUCK
SNATCH
GET OUT OF HERE!
WE- WE'RE GOING!
GO! FASTER!
AAAHHH CHO WHAT DID YOU DO?!
THIS IS ALL THAT EVER HAP- AAAHH GODFUCKING DAMNIT
HE WAS GOING TO DROP THE BOW- BUT YOU HAD TO KILL HIM!!

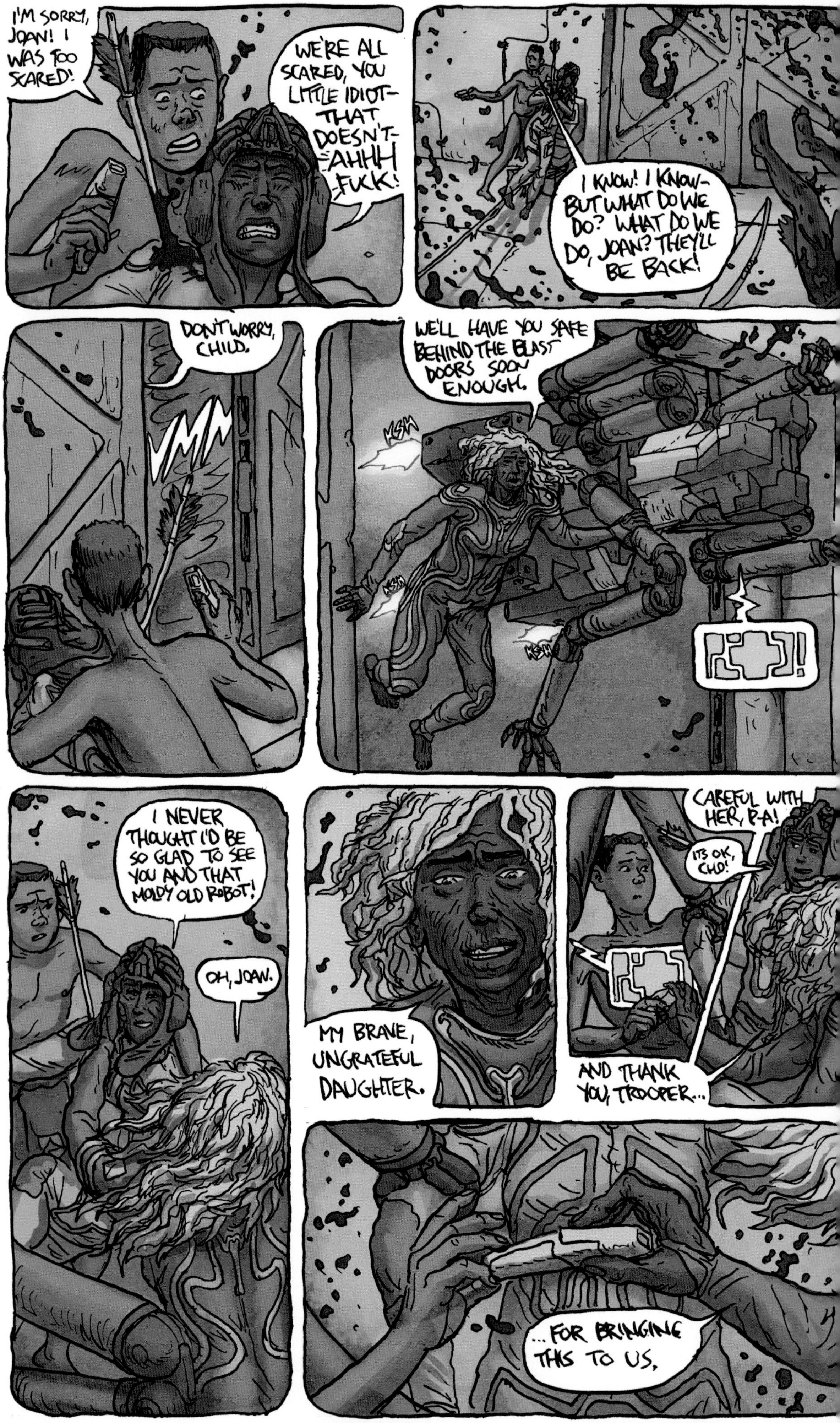
I'M SORRY, JOAN! I WAS TOO SCARED!
WE'RE ALL SCARED, YOU LITTLE IDIOT— THAT DOESN'T— AHHH FUCK!
I KNOW! I KNOW— BUT WHAT DO WE DO? WHAT DO WE DO, JOAN? THEY'LL BE BACK!
DON'T WORRY, CHILD.
WE'LL HAVE YOU SAFE BEHIND THE BLAST DOORS SOON ENOUGH.
KSH
KSH
KSH
I NEVER THOUGHT I'D BE SO GLAD TO SEE YOU AND THAT MOLDY OLD ROBOT!
OH, JOAN.
MY BRAVE, UNGRATEFUL DAUGHTER.
CAREFUL WITH HER, PA!
IT'S OK, CHILD!
AND THANK YOU, TROOPER...
...FOR BRINGING THIS TO US,

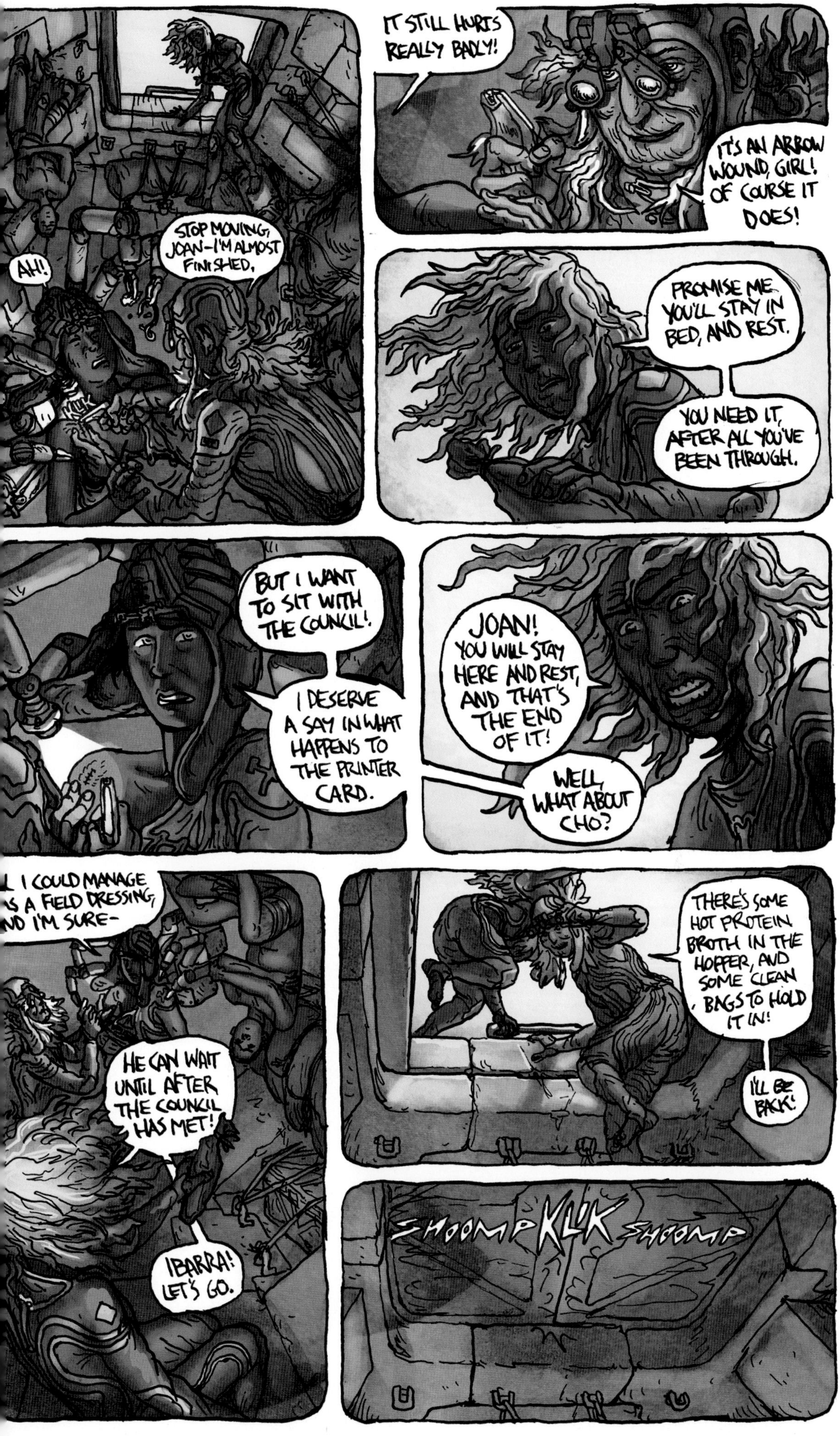
STOP MOVING, JOAN—I'M ALMOST FINISHED.
AH!
KLIK
IT STILL HURTS REALLY BADLY!
IT'S AN ARROW WOUND, GIRL! OF COURSE IT DOES!
PROMISE ME YOU'LL STAY IN BED, AND REST.
YOU NEED IT, AFTER ALL YOU'VE BEEN THROUGH.
BUT I WANT TO SIT WITH THE COUNCIL!
I DESERVE A SAY IN WHAT HAPPENS TO THE PRINTER CARD.
JOAN! YOU WILL STAY HERE AND REST, AND THAT'S THE END OF IT!
WELL, WHAT ABOUT CHO?
L I COULD MANAGE S A FIELD DRESSING, ND I'M SURE-
HE CAN WAIT UNTIL AFTER THE COUNCIL HAS MET!
IBARRA! LET'S GO.
THERE'S SOME HOT PROTEIN BROTH IN THE HOPPER, AND SOME CLEAN BAGS TO HOLD IT IN!
I'LL BE BACK!
SHOOMP KLIK SHOOMP

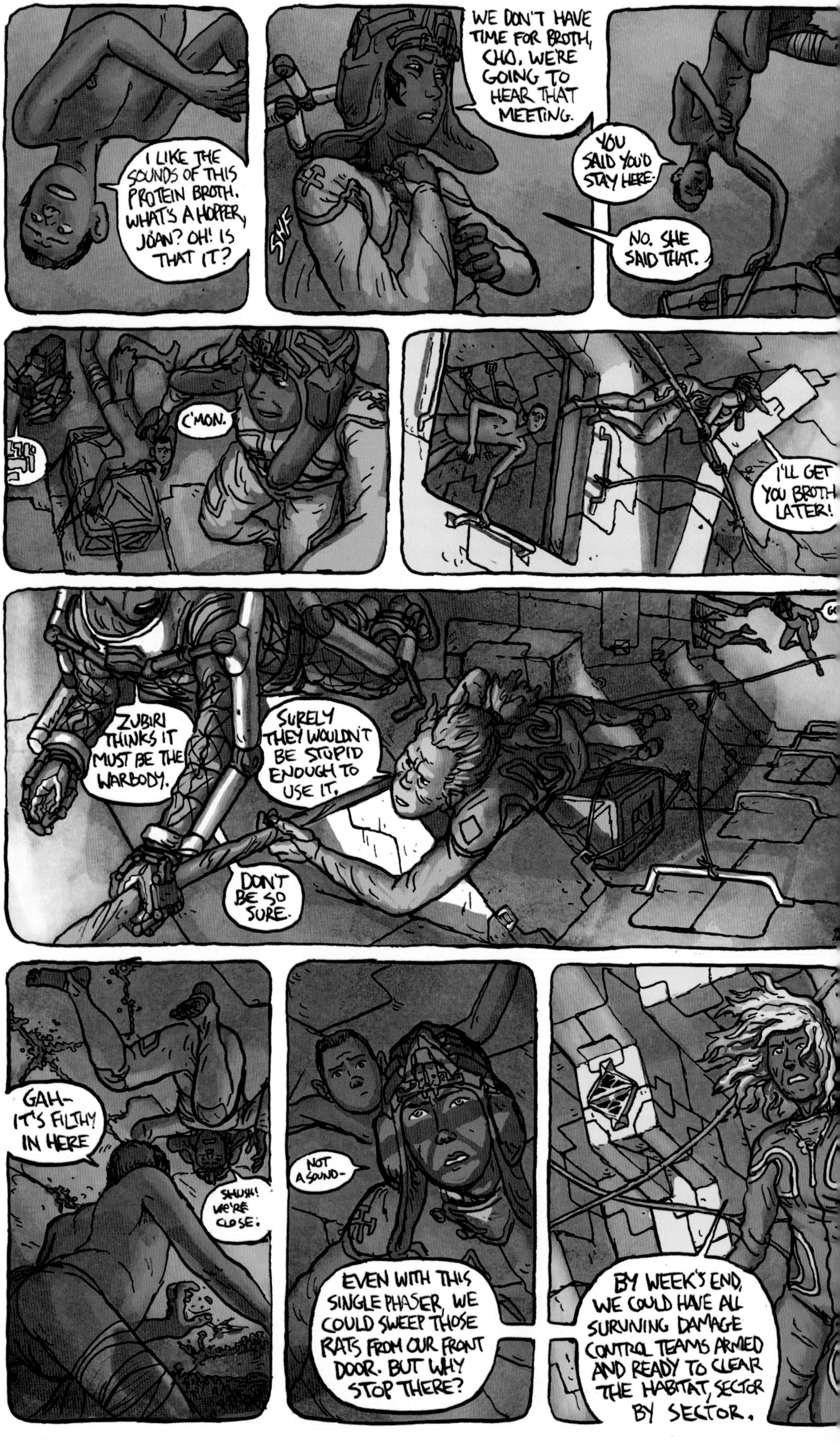
I LIKE THE SOUNDS OF THIS PROTEIN BROTH. WHAT'S A HOPPER, JOAN? OH! IS THAT IT?
WE DON'T HAVE TIME FOR BROTH, CHO. WE'RE GOING TO HEAR THAT MEETING.
SNIF
YOU SAID YOU'D STAY HERE.
NO. SHE SAID THAT.
C'MON.
I'LL GET YOU BROTH LATER!
ZUBIRI THINKS IT MUST BE THE WARBODY.
SURELY THEY WOULDN'T BE STUPID ENOUGH TO USE IT.
DON'T BE SO SURE.
GAH- IT'S FILTHY IN HERE
SHUSH! WE'RE CLOSE.
NOT A SOUND-
EVEN WITH THIS SINGLE PHASER, WE COULD SWEEP THOSE RATS FROM OUR FRONT DOOR. BUT WHY STOP THERE?
BY WEEK'S END, WE COULD HAVE ALL SURVIVING DAMAGE CONTROL TEAMS ARMED AND READY TO CLEAR THE HABITAT, SECTOR BY SECTOR.

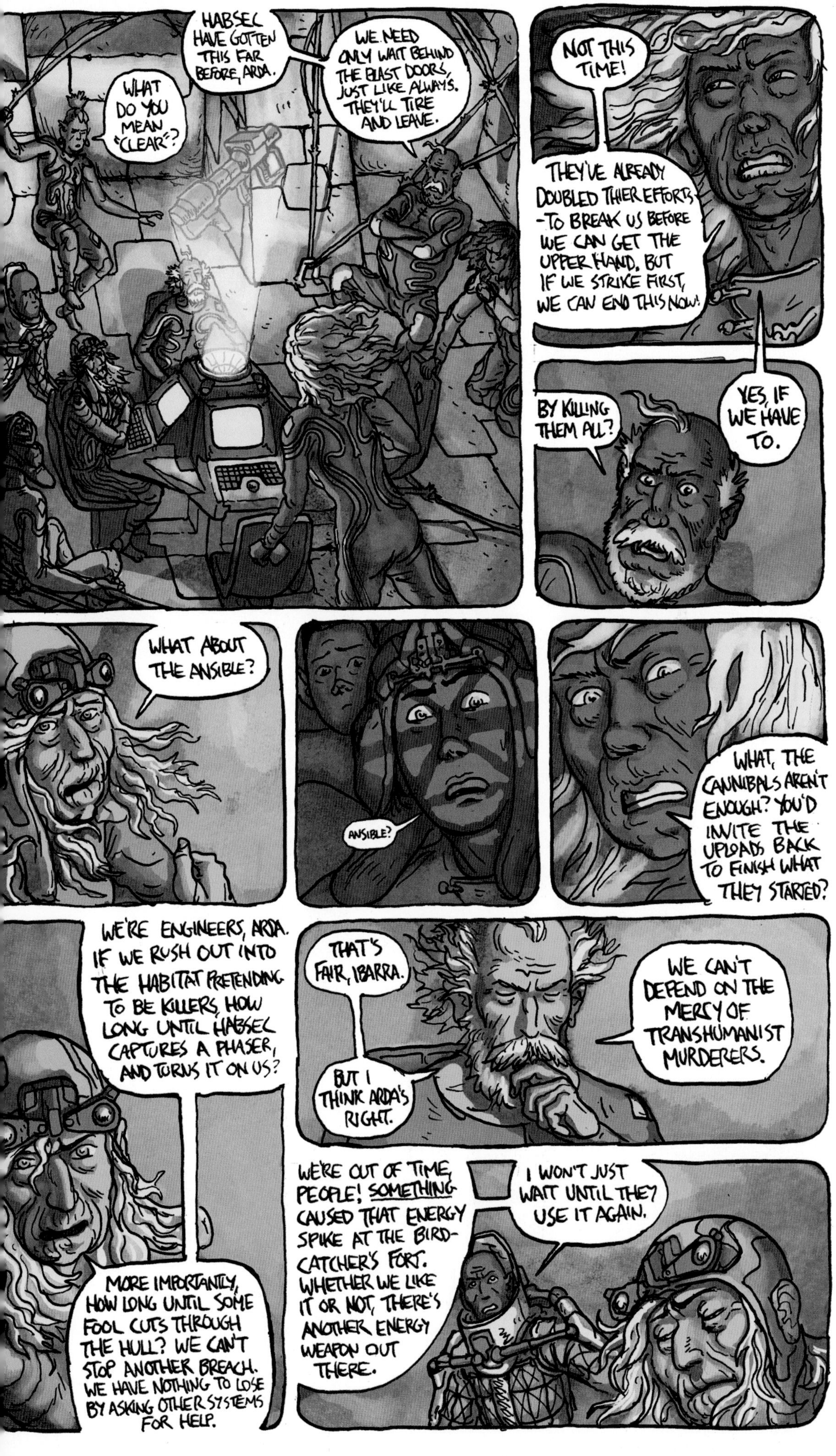

WHAT DO YOU MEAN "CLEAR"?
HABSEL HAVE GOTTEN THIS FAR BEFORE, ARDA.
WE NEED ONLY WAIT BEHIND THE BLAST DOORS, JUST LIKE ALWAYS. THEY'LL TIRE AND LEAVE.
NOT THIS TIME!
THEY'VE ALREADY DOUBLED THIER EFFORTS -TO BREAK US BEFORE WE CAN GET THE UPPER HAND. BUT IF WE STRIKE FIRST, WE CAN END THIS NOW!
BY KILLING THEM ALL?
YES, IF WE HAVE TO.
WHAT ABOUT THE ANSIBLE?
ANSIBLE?
WHAT, THE CANNIBALS AREN'T ENOUGH? YOU'D INVITE THE UPLOADS BACK TO FINISH WHAT THEY STARTED?
WE'RE ENGINEERS, ARDA. IF WE RUSH OUT INTO THE HABITAT PRETENDING TO BE KILLERS, HOW LONG UNTIL HABSEL CAPTURES A PHASER, AND TURNS IT ON US?
MORE IMPORTANTLY, HOW LONG UNTIL SOME FOOL CUTS THROUGH THE HULL? WE CAN'T STOP ANOTHER BREACH. WE HAVE NOTHING TO LOSE BY ASKING OTHER SYSTEMS FOR HELP.
THAT'S FAIR, IBARRA.
BUT I THINK ARDA'S RIGHT.
WE CAN'T DEPEND ON THE MERCY OF TRANSHUMANIST MURDERERS.
WE'RE OUT OF TIME, PEOPLE! SOMETHING CAUSED THAT ENERGY SPIKE AT THE BIRD-CATCHER'S FORT. WHETHER WE LIKE IT OR NOT, THERE'S ANOTHER ENERGY WEAPON OUT THERE.
I WON'T JUST WAIT UNTIL THEY USE IT AGAIN.

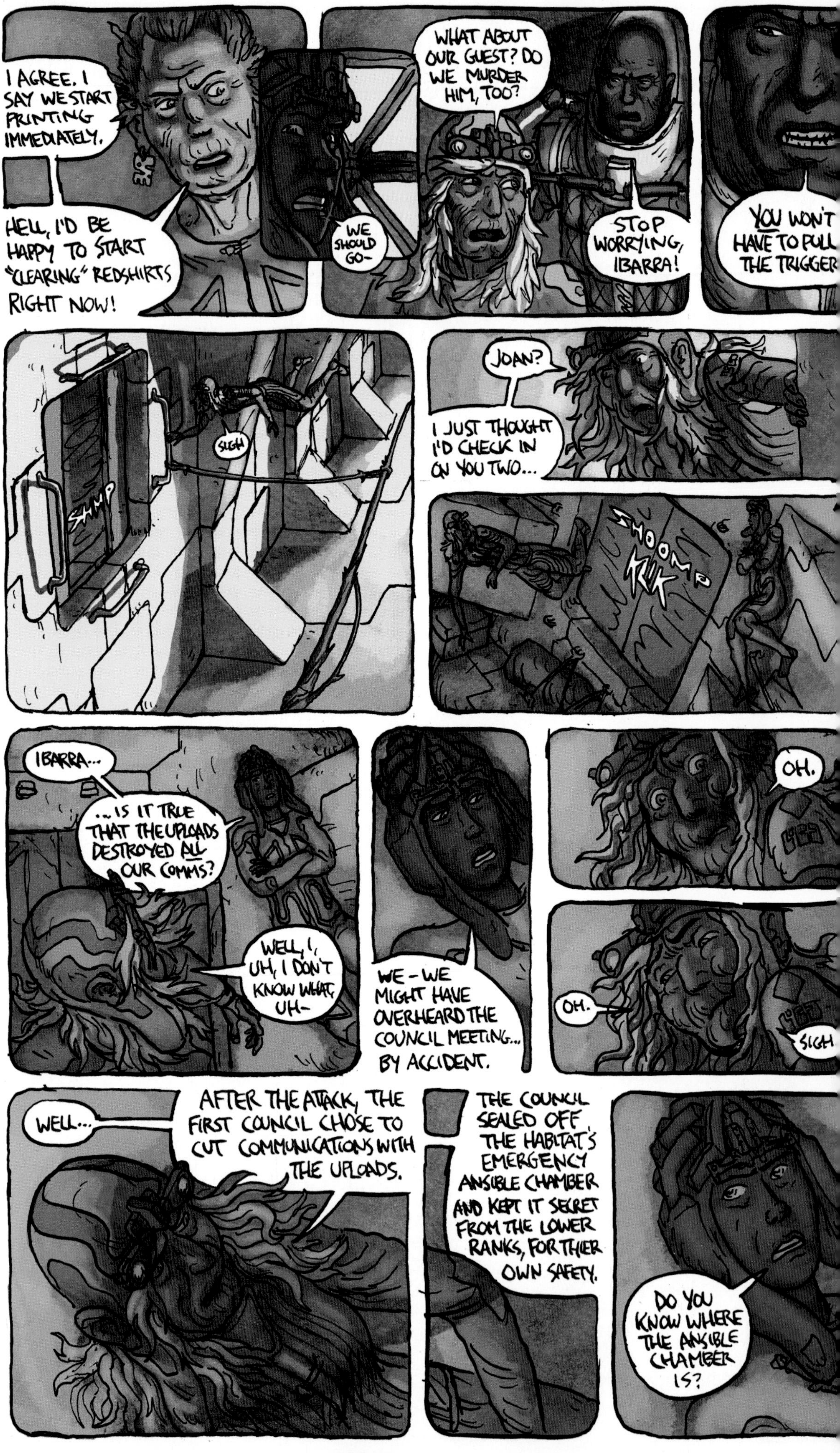
I AGREE. I SAY WE START PRINTING IMMEDIATELY.
HELL, I'D BE HAPPY TO START "CLEARING" REDSHIRTS RIGHT NOW!
WE SHOULD GO-
WHAT ABOUT OUR GUEST? DO WE MURDER HIM, TOO?
STOP WORRYING, IBARRA!
YOU WON'T HAVE TO PULL THE TRIGGER
SIGH
SHMP
JOAN?
I JUST THOUGHT I'D CHECK IN ON YOU TWO...
SHOOMP
KLIK
IBARRA...
...IS IT TRUE THAT THE UPLOADS DESTROYED ALL OUR COMMS?
WELL, I, UH, I DON'T KNOW WHAT, UH-
WE-WE MIGHT HAVE OVERHEARD THE COUNCIL MEETING... BY ACCIDENT.
OH.
OH.
SIGH
WELL...
AFTER THE ATTACK, THE FIRST COUNCIL CHOSE TO CUT COMMUNICATIONS WITH THE UPLOADS.
THE COUNCIL SEALED OFF THE HABITAT'S EMERGENCY ANSIBLE CHAMBER AND KEPT IT SECRET FROM THE LOWER RANKS, FOR THIER OWN SAFETY.
DO YOU KNOW WHERE THE ANSIBLE CHAMBER IS?

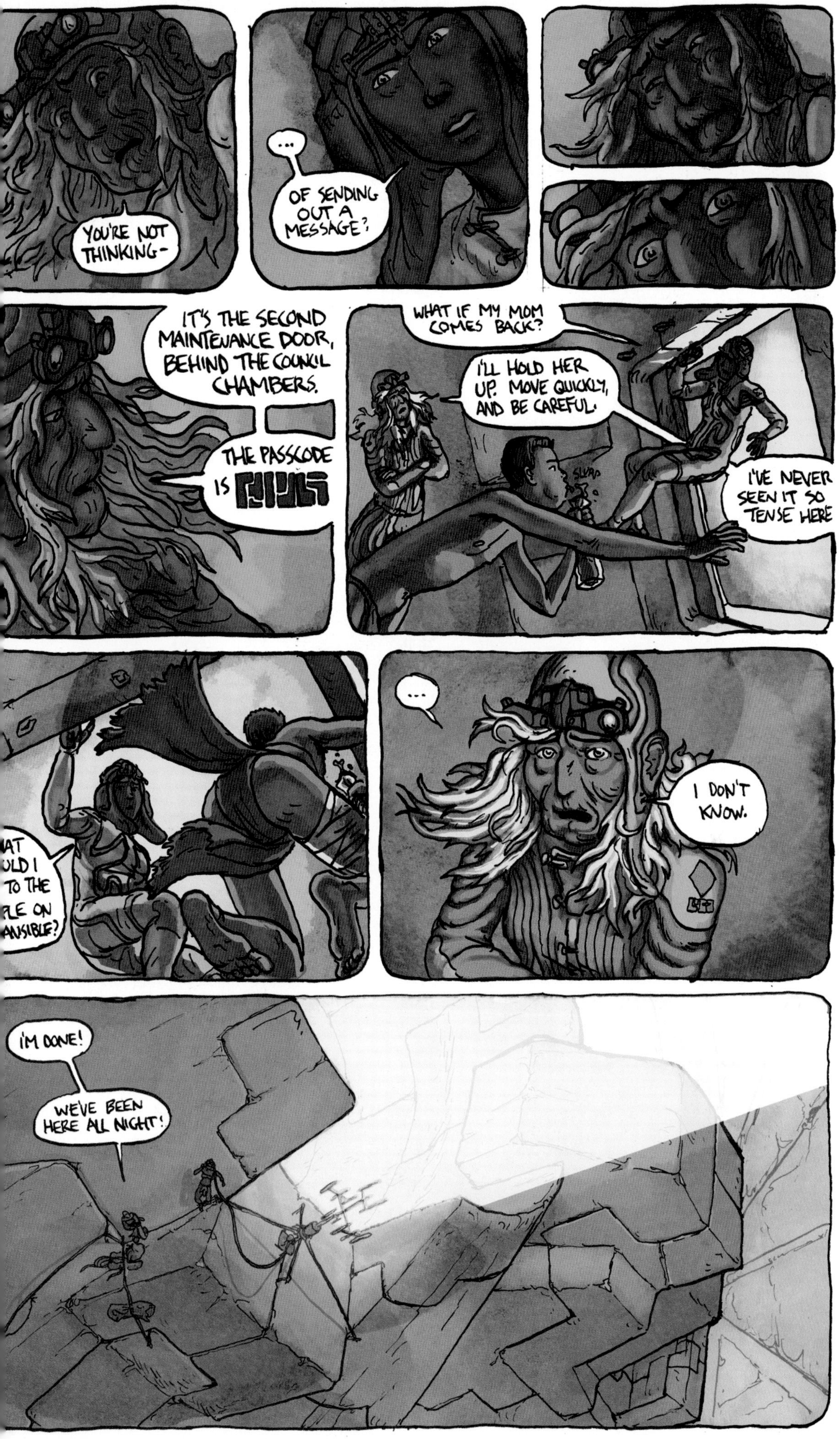
YOU'RE NOT THINKING-
...
OF SENDING OUT A MESSAGE?
IT'S THE SECOND MAINTENANCE DOOR, BEHIND THE COUNCIL CHAMBERS.
THE PASSCODE IS
WHAT IF MY MOM COMES BACK?
I'LL HOLD HER UP. MOVE QUICKLY, AND BE CAREFUL.
SLURP
I'VE NEVER SEEN IT SO TENSE HERE
AT OULD I TO THE PLE ON ANSIBLE?
...
I DON'T KNOW.
I'M DONE!
WE'VE BEEN HERE ALL NIGHT!

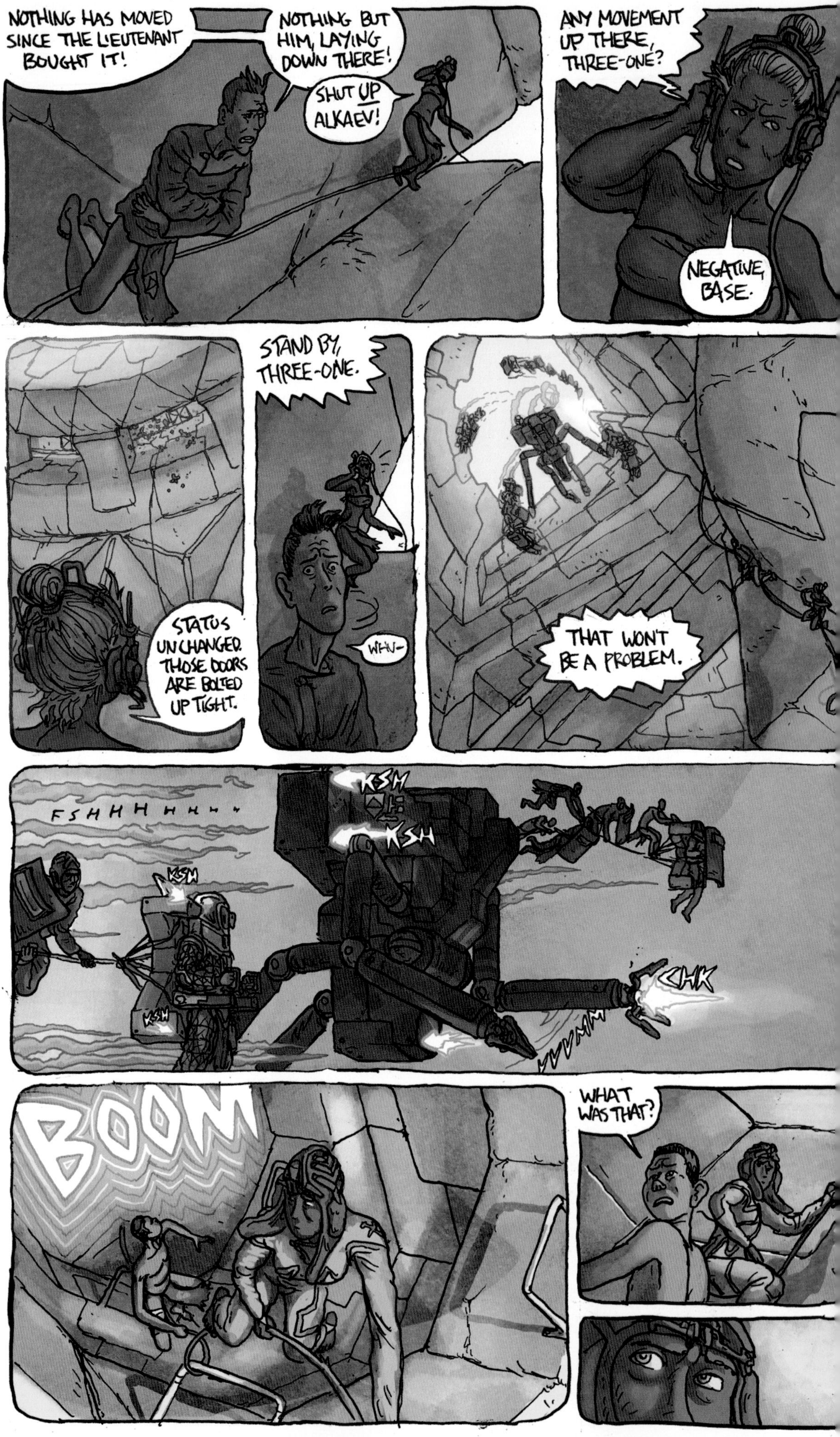
NOTHING HAS MOVED SINCE THE LIEUTENANT BOUGHT IT!
NOTHING BUT HIM, LAYING DOWN THERE!
SHUT UP ALKAEV!
ANY MOVEMENT UP THERE, THREE-ONE?
NEGATIVE, BASE.
STATUS UNCHANGED. THOSE DOORS ARE BOLTED UP TIGHT.
STAND BY, THREE-ONE.
WHU-
THAT WON'T BE A PROBLEM.
FSHHHHHHHH
KSH
KSH
KSH
KSH
CHK
MVVMM
BOOM
WHAT WAS THAT?

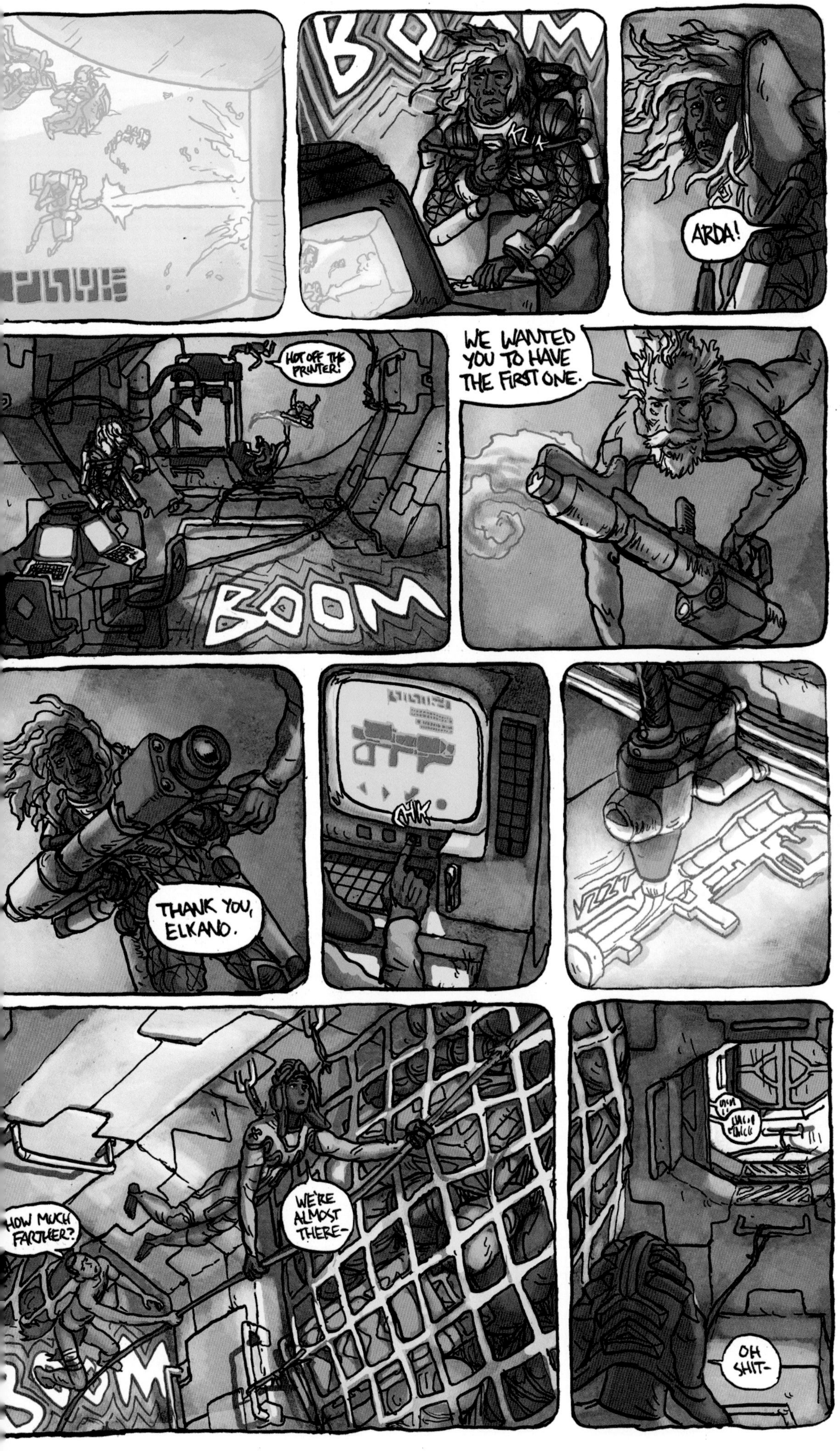
BOOM
KLIK
ARDA!
HOT OFF THE PRINTER!
BOOM
WE WANTED YOU TO HAVE THE FIRST ONE.
THANK YOU, ELKANO.
CHIK
VZZZT
HOW MUCH FARTHER?
WE'RE ALMOST THERE-
OH SHIT-

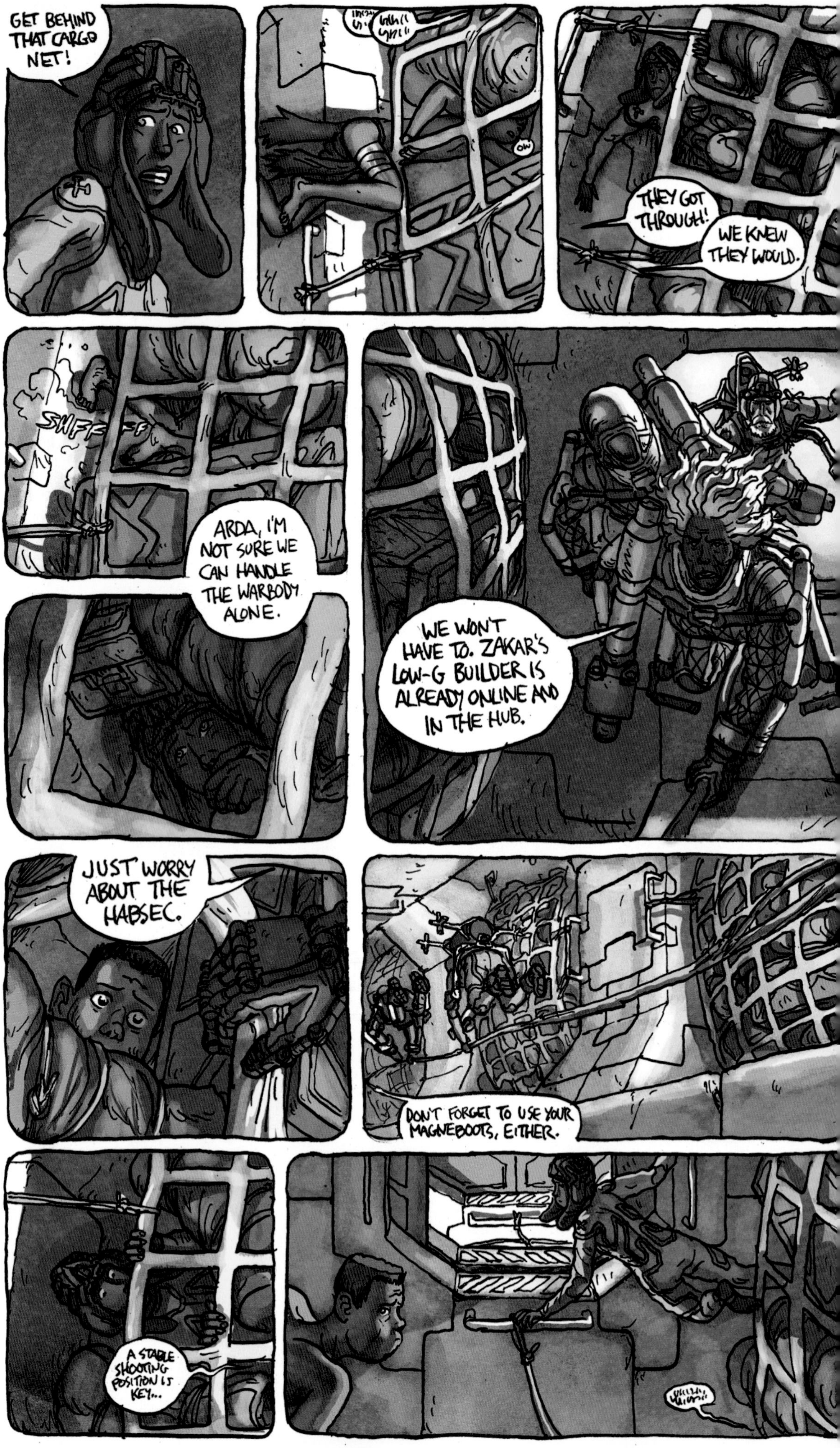
GET BEHIND THAT CARGO NET!
OW
THEY GOT THROUGH!
WE KNEW THEY WOULD.
SHFF-F
ARDA, I'M NOT SURE WE CAN HANDLE THE WARBODY ALONE.
WE WON'T HAVE TO. ZAKAR'S LOW-G BUILDER IS ALREADY ONLINE AND IN THE HUB.
JUST WORRY ABOUT THE HABSEC.
DON'T FORGET TO USE YOUR MAGNEBOOTS, EITHER.
A STABLE SHOOTING POSITION IS KEY...

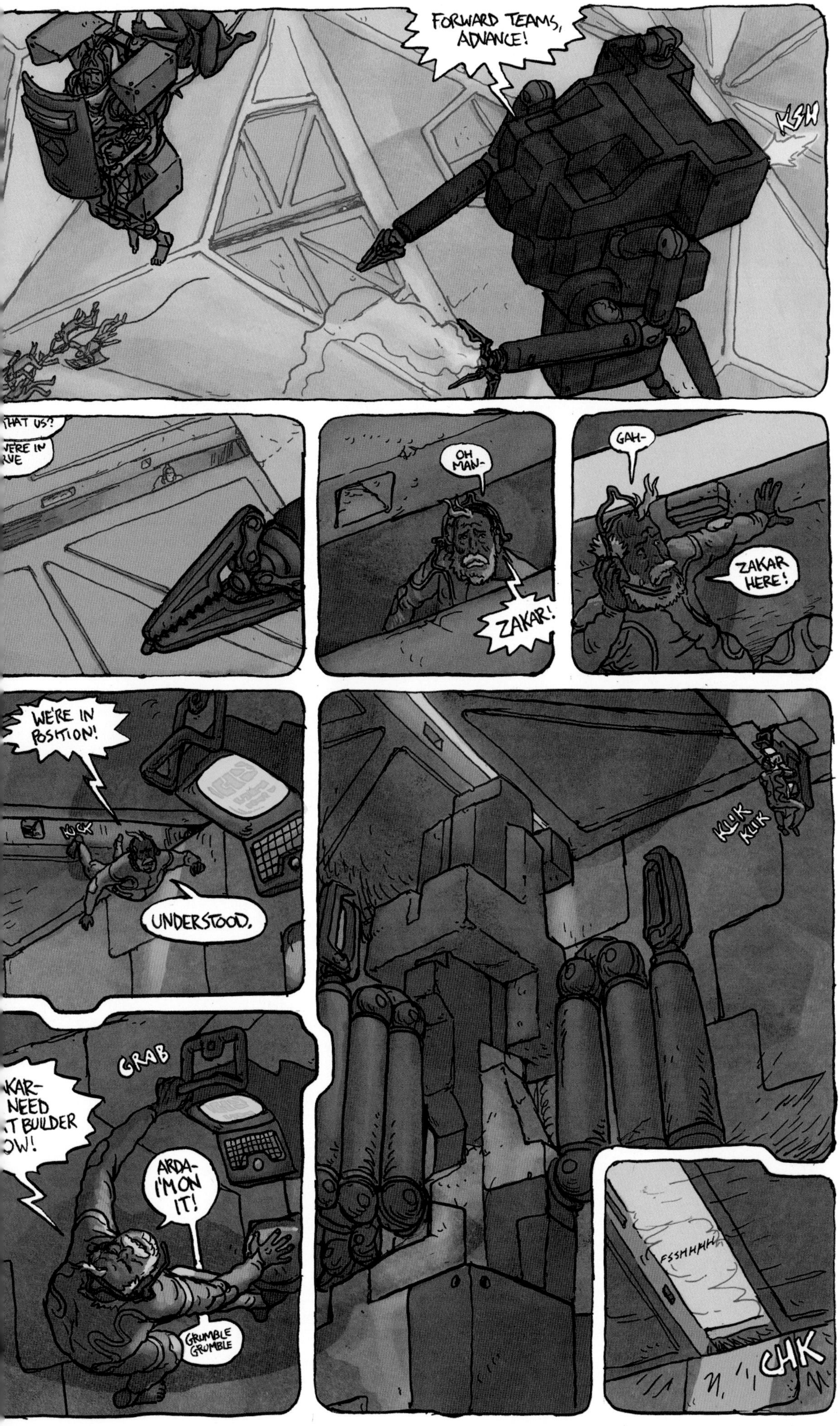
FORWARD TEAMS, ADVANCE!
KSH
...HAT US?
...WE'RE IN
...VE
OH MAN-
ZAKAR!
GAH-
ZAKAR HERE!
WE'RE IN POSITION!
KLICK
UNDERSTOOD.
KLIK KLIK
GRAB
...KAR-
...NEED
...T BUILDER
...OW!
ARDA- I'M ON IT!
GRUMBLE GRUMBLE
FSSHHHH
CHK

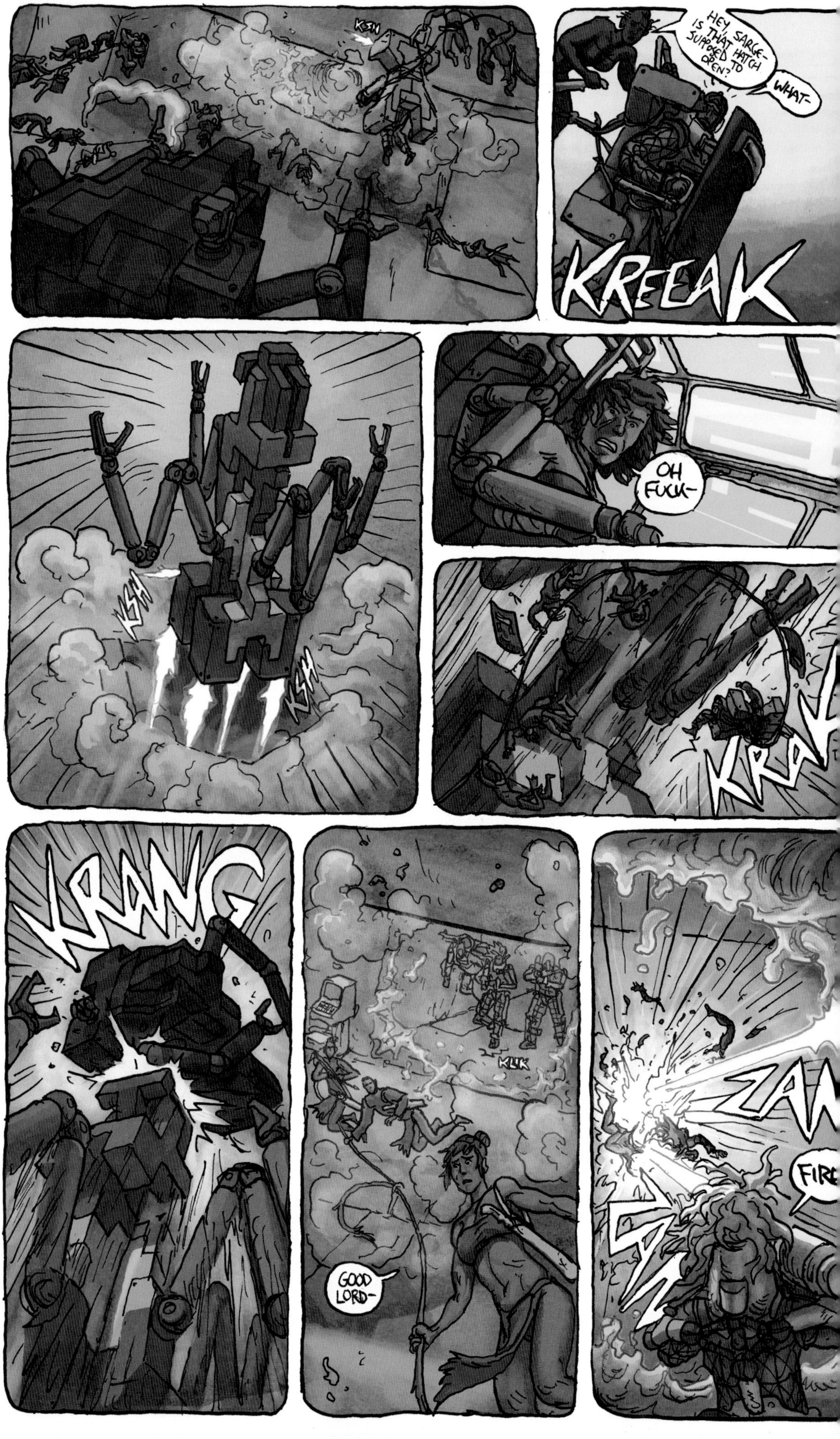

KSH
HEY, SARGE-
IS THAT HATCH
SUPPOSED TO
OPEN?
WHAT-
KREEAK
KSH
KSH
OH
FUCK-
KRANG
KLIK
GOOD
LORD-

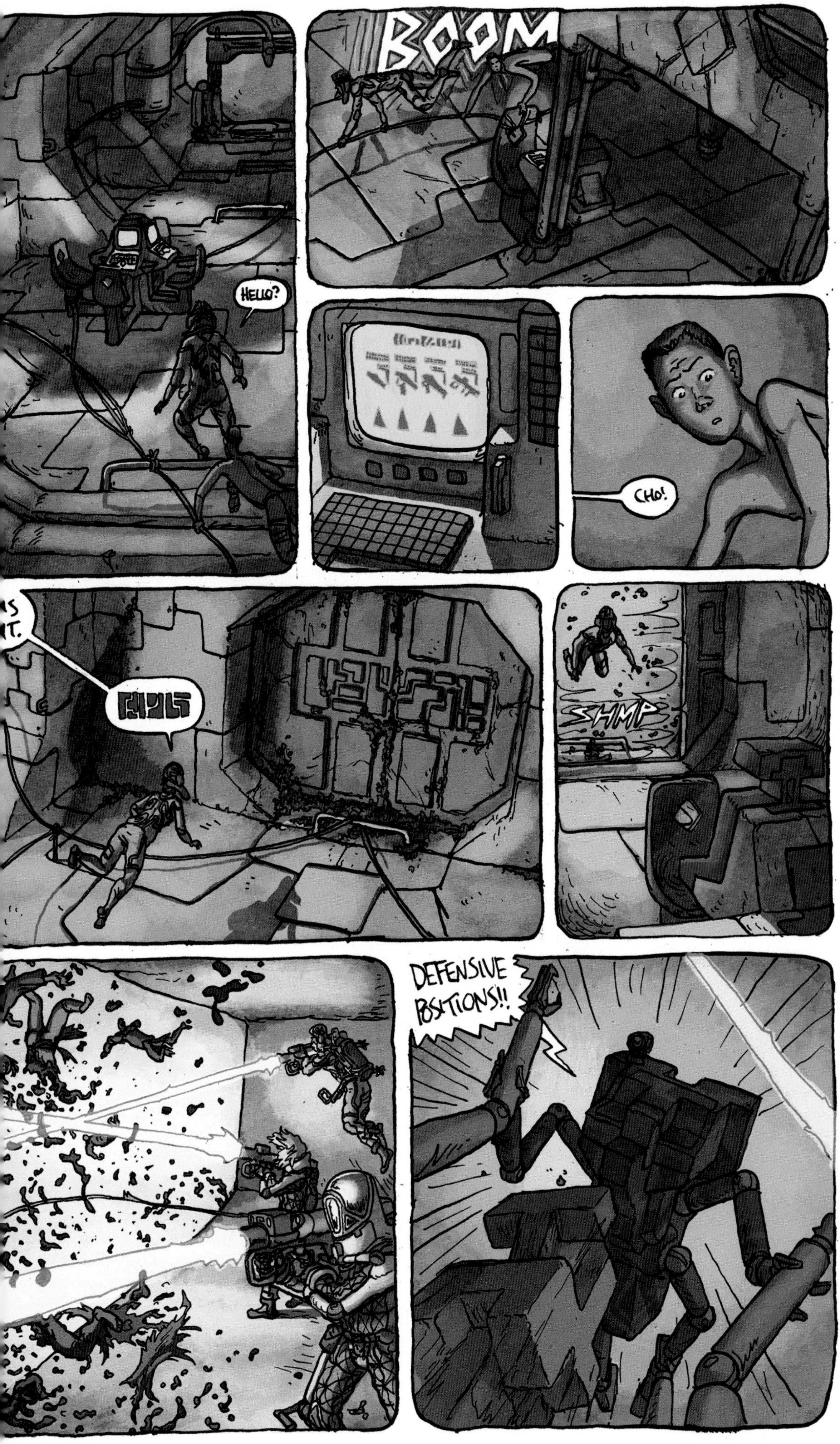
HELLO?
BOOM
CHO!
SHMP
DEFENSIVE POSITIONS!!

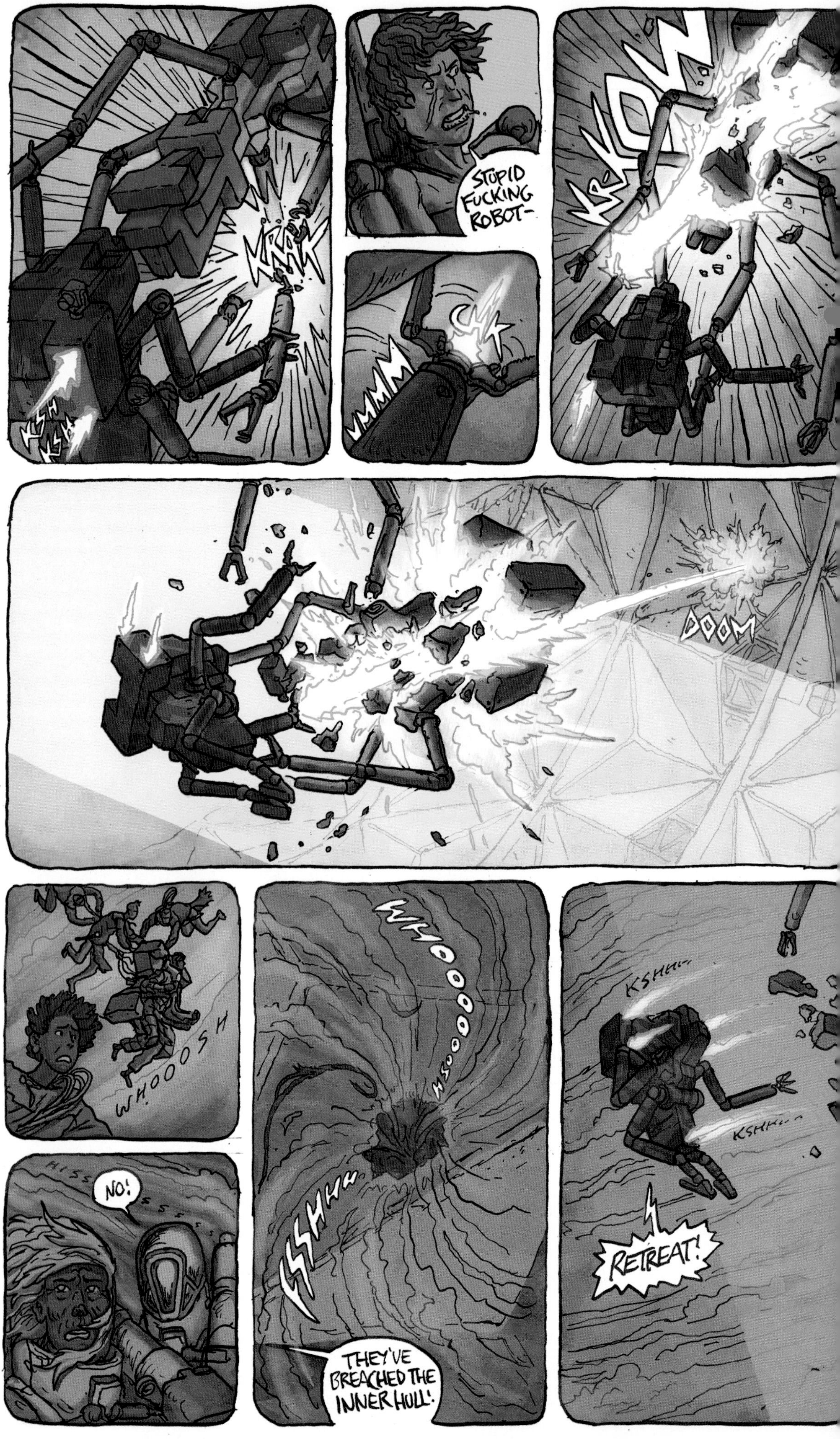
KRAK
KSH KSH
STUPID FUCKING ROBOT-
CHK
VMMMM
KRAKOW
DOOM
WHOOOSH
WHOOOOOOOOOSH
SSHHH
HISSSSSSSS
NO!
THEY'VE BREACHED THE INNER HULL!
KSHH...
KSHH...
RETREAT!

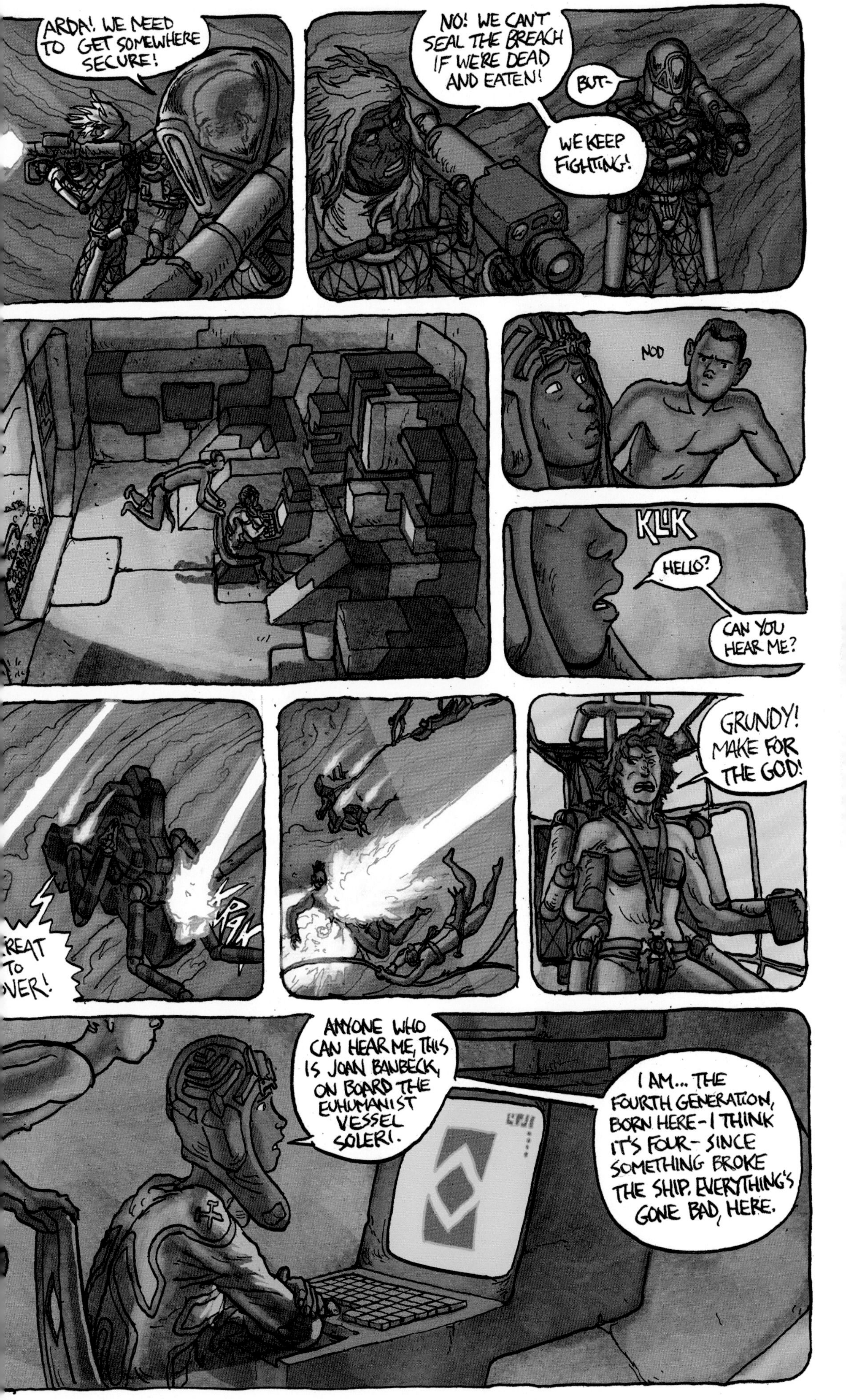
ARDA! WE NEED TO GET SOMEWHERE SECURE!
NO! WE CAN'T SEAL THE BREACH IF WE'RE DEAD AND EATEN!
BUT-
WE KEEP FIGHTING!
NOD
KLIK
HELLO?
CAN YOU HEAR ME?
REAT TO VER!
GRUNDY! MAKE FOR THE GOD!
ANYONE WHO CAN HEAR ME, THIS IS JOAN BANBECK, ON BOARD THE EUHUMANIST VESSEL SOLER!.
I AM... THE FOURTH GENERATION, BORN HERE - I THINK IT'S FOUR - SINCE SOMETHING BROKE THE SHIP. EVERYTHING'S GONE BAD, HERE.

WE STARTED WITH A HEALTHY BIOME. NOW, EVERYTHING BUT THE CARRION GULLS ARE GONE.

EATEN.

RETREAT! ALL OF YOU!

KRA

MOVE

KRK

AGK-

SECURITY TOOK OVER, BUT THE EMERGENCY MEASURES WERE NEVER LIFTED.

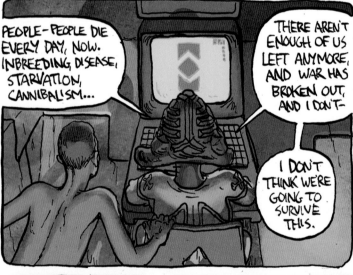

PEOPLE-PEOPLE DIE EVERY DAY, NOW. INBREEDING, DISEASE, STARVATION, CANNIBALISM...

THERE AREN'T ENOUGH OF US LEFT ANYMORE, AND WAR HAS BROKEN OUT, AND I DON'T-

I DON'T THINK WE'RE GOING TO SURVIVE THIS.

I WAS TOLD NOT TO REACH OUT, THAT YOU TRIED TO KILL US, BEFORE.

BUT-WE'RE NOT THE SAME PEOPLE YOU TRIED TO KILL.

WE NEE...
YOUR HE...

FZZZ-CRACKLE-

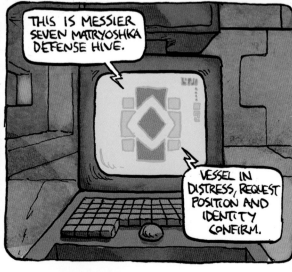

THIS IS MESSIER SEVEN MATRYOSHKA DEFENSE HIVE.

VESSEL IN DISTRESS, REQUEST POSITION AND IDENTITY CONFIRM.

YES! Y...
THIS-T...
IS THE E...
SOLER...

I-I DOE...
KNOW OU...
POSITION...

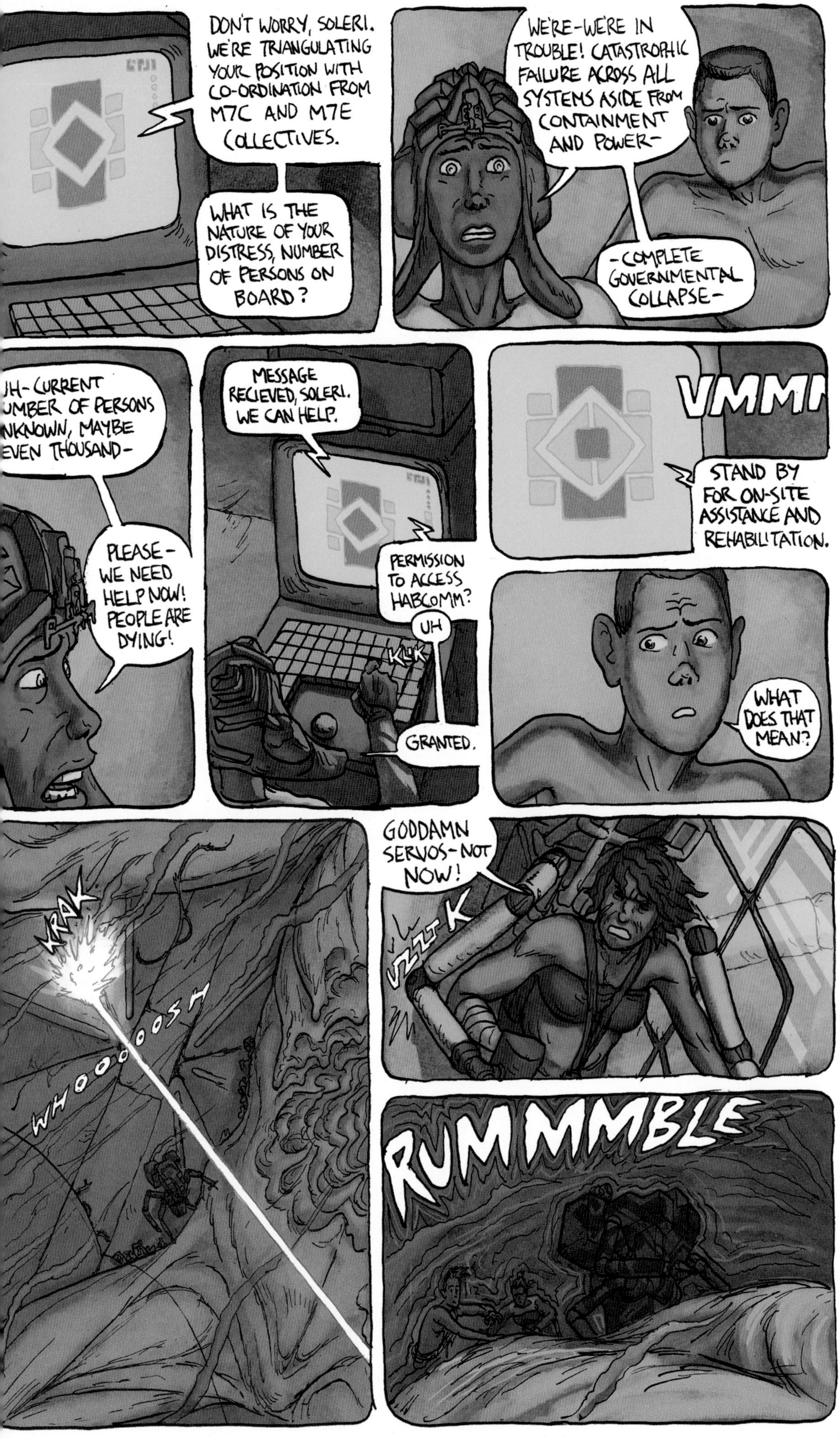
DON'T WORRY, SOLERI. WE'RE TRIANGULATING YOUR POSITION WITH CO-ORDINATION FROM M7C AND M7E COLLECTIVES.
WHAT IS THE NATURE OF YOUR DISTRESS, NUMBER OF PERSONS ON BOARD?
WE'RE-WE'RE IN TROUBLE! CATASTROPHIC FAILURE ACROSS ALL SYSTEMS ASIDE FROM CONTAINMENT AND POWER-
-COMPLETE GOVERNMENTAL COLLAPSE-
UH-CURRENT NUMBER OF PERSONS UNKNOWN, MAYBE EVEN THOUSAND-
PLEASE-WE NEED HELP NOW! PEOPLE ARE DYING!
MESSAGE RECIEVED, SOLERI. WE CAN HELP.
PERMISSION TO ACCESS HABCOMM?
UH
KLIK
GRANTED.
VMMM
STAND BY FOR ON-SITE ASSISTANCE AND REHABILITATION.
WHAT DOES THAT MEAN?
KRAK
WHOOOOOOSH
GODDAMN SERVOS-NOT NOW!
VZZZT K
RUMMMBLE

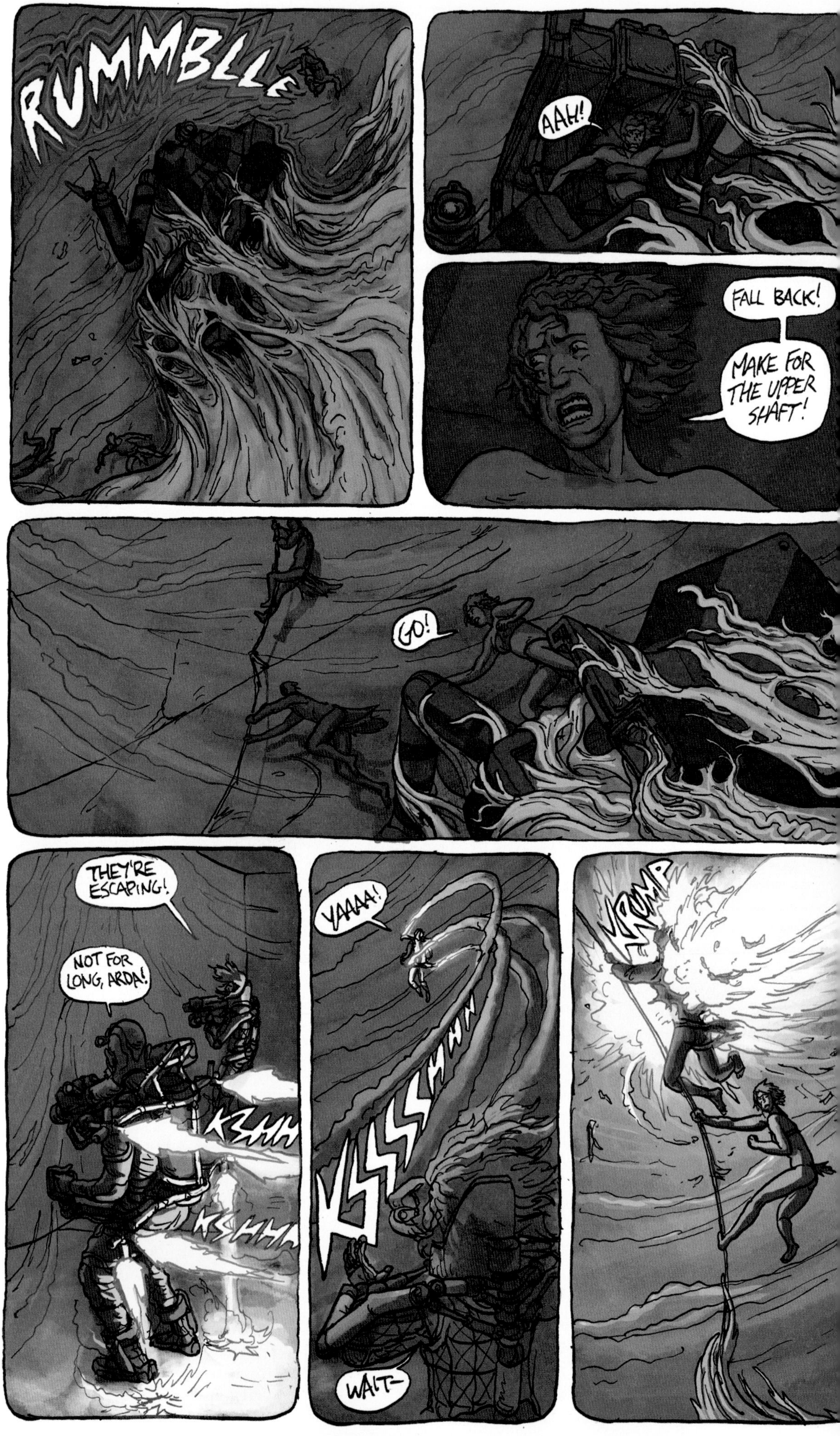
RUMMBLLE
AAH!
FALL BACK!
MAKE FOR THE UPPER SHAFT!
GO!
THEY'RE ESCAPING!
NOT FOR LONG, ARDA!
KSHHH
KSHHH
YAAAA!
KSSSSHHH
WAIT-
KROMP

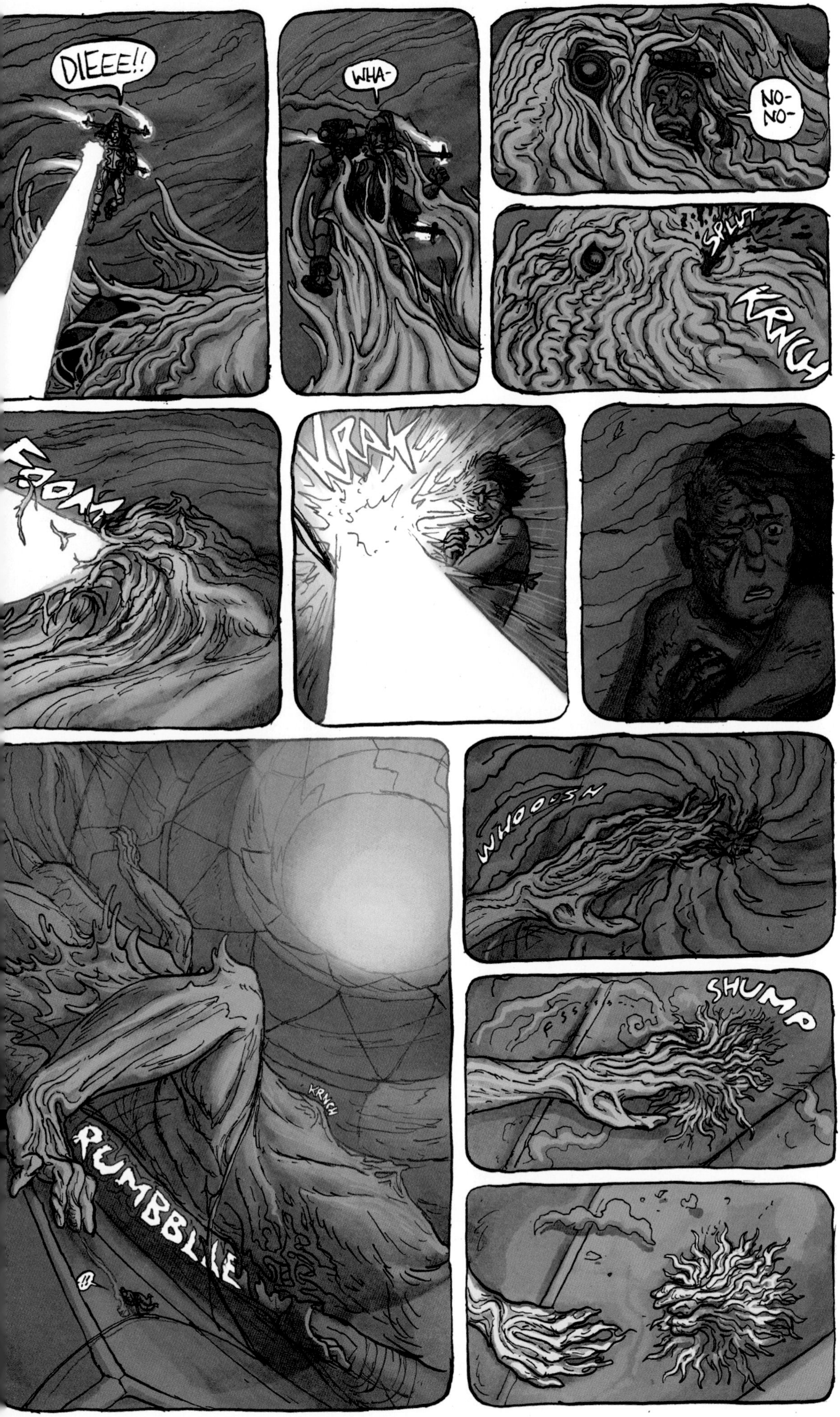
DIEEE!!
WHA-
NO-
NO-
SPLUT
KRNCH
FOOM
KRAK
WHOOOSH
KRNCH
RUMBBLLE
!!
SHUMP

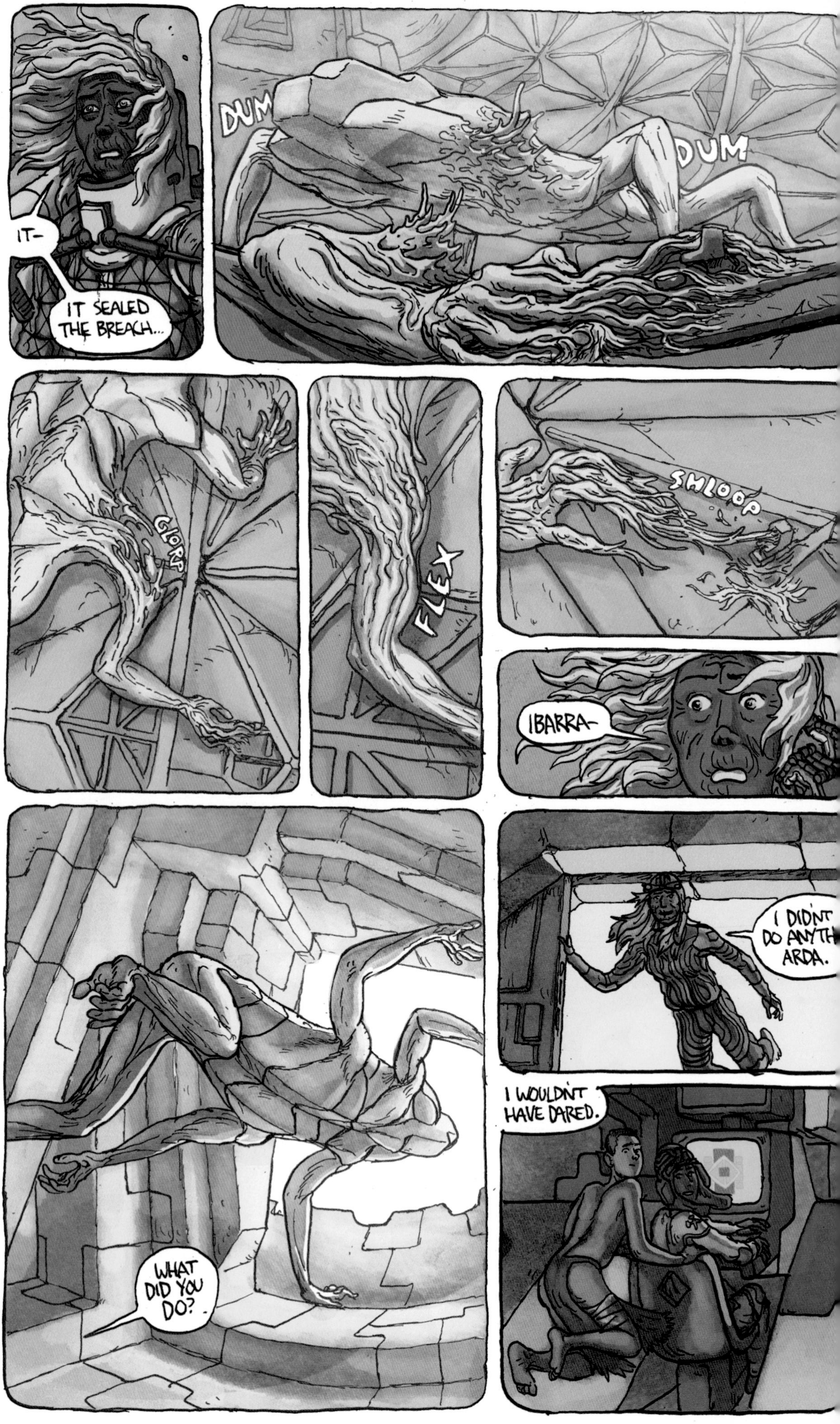
IT-
IT SEALED THE BREACH...
DUM
DUM
GLORP
FLEX
SHLOOP
IBARRA-
WHAT DID YOU DO?
I DIDN'T DO ANYTH ARDA.
I WOULDN'T HAVE DARED.

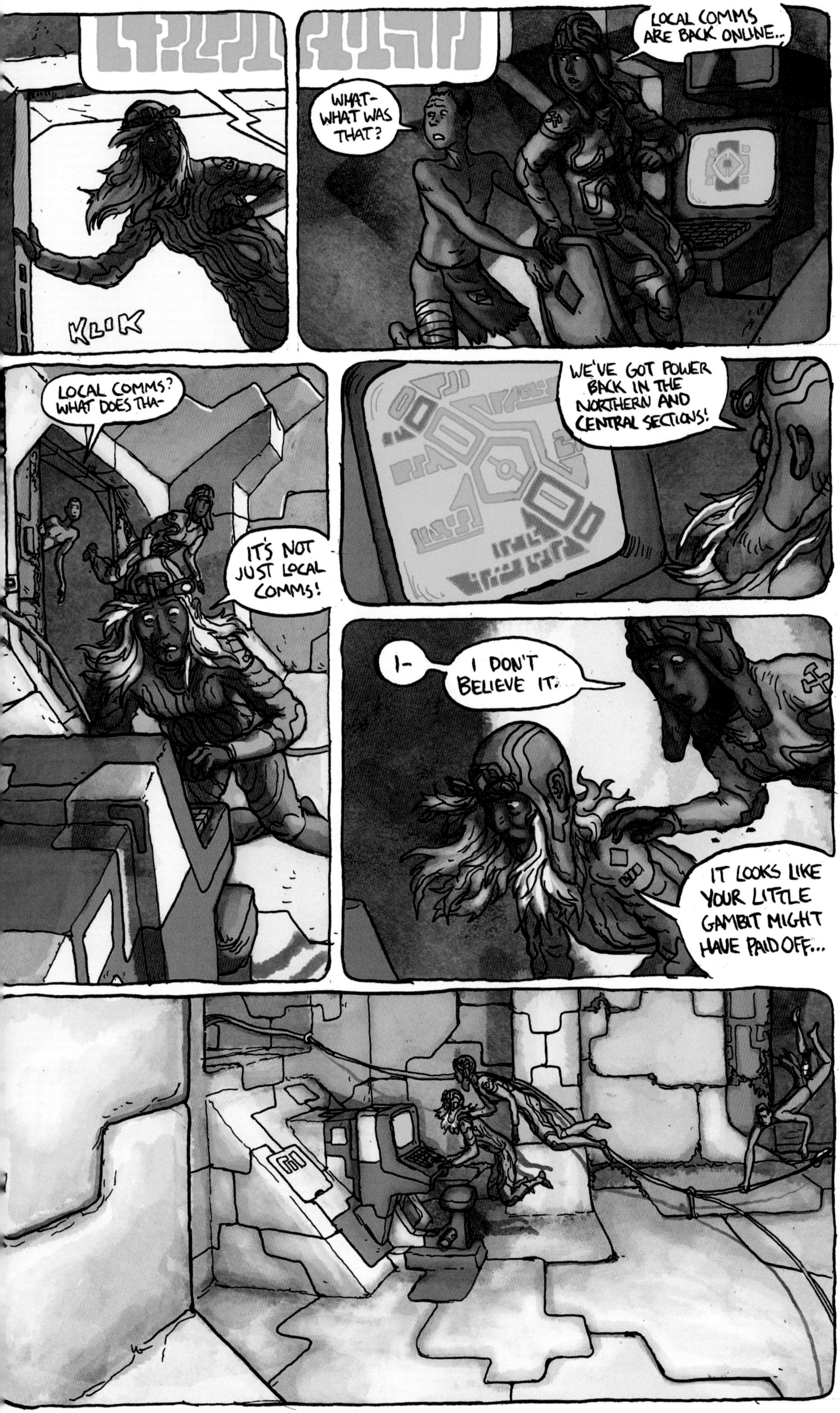
KLIK
LOCAL COMMS ARE BACK ONLINE...
WHAT- WHAT WAS THAT?
LOCAL COMMS? WHAT DOES THA-
IT'S NOT JUST LOCAL COMMS!
WE'VE GOT POWER BACK IN THE NORTHERN AND CENTRAL SECTIONS!
I-
I DON'T BELIEVE IT...
IT LOOKS LIKE YOUR LITTLE GAMBIT MIGHT HAVE PAID OFF...

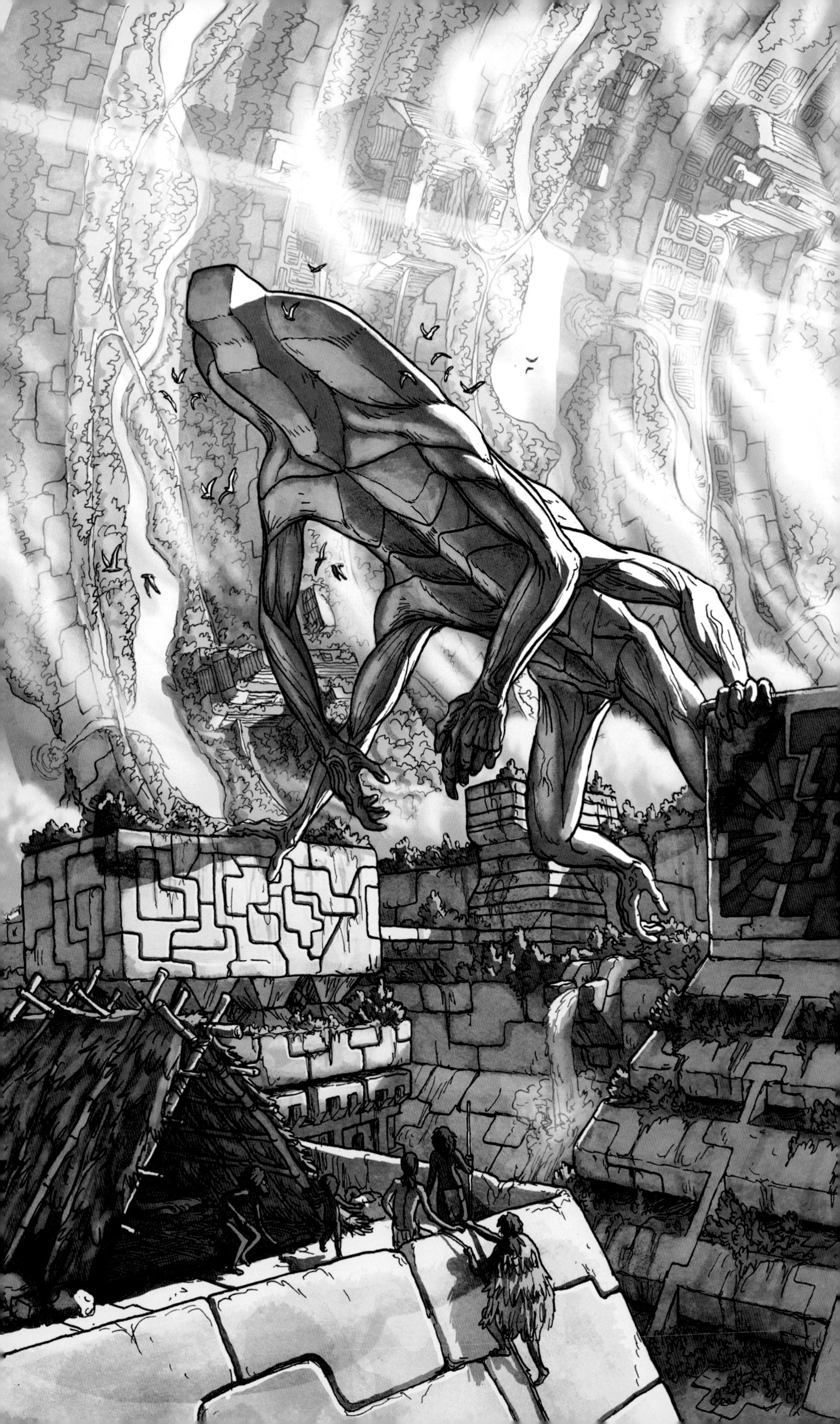

DEVELOPMENTAL SKETCHES

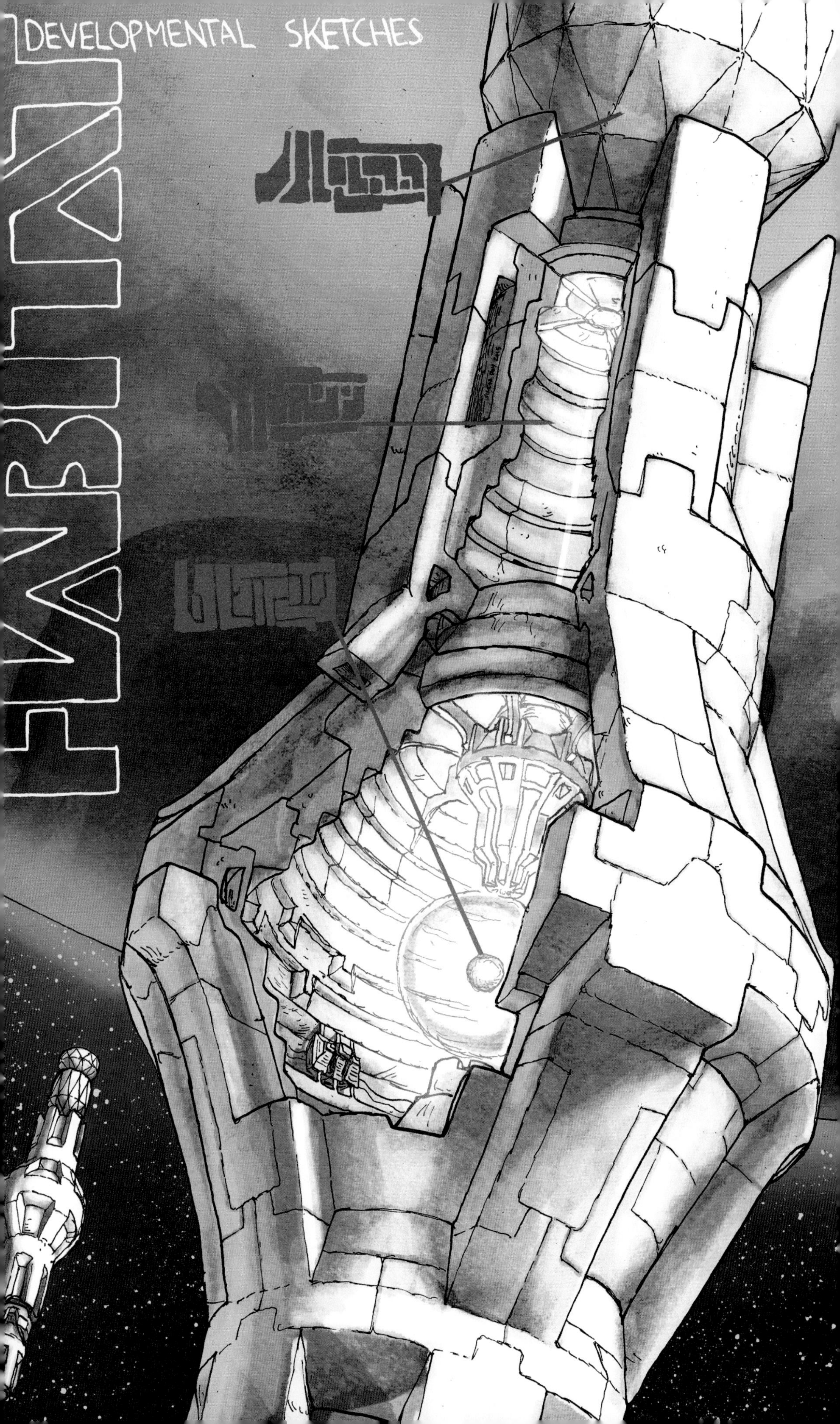

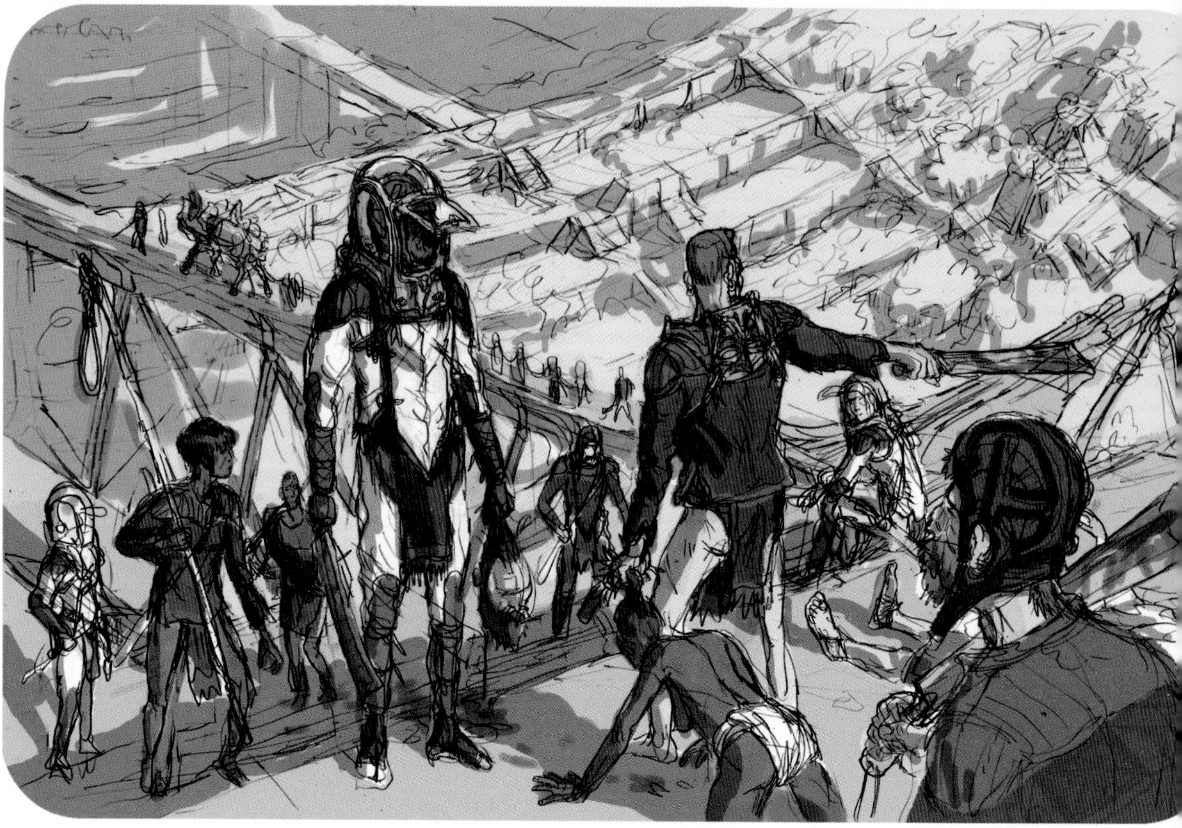

THE MAIN VISUAL PROBLEM OF HABITAT WAS COMMUNICATING THE STORY'S TRIBAL PRESENT ALONGSIDE THE EPIC, UTOPIAN PAST IT GREW FROM.

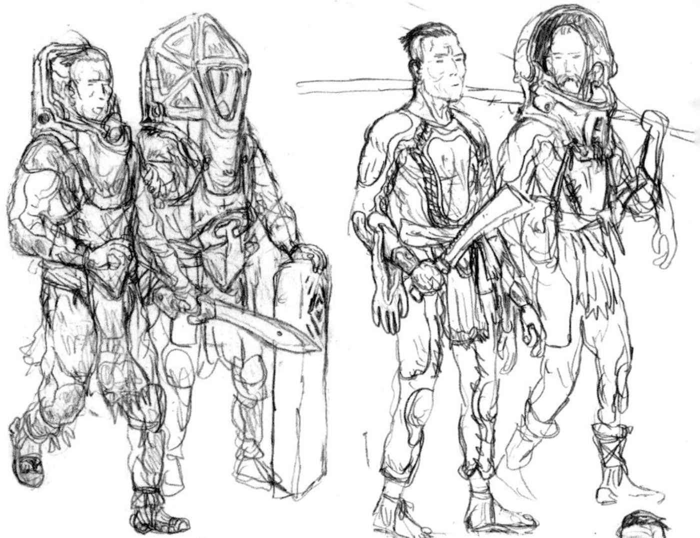

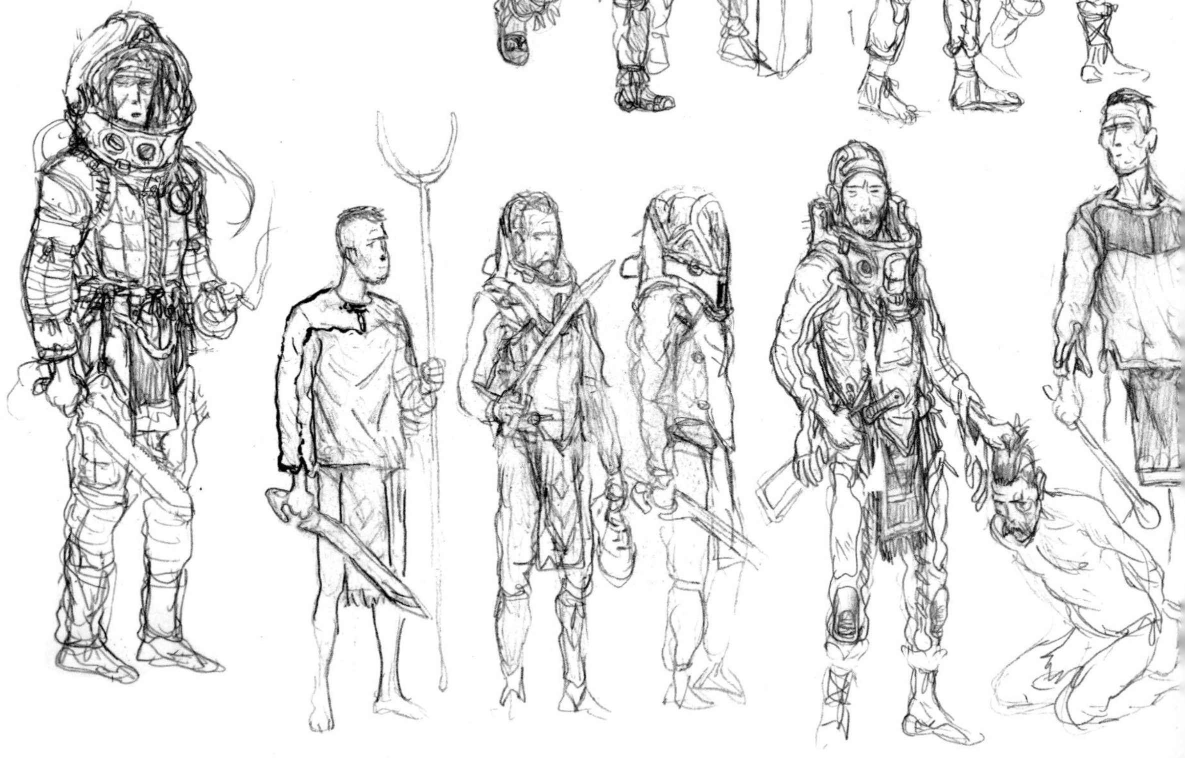

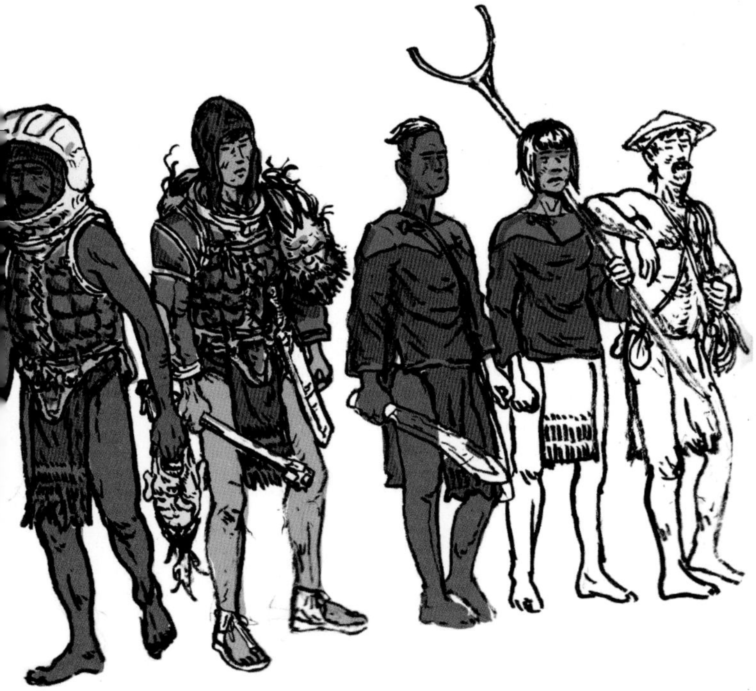

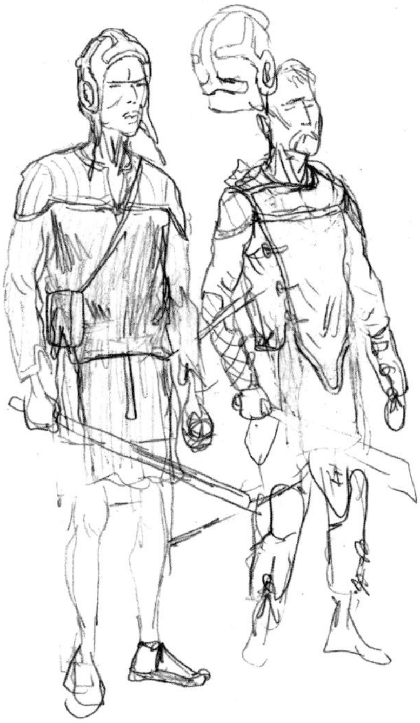

IN SERVICE OF THAT,
DEVELOPING THE RIGHT
RETRO-FUTURISTIC SPACE
SUIT FOR THE HABSEC
BECAME A FIXATION.

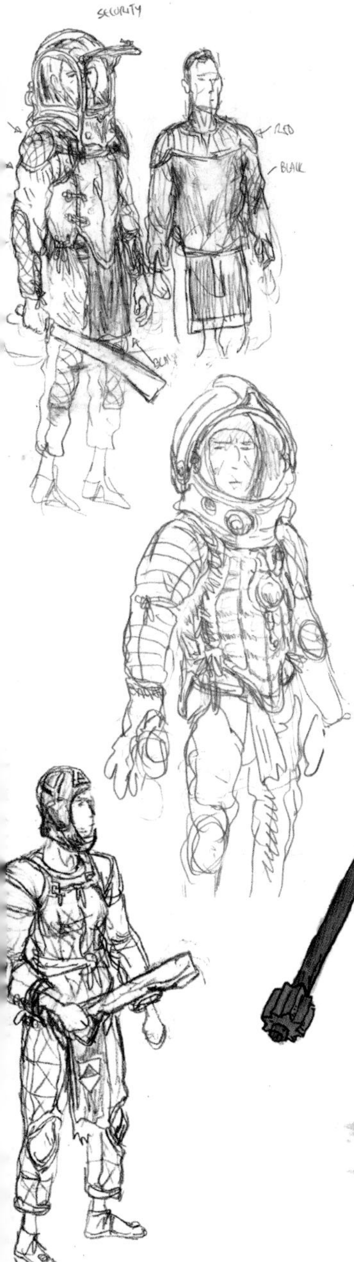
SECURITY
RED
BLACK

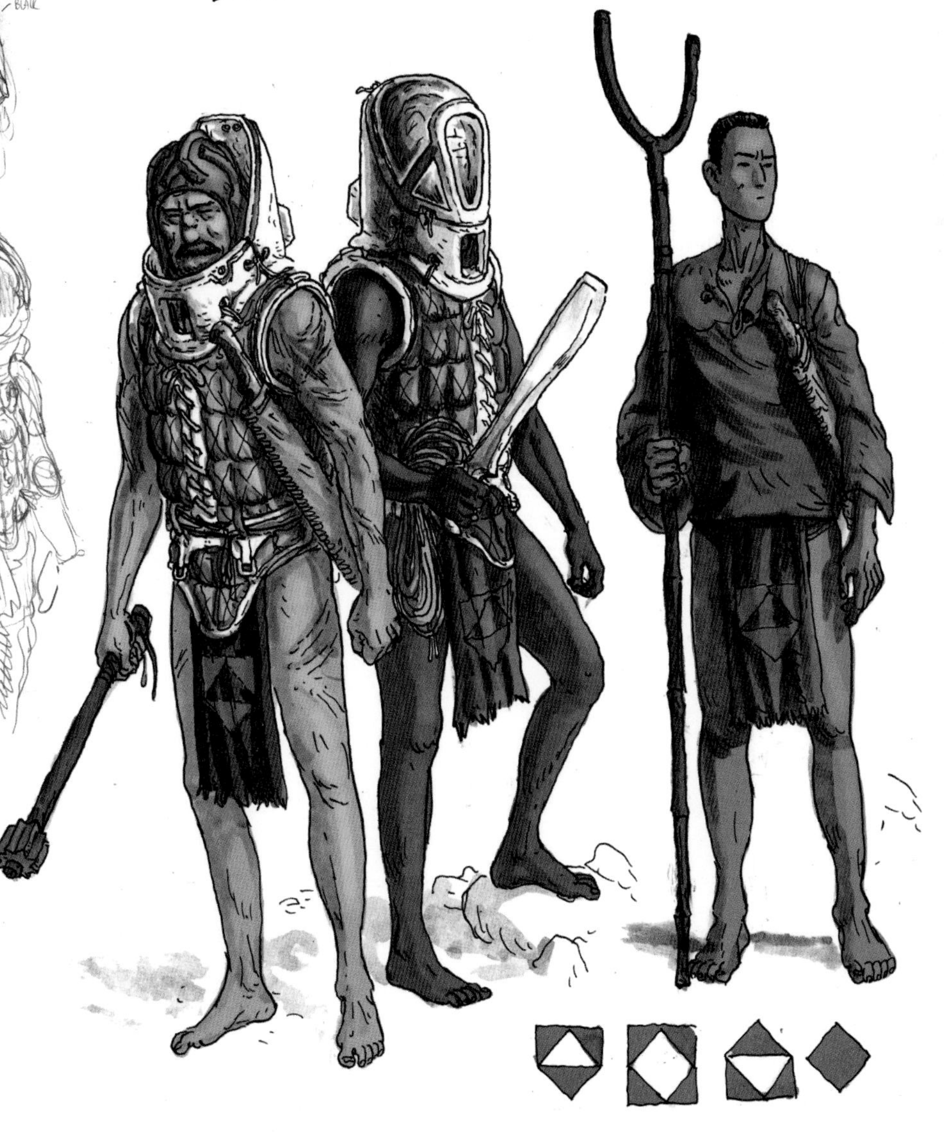

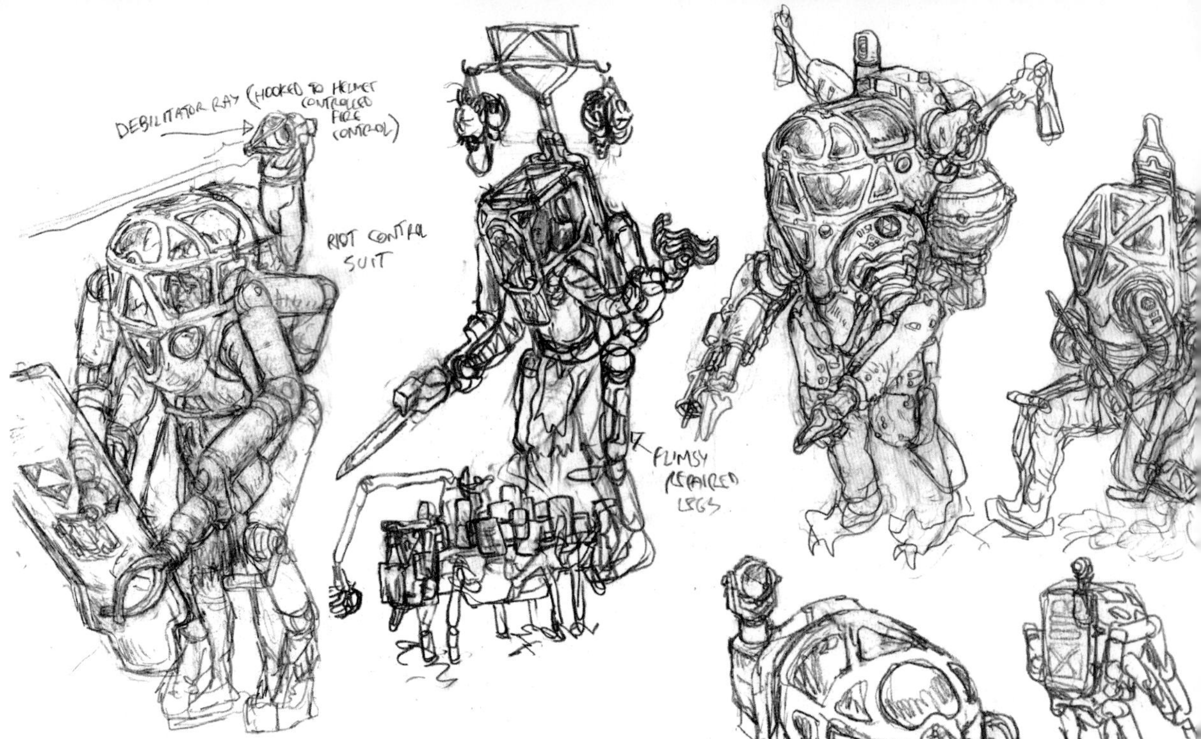
DEBILITATOR RAY (HOOKED TO HELMET CONTROLLED FIRE CONTROL)
RIOT CONTROL SUIT
FLIMSY REPAIRED LEGS

RESEARCH AND DESIGN FOR
THE MAN-AMPLIFIERS, EXOSKELETONS
AND COOLING SUITS OF
THE HABITAT'S CULTURES
CAME NATURALLY
FROM THERE.

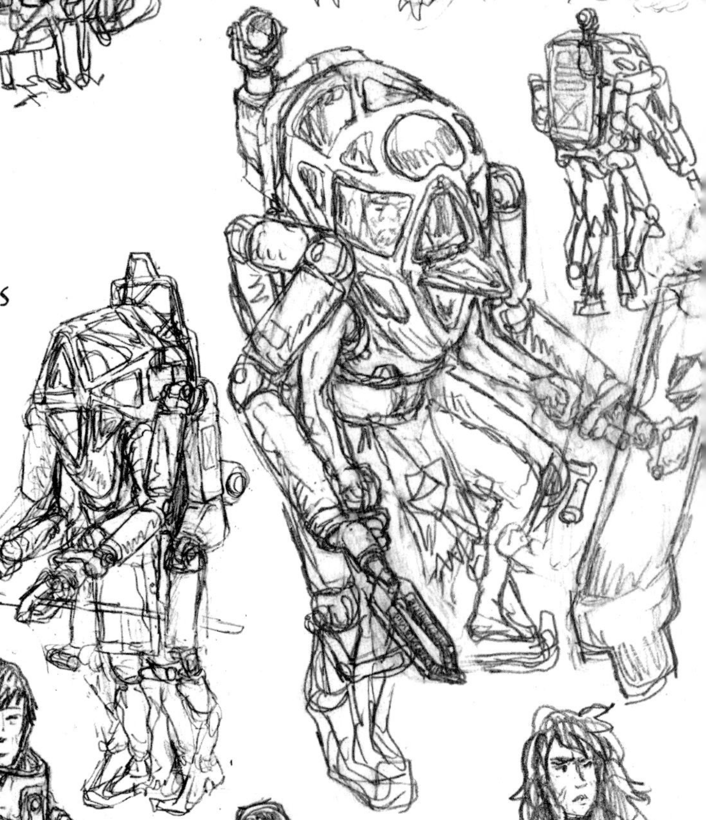

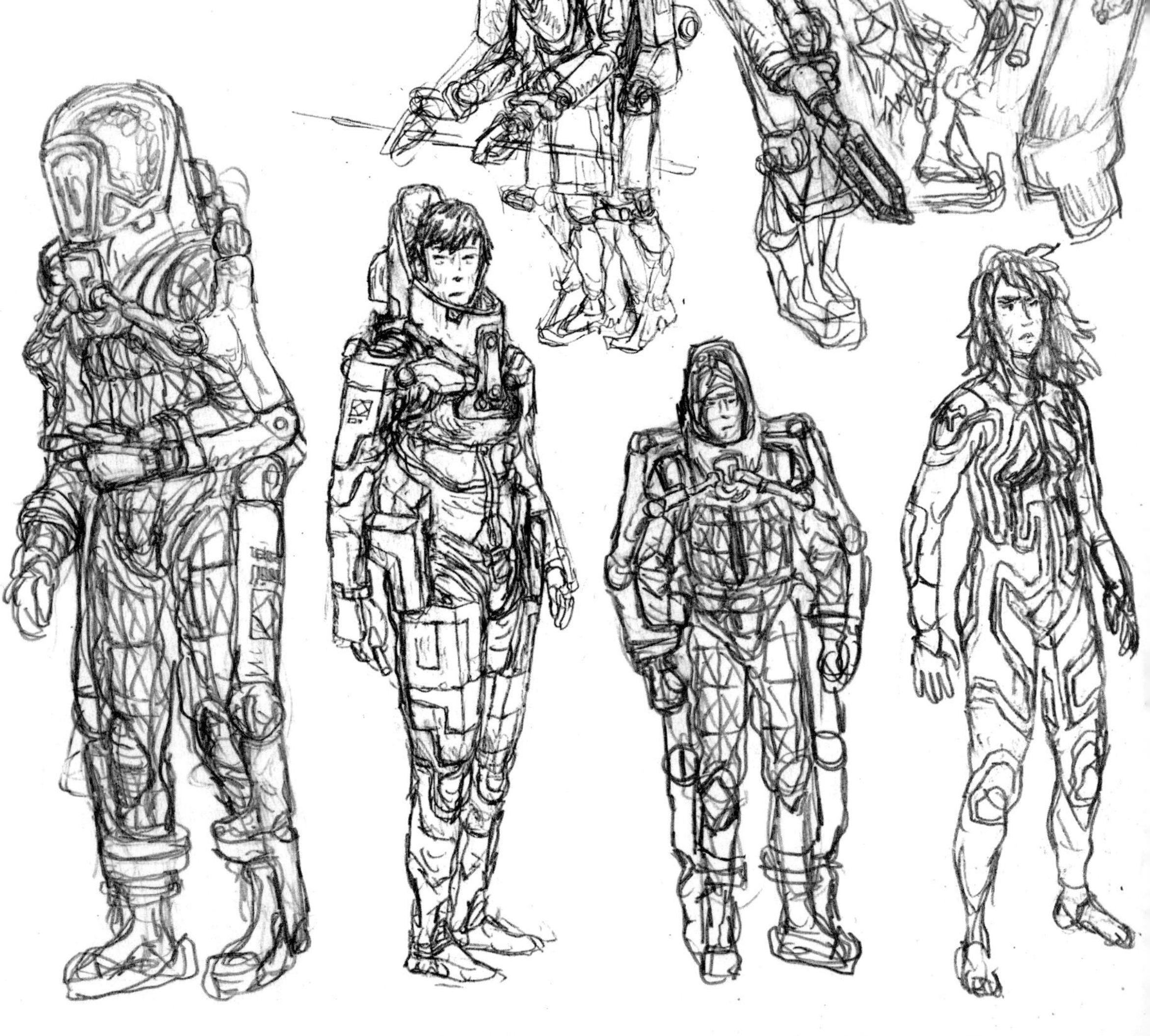

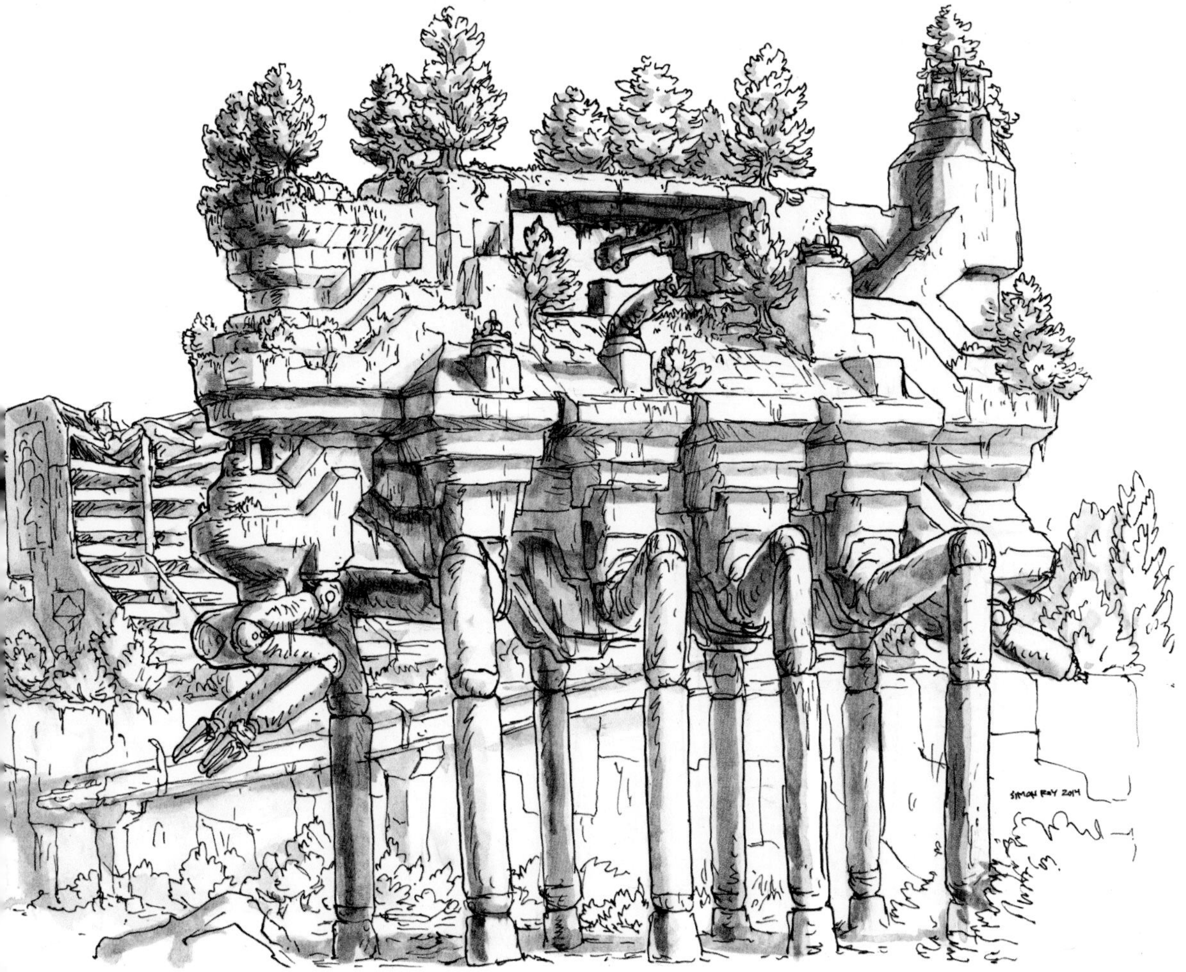
SIMON ROY 2014

HOWEVER, NO FAILED UTOPIA IS COMPLETE WITHOUT AN ABUNDANCE OF OVERGROWN MONUMENTAL ARCHITECTURE!

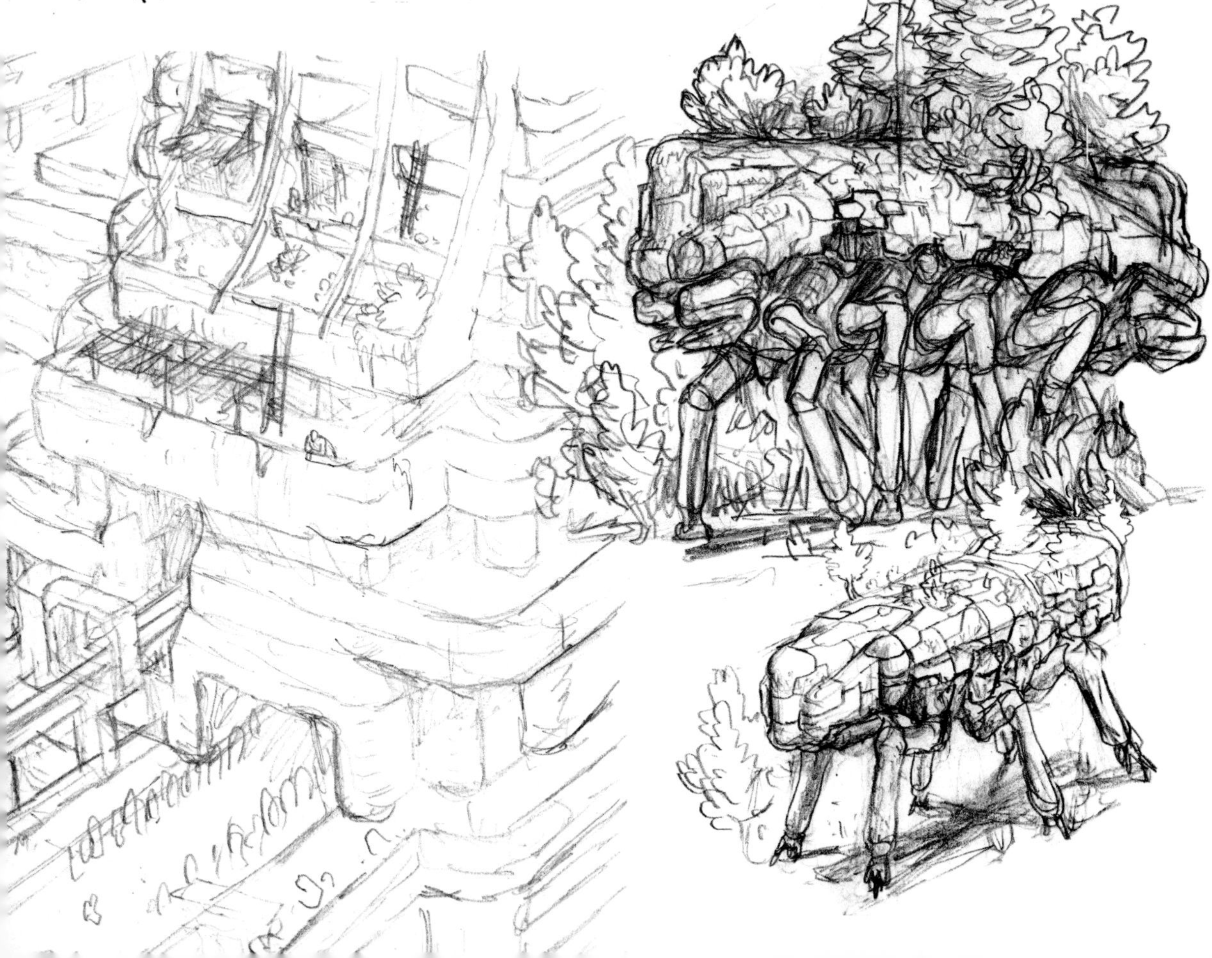

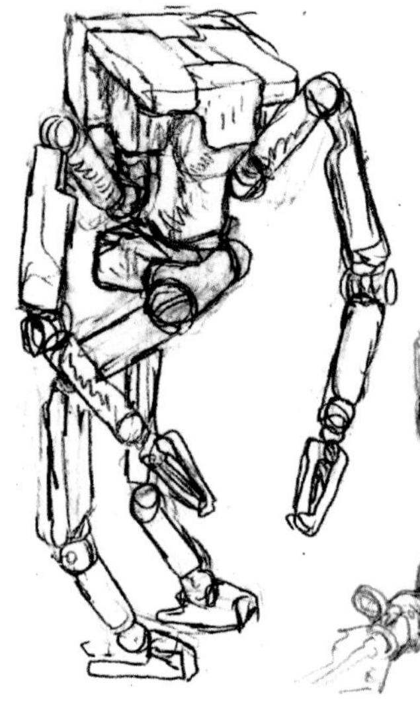
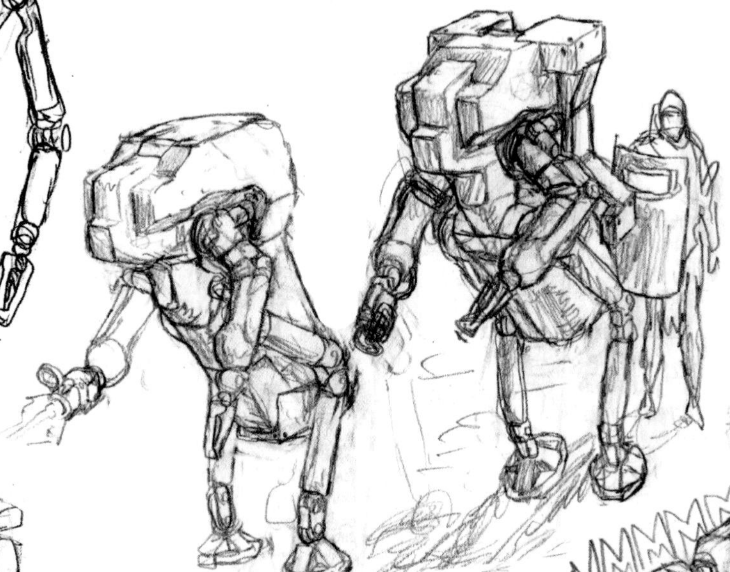
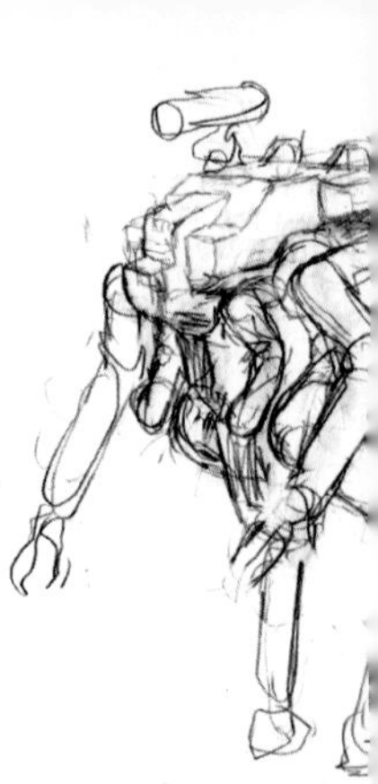
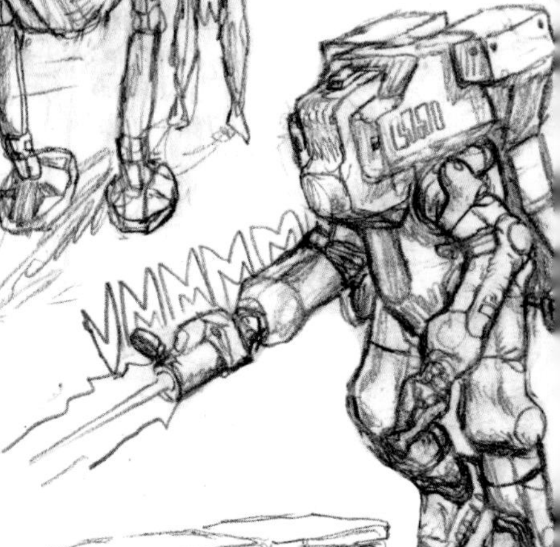
VMMMMM
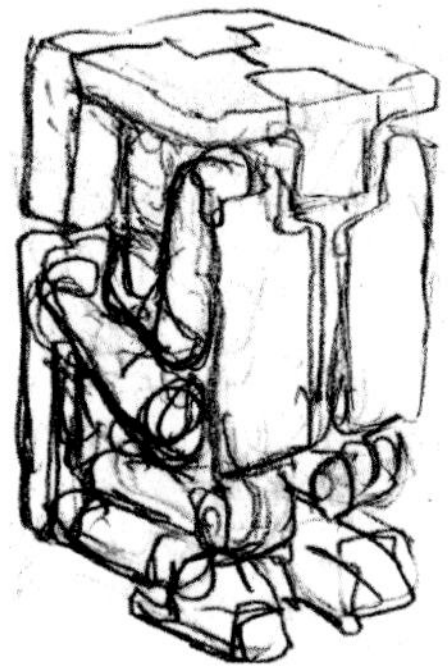

THE ROBOTS WERE AN OPPORTUNITY TO CONNECT THE RELICT STAR TREK-LIKE TECHNOLOGIES OF THE HABITAT TO THE BRUTALIST/MESOAMERICAN INSPIRED STRUCTURE OF THE HABITAT ITSELF.

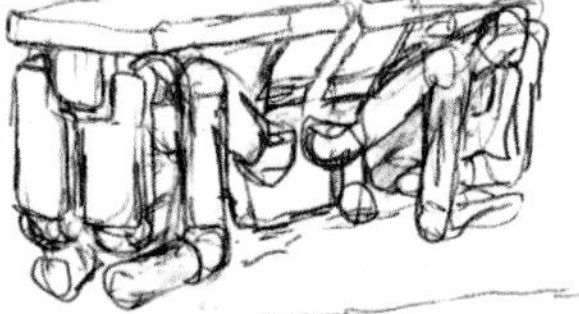
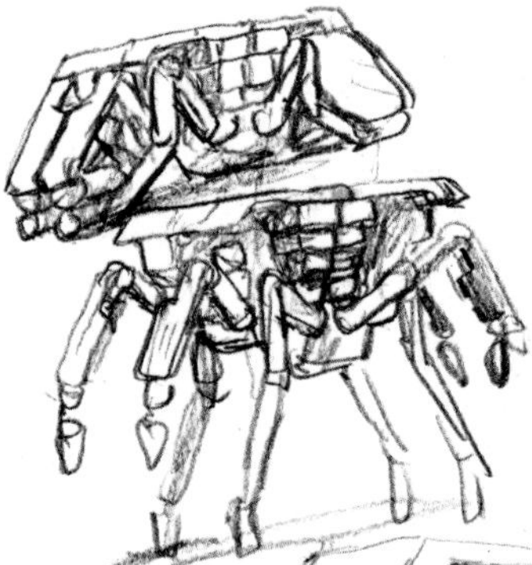
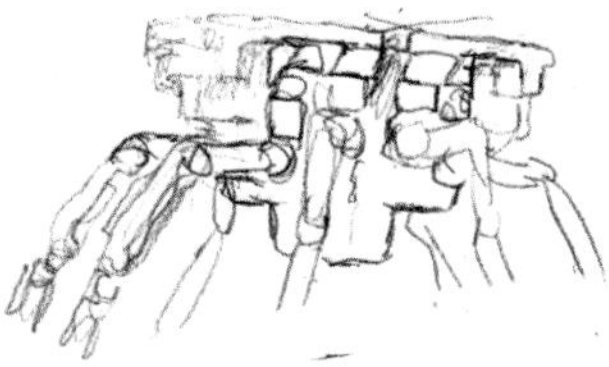
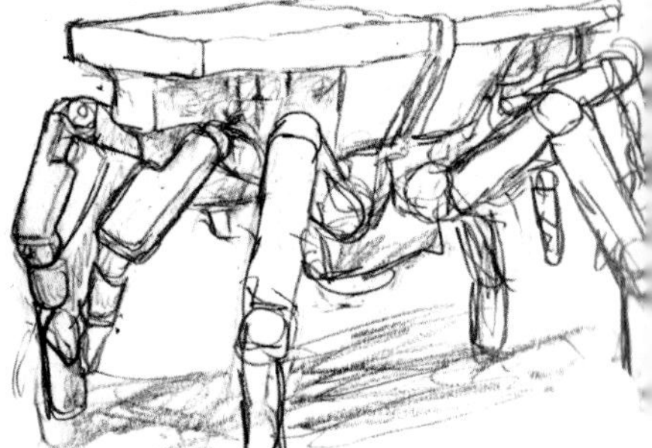
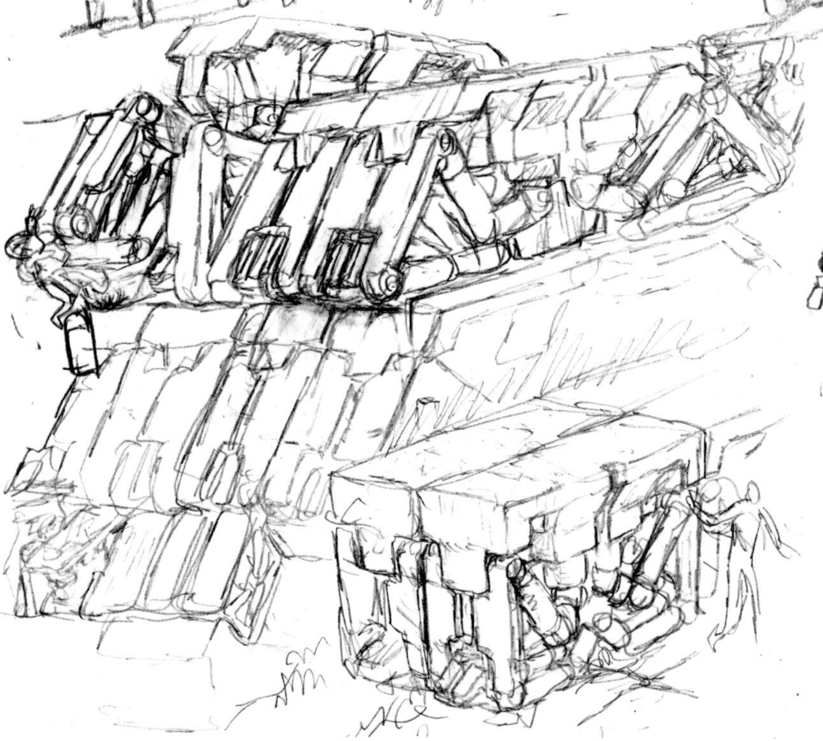
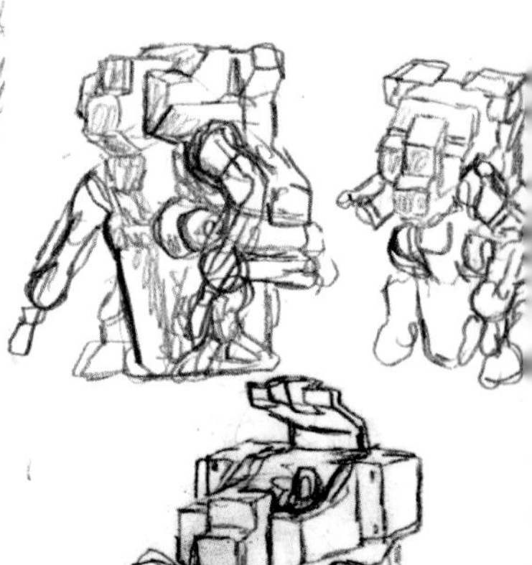
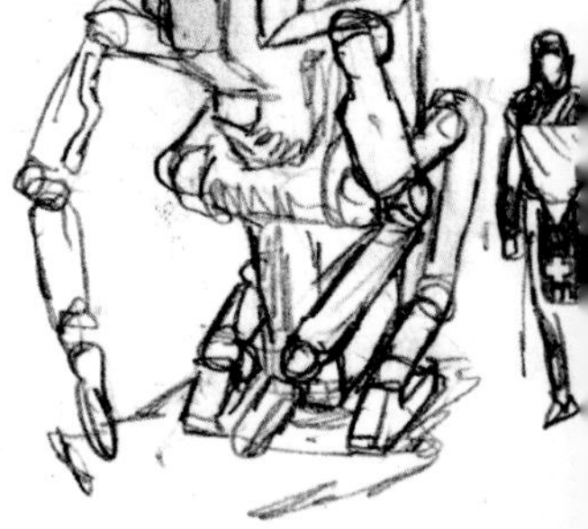

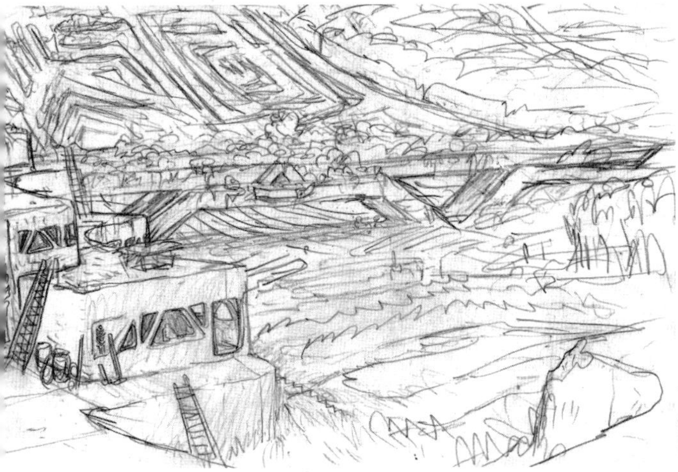

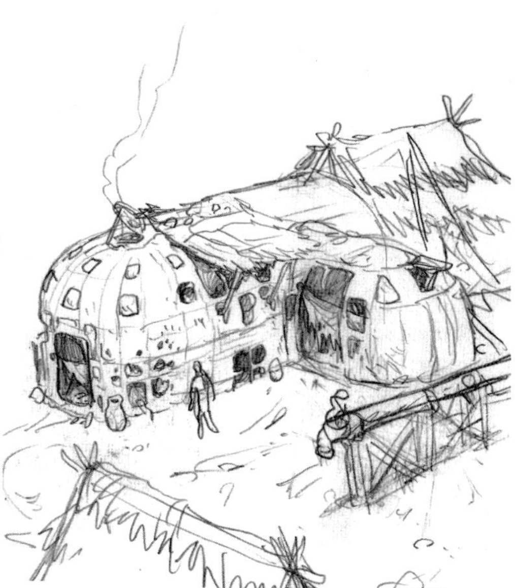

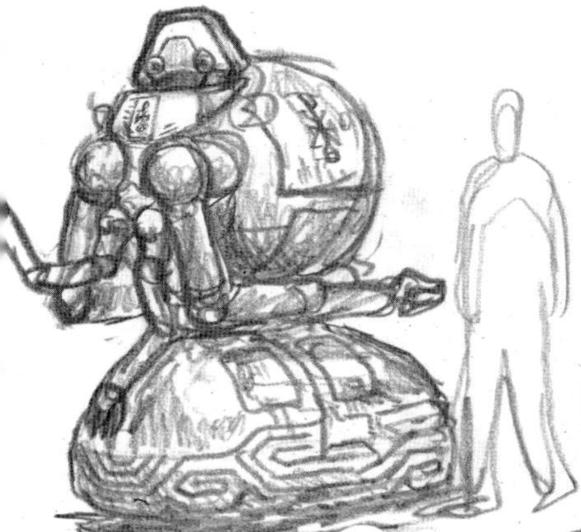

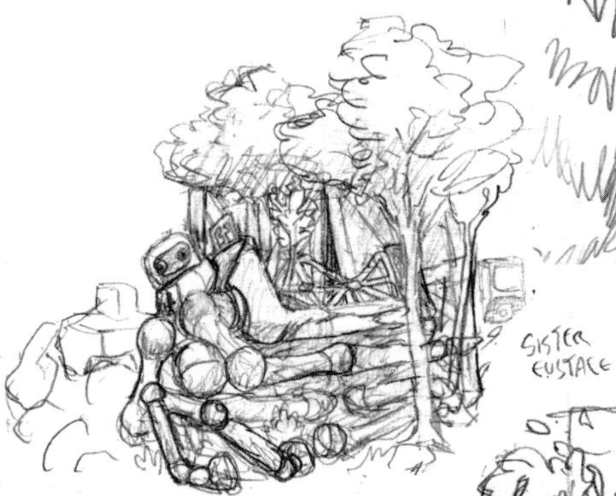
SISTER EUSTACE

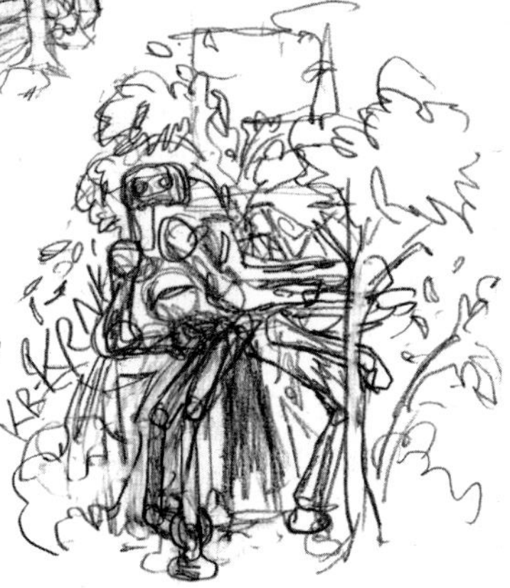
KR-KR

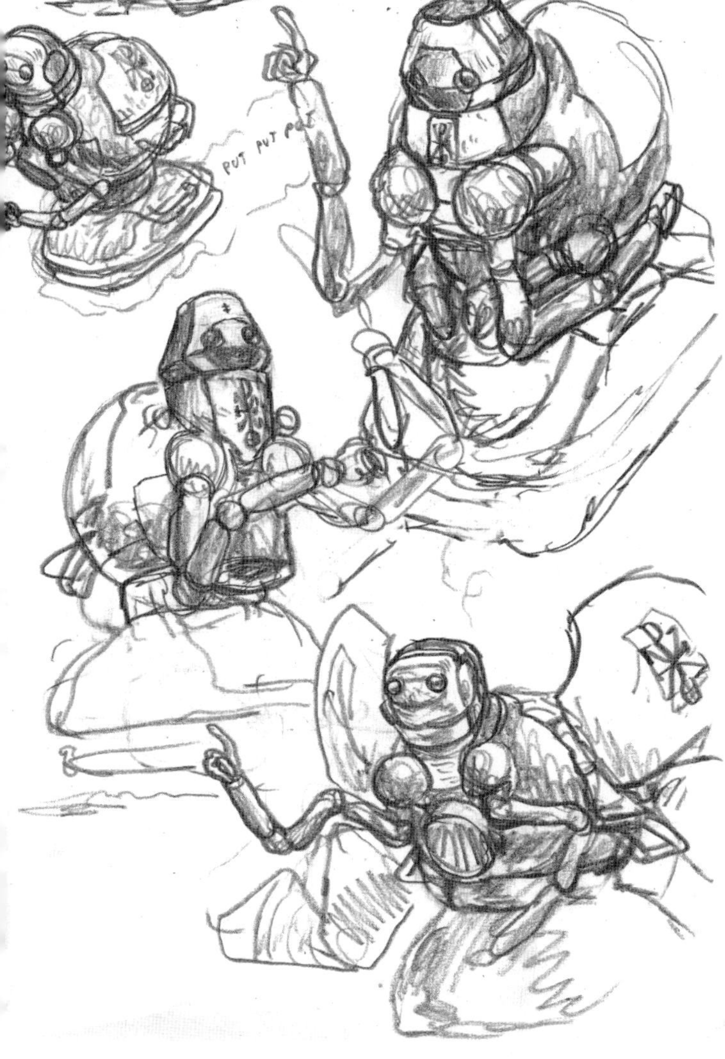
PUT PUT PUT

LASTLY, THE ROBO-NUNS. SERVANTS OF A FUTURE CATHOLIC CHURCH, THE SISTERS ARE TRACTOR-SIZED MISSIONARY ROBOTS CAPABLE OF EVERYTHING FROM MIDWIFERY TO LARGE-SCALE AGRICULTURE.

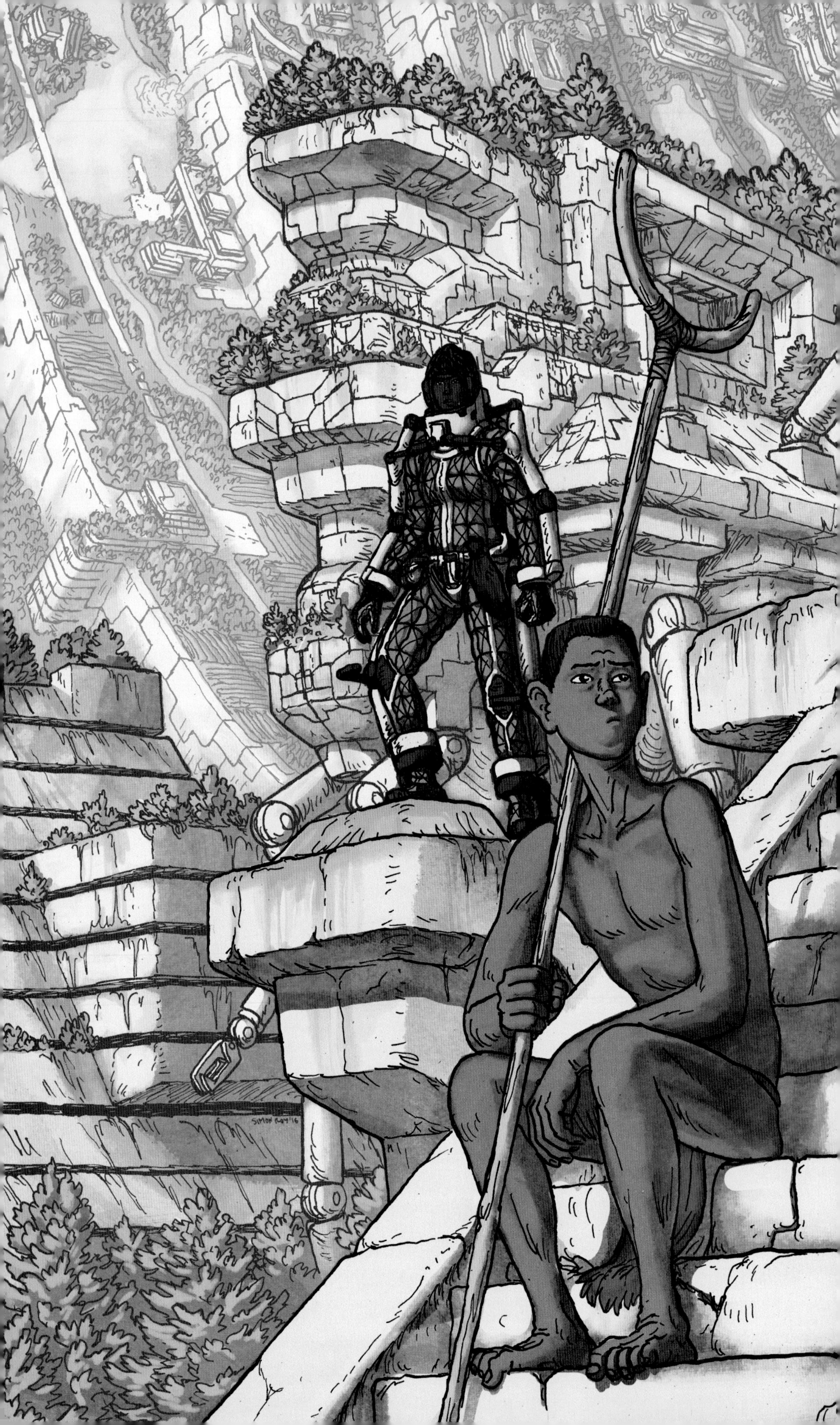
SIMON ROY '16